DESERT DIPLOMAT

Desert Diplomat

Inside Saudi Arabia Following 9/11

ROBERT W. JORDAN
with STEVE FIFFER

Foreword by
JAMES A. BAKER III

Potomac Books
An imprint of the University of Nebraska Press

Library of Congress Cataloging-in-Publication Data
Jordan, Robert W., 1945–
Desert diplomat: inside Saudi Arabia following 9/11 /
Robert W. Jordan with Steve Fiffer; foreword by James
A. Baker III.
pages   cm
Includes bibliographical references.
ISBN 978-1-61234-670-0 (cloth: alk. paper)
ISBN 978-1-61234-740-0 (epub)
ISBN 978-1-61234-741-7 (mobi)
ISBN 978-1-61234-671-7 (pdf)
1. Jordan, Robert W., 1945– 2. Ambassadors—
United States—Biography. 3. United States—Foreign
relations—Saudi Arabia. 4. Saudi Arabia—Foreign
relations—United States. 5. United States—
Foreign relations—2001–2009. 6. September 11
Terrorist Attacks, 2001—Influence. 7. Iraq War,
2003–2011—Diplomatic history. I. Fiffer, Steve. II.
Title.
E901.1.J67A3 2015
327.2092—dc23
[B]
2015002747

Set in Fanwood Text by M. Scheer.

For Kathy and our family, and for the brave men and women who serve in America's embassies and consulates abroad

FOREWORD

AMBASSADORS ARE THE Swiss Army knives of America's diplomatic ranks. They are multitools—part diplomat, part analyst, and part politician. And, yes, from time to time, they are part spy. They must display the skills and characteristics required to confront challenging tasks, often during trying times. They must have voracious appetites for information yet be discrete when sharing it. They must be as equally charming as they are tough. Above all, they must be smart. An ambassador, as the U.S. Diplomacy Center defines it, is the president's highest-ranking representative to a specific nation or international organization abroad. They must act accordingly.

The day following the 9/11 attacks on New York City and Washington, President George W. Bush selected exactly the right man when he formally nominated Robert W. Jordan to became the U.S. ambassador to Saudi Arabia. Jordan had already gone through a background check. But by September 12, a lot more was riding on the appointment. America's relationship with Saudi Arabia would face inevitable strains amid backlash at the Islamic extremists responsible for the terrible bombings that shook the world. Osama bin Laden, after all, was a member of the House of Saud. Having a cool hand in Riyadh would be critical if the United States were to maintain Saudi Arabia as a close ally in this important part of the world. As events in the Middle East unfolded during the two years Jordan was stationed there, that bilateral relationship would be tested time and time again.

Although Jordan had no prior foreign service experience, he had many of the qualities needed to be a model ambassador to the Kingdom. He was intelligent, savvy, and street smart. He was a good negotiator. But above all, he had strong professional and personal ties with the president. An accomplished trial lawyer from Dallas, Jordan had represented Bush when he was a Texas businessman. Although not a part of the president's inner circle, Jordan and his wife socialized with George and Laura Bush, and he played a key role in Bush's victory over Ann Richards to become governor of Texas. Jordan was his own man with his own code. The president knew that he would always get the skinny from Jordan, and not merely the bureaucratic buttering up that sometimes comes with being the leader of the free world. As the president told Jordan three months after the attacks, the new ambassador would be his "point man" in Saudi Arabia.

In his memoir Jordan has done a stellar job of telling the compelling story about much of the diplomatic activity that swept the Middle East after 9/11. Saudi Arabia, of course, played a key role. In order for the United States to successfully invade Iraq and oust Saddam Hussein, assistance from neighboring Saudi Arabia was critical—particularly in using the country's assets, such as military bases, border crossings, intelligence, and logistics. But more was at stake. It was also critical that Saudi Arabia be viewed by others in the region as supporting the invasion of another Islamic country. This was a pivotal two years for both countries.

Jordan writes with unflinching acuity, providing keen insight into the Arab world as well as the inner workings of American diplomacy during his time as ambassador. He tells about the first meeting between President Bush and Saudi crown prince Abdullah during the Crawford Summit at the president's Central Texas ranch in April 2002 in the lead-up to the second Gulf War. He tells about the 2003 terrorist bombings at three compounds in Riyadh that left 39 people dead and more than 160 wounded. And he tells of his personal role in helping save the life of Michael Baba Yemba, a Christian pastor from South Sudan who was being persecuted for his faith before Jordan assisted his immigration to Dallas, Texas.

Simply put, *Desert Diplomat* is an intriguing tale of an interesting man serving his country during an important time in history.

James A. Baker III
Sixty-First U.S. Secretary of State

ACKNOWLEDGMENTS

THIS BOOK TOOK a long time to write. When I left government I spent hours outlining it and doing research to get the facts and historical context right. But I soon realized that I was writing it as a term paper, not as my personal story. My wife Kathy Donovan helped me realize that I needed to make it a more intimate account of my life at a crucial time for me and for our nation. My friend Jim Hime then introduced me to Steve Fiffer, who had helped former secretary of state James A. Baker III write his terrific memoir. Steve and I immediately clicked. Working from my outline and through countless evenings talking with him in Chicago via Skype from my home in Dubai, Steve helped me add texture and detail to these stories, and he also provided further research. He pressed me on nuances and descriptive elements that I never would have included if left to my own devices. He added a lively and conversational tone to the stories and was a joy to work with. This book would never have been written without Steve's enormous contribution.

I am also indebted to many friends, colleagues, and associates. Secretary Baker was a continuing inspiration, and I greatly appreciate his contribution of the foreword to this book. My colleagues at the State Department and Embassy Riyadh were uniformly supportive, and I cannot thank them enough. They and their counterparts around the world often serve in dangerous places with minimal protection to advance our country's interests, and all Americans owe them a debt of gratitude. My deputy, Margaret Scobey, deserves special recognition for her steadfast judgment, leadership, and friendship. My friends in Saudi Arabia and the United Arab Emirates also provided wonderful encouragement and support. The lawyers at Baker Botts LLP were also extremely helpful when I returned to the firm after my time as ambassador. Baker Botts's managing partners Walt Smith and Andy Baker generously granted me time to work on the book and to provide commentary in the media on events in the Middle East.

Writing a book involves many people whose efforts often go unnoticed. Nicolas Schuepbach helped me greatly with early research assistance, and Abigail Swetz provided excellent comments on the first draft. HRH Prince Alwaleed bin Talal and Jacqueline Visser provided valuable photographs, and Vern Cassin helped coordinate use of the cover photograph. Emily Heppard spent hours transcribing my conversations with Steve Fiffer. My agent, Gail Hochman, found the perfect publisher. The staff and editors at Potomac Books provided superb assistance, especially Sabrina Stellrecht, Alicia Christensen, and Marguerite Boyles. I am indeed fortunate to be surrounded by such professionals.

ALL STATEMENTS OF fact, opinion, or analysis expressed are those of the author and do not reflect the official positions or views of any U.S. government agency. Nothing in the contents should be construed as asserting or implying U.S. government authentication of information or endorsement of the author's views. This material has been reviewed by the U.S. government to prevent the disclosure of classified information.

Many of the events and conversations related on the following pages took place several years ago. I have done my best to faithfully re-create them to the best of my memory and ability. In certain cases I have put conversations in italics to avoid giving the appearance that these are exact quotations. I have also changed the names of a few key aides to protect their identities.

DESERT DIPLOMAT

Prologue

SOMEWHERE—IN A FILE cabinet, or a desk, or a shoebox or an old coat pocket—is a note card with the date December 11, 2002, and several words penned by my shaky hand.

Here's what I remember of that day:

I left the State Department's Near East Bureau, a nondescript set of offices where I temporarily worked when in Washington DC. At the motor pool in the building's underground garage, the dispatcher located my assigned driver. He pulled up in a Ford Crown Victoria, the vehicle of choice for U.S. motor pools around the world. "Good morning, Mr. Ambassador," the driver said.

The cold December gray offered little of the beauty of Washington in nice weather, and I thought of President Kennedy's ironic quip that Washington is a city of southern efficiency . . . and northern charm. We headed down Constitution Avenue, then turned and pulled up to the White House's West Wing entrance.

I showed my diplomatic passport to the guard. He made a call. After a short wait, he gave me a badge hanging on a chain. I put the chain, which had a plastic badge with a big "A" on it, around my neck.

I turned off my cell phone and handed it to security. On a prior visit, I had forgotten to do so, and my ring tone—Norah Jones's *Come Away with Me*—had interrupted a meeting with Dick Cheney. The vice president had not been amused.

After passing through a metal detector, I was directed down the sidewalk from the guardhouse to the door leading to the reception area for the West Wing, not far from the White House Situation Room.

The waiting room, lined with a few sofas and a couple of chairs, was not large. Its warmth was a relief from the chill of the short walk from the guardhouse. People spoke in hushed voices. Occasionally a staff person would walk by carrying binders or stacks of papers.

After about half an hour, a staff assistant came and said, "Just a few more minutes." Finally, I heard the words, "Ambassador, please come in," and I walked into the Oval Office.

President Bush was wearing his suit coat, an American flag pin in his lapel. He offered a hearty handshake and said, "Jourdaaan, welcome"— purposely twisting my name into the French-sounding nickname he had bestowed on me several years earlier—after Louis Jourdan, a once-famous French actor from the 1950s and '60s. At least it was better than the moniker he gave Karl Rove: "Turd Blossom."

The president gestured to the two striped Queen Anne–style chairs in front of the Oval Office fireplace, and we sat down. I hadn't seen him in several months. The youthful, athletic look of the days before 9/11 was giving way to graying hair, wrinkles, and a pale complexion.

After asking me about the state of affairs in Saudi Arabia, the president turned to the need to secure Saudi support for U.S. opposition to Saddam Hussein. The Kingdom exerted tremendous influence in the region. Moreover, we occupied a military base there with troops and support aircraft. Looking me straight in the eye, he announced, "Bob, we're fixin' to do a regime change in Iraq."

The pronouncement was not a complete surprise, and there was no indication of how soon the shooting would start, but I felt a need for air. War was inevitable.

The president said that he felt that the inspectors looking for weapons of mass destruction in Iraq were getting nowhere and likely would not be allowed to complete their task. In his view the United Nations probably would not take decisive action, although there was still some time to pursue a diplomatic course.

My verbal response? "You have my support."

My mental response? *Can't the weapons inspectors have more time?*

The president's question? "How do you think the Saudis will respond?"

My answer? "Like the Rolling Stones say, 'You can't always get what you want, but you can get what you need.'"

The president had doubts that the Saudis would support an invasion, doubts that I suspected had been passed on to him by the leadership in Donald Rumsfeld's Defense Department. I disagreed and shared what the Saudis had privately expressed to me: while they didn't believe we understood what an invasion would mean to the region and to their own standing as a U.S. ally, they would be there for us when we needed them. They might condemn us in public, but in private we would get assistance in using bases, logistics, border crossings, and intelligence.

The president thanked me for my views, told me to keep my ear to the ground, and said he would need my help in getting the Saudis to follow through when the time came. I would be his "point man."

My scribbled card of December 11 includes this notation: "I'm running the show, not Rumsfeld or Cheney." During the visit, the president had asked me how the Saudis viewed Secretary of State Colin Powell. I said they liked him a lot but believed Cheney and Rumsfeld were "running the show." In one of the few times I have seen George W. Bush visibly angry, he whirled around to me, pointed his finger, and said, "You tell 'em *I'm* running the show!"

When our meeting was over, the president rose from his chair and then walked me through an adjoining office full of word processors and high-speed printers to the reception room door. We shook hands, and I thanked him for seeing me.

Leaving the Oval Office, I thanked the receptionist and headed out to the guardhouse to retrieve my cell phone and turn in my visitor's badge, depositing it into a slot that opened the gate to allow me to exit.

I returned to the State Department car that was waiting for me in the West Wing parking lot. I sat alone in the back seat—light-headed, hyperventilating, trying to process what had just happened. In a one-on-one meeting, the president of the United States had just confided something that very few people knew, but many suspected: he planned to go to war in Iraq.

Yes, we were already at war in Afghanistan. But we had a limited number of forces on the ground there. Equally important, in that country, we weren't trying to topple a regime run by a madman—a regime that, if in possession of weapons of mass destruction, would likely use them against our troops and our allies in the region—namely Saudi Arabia.

My heart racing, I pulled that note card from my pocket and wrote down, "Pres. (12/11/02) If attack SH [Saddam Hussein] we'll win. Fixing to do so in March."

Holy shit, I said to myself, knowing I could never share this secret with anyone, *I can't believe what I just heard.*

Just fifteen months earlier, I'd been a Dallas trial lawyer whose biggest worry was paying for the college educations of my three sons. I'd had no diplomatic experience, knew very little about the Kingdom of Saudi Arabia. Now *my* help would be needed in dealing with the government of the nation most important to our success in prosecuting that regime change.

"Point man"? How the hell had that happened?

1

IN MARCH 1949, J. Rives Childs, the fifth U.S. ambassador to Saudi Arabia, flew to Riyadh to present his credentials to King Abdulaziz ibn Saud and establish our first embassy in the capital city. Childs was an interesting character. Although a career foreign service officer, he was known for his literary accomplishments as much as his diplomatic ones. He wrote four books on the eighteenth-century Italian libertine Casanova and corresponded regularly with the groundbreaking American novelist Henry Miller.

A year before his trip to Riyadh, Childs had published *American Foreign Service*, a book about the traditions and operations of the U.S. diplomatic corps. The new ambassador was, however, ill-prepared for his meeting with Abdulaziz. Outfitted in Arab robes, as was the custom, Childs and two of his aides entered the royal palace's receiving room. After a brief conversation through an interpreter, Childs shook hands with the monarch, bowed, and backed out of the room. While this kind of exit is de rigueur when meeting the king or queen of England, it is not the preferred method in Saudi Arabia. Childs's aides knew this, but they did not want to embarrass their superior. They left in the same fashion as the ambassador.

Unfortunately, before Childs could make it out of the hall, he backed into a pillar and tumbled to the floor. Moments later, the aides—their eyes forward—tripped over him and also fell. Their robes tangled, the not-so-quiet Americans lay on the ground until Abdulaziz's son Prince Faisal helped them up.[1]

As I flew to Riyadh in early October 2001 to take my post as the twenty-fifth U.S. ambassador to Saudi Arabia, I knew how to enter and exit audiences with the king, but I felt almost as ill-prepared as J. Rives Childs. Today the Kingdom insists that the U.S. ambassador be a political appointee and refuses to grant diplomatic credentials (called *agrément*) to a career foreign service officer. The Saudis want the ambassador to be a friend of the president who can get the White House on the phone at a moment's notice. They also want someone who can go over the heads of the bureaucrats and who has no government career to protect.

I was not a diplomat familiar with the ways of the region but rather a litigator familiar with the ways of the state and federal courts. I'd received some training in advance of my departure, but world events had intervened to cut short such schooling and hasten my departure. I did not speak Arabic.

It's fair to ask what qualified me, or any other political appointee for that matter, to be an ambassador. Thomas Jefferson strongly believed in "citizen diplomats," people from different walks of life who would bring their private-sector experience to a temporary government role and then ultimately return home to enrich their communities with their added experience and perspective. This seemed like a noble purpose, and I hoped that my background might add something to the effort.

A little about that background:

I was born in 1945 and grew up in Tulsa, Oklahoma. We were a family of modest means. My father worked for oil companies and the U.S. Agency for International Development. Often he lived abroad—in Venezuela, Peru (where I lived when I was a young boy), Libya, Hong Kong (where I lived during one college summer), and Vietnam (during the war). I went to college at Duke on a partial scholarship, graduating in 1967.

Just before receiving my military draft notice at the height of the Vietnam conflict, I was accepted into Navy Officer Candidate School, and then I volunteered for the Naval Security Group, a code-breaking, intercept operation. Because I had studied Russian, I expected to be sent to a minesweeper in the Gulf of Tonkin to monitor Soviet communications. Instead I spent 3½ years in the group's Washington headquarters as the administrative officer, effectively the assistant to the station's commanding officer.

During this time, I took night classes at the University of Maryland and received a master's in international relations. My major research project focused on the U.S. Senate's Foreign Relations Committee. Here I learned how important staff is in influencing policy—a lesson that would serve me well when dealing with visiting senators and congresspersons in Saudi Arabia.

After the navy, I went back home to the University of Oklahoma Law School on the GI Bill. I worked my way through school as a clerk in a firm and was honored to become editor in chief of the law review. After graduating from law school in 1974, I became a trial lawyer in a Dallas firm. A dozen years later, I helped found the newly opened Dallas office of the Houston-based law firm Baker Botts.

In January 1989, I first met George W. Bush in passing at a Washington reception that my firm hosted on the occasion of his father's inauguration. Two years later our paths crossed again, as I successfully represented him in a federal securities investigation that could have derailed his political career before it started.

When Bush ran for governor of Texas and then president, he asked if I would be on call to explain the investigation to the media. In the race for governor, it was a hot topic in the closing weeks of the campaign. Both Bush and his opponent, the incumbent Ann Richards, flooded the airwaves with television ads that featured the letter I received from the Securities and Exchange Commission closing the investigation. Bush highlighted the fact that the investigation was over, calling it an "exoneration." Richards highlighted other words and argued that the matter was simply being closed and was not an exoneration. Bush won in a major upset. In the presidential campaign, the investigation rarely came up.

During this time period, my wife, Ann, and I periodically socialized with the Bush family. We enjoyed a few overnight stays in the governor's mansion and went to some Texas Rangers baseball games together. I was not, however, part of his inner circle.

After the 2000 presidential election was finally resolved, I thought that, at age fifty-five, it might be interesting to work in government for a few years. The president-elect told me he'd like me to serve but that I should be very specific in saying what position I would like. He didn't want to have to figure it out for me.

Having been an attorney for over twenty-five years, served as president of the Dallas Bar Association, and previously represented our new commander in chief, I suggested that perhaps White House counsel would be a fit. But the president-elect told me that he had already penciled in Alberto Gonzales for that post. Since I'd thoroughly enjoyed my time as a naval security officer and my father had served in the navy at Normandy, my second choice was secretary of the navy. Unfortunately, the president indicated he wanted that position to go to what he called a "procurement jock," someone steeped in the arcane ways of military procurement.

There was an opening for associate attorney general, the number-three spot in the Justice Department. But my one-on-one with Attorney General John Ashcroft did not go well. We did not see the world the same way, and he clearly wanted his own people under him, not a Bush guy. That was fine with me.

By spring 2001 I was happily resigned to remaining in the private sector. Then a call came from the White House: Would I be interested in serving as U.S. ambassador to Saudi Arabia? (Or, to be precise, ambassador extraordinary and plenipotentiary.) Hmm. I had lived abroad as a child, had studied a few languages, though not Arabic, and had that master's in international relations. A year or two overseas might be interesting.

But Saudi Arabia? Although I grew up in Oklahoma and practiced litigation involving energy companies in the Lone Star State, I was not a transactional oil lawyer. I knew little about the country. What I thought I knew, however, was closer to the stereotypical view of an intolerant regime that did not treat women well. I was concerned.

Instead of accepting on the spot, I asked for time to think it over. And I took more time than normal, two or three weeks. During one conversation with White House Chief of Staff Andy Card, I expressed my reservations.

Andy replied, "Bob, can you do a year? If you can't do a year, then don't do it; if you can, then any additional time you spend will just be on the plus side." I figured I could do anything for a year but still wasn't ready to commit.

Ann was also unenthusiastic. She shared my concerns about the image of how women were treated in the Kingdom, and she thought her own career as a professor of anthropology at the University of North Texas would suffer if she had to take a year or two off from her research. Her specialty was American Indians, and she spent several weeks each summer living on a Sioux Indian reservation in South Dakota.

Our twenty-two-year-old son, Peter, however, provided an insightful view. It wasn't that he wanted his old man out of his hair halfway across the world. "Dad," he said, "when the president of the United States asks you to serve, you can't say no." I knew he was right.

My law partners also encouraged me to say yes. The counsel I received from one of them, Jim Baker, the U.S. secretary of state under President George H. W. Bush, influenced my decision. He said he that of all the political ambassadorial appointments, Saudi Arabia was the most important in terms of having a real impact and a real job to do.

Ray Mabus, a former ambassador to the Kingdom (and later secretary of the navy) whom I consulted, agreed. He said that I'd become the second most important person in Saudi Arabia next to the king, that I would have instant access to the monarch, and that I would be involved in some very important bilateral relationship issues and have a lot of autonomy and independence.

In April 2001 I accepted the offer. Three months later—after I'd filled out all the proper forms and been vetted by the FBI—the president announced my appointment, telling the press, "Bob Jordan is a leader in his profession and in his community. He understands the important relationship that exists between the United States and Saudi Arabia, and I am confident he will be an outstanding ambassador."[2]

At the time of my nomination, we didn't have an ambassador to the Kingdom; my predecessor, Wyche Fowler Jr., had resigned in March. But I was told that most of the ambassadorial confirmation hearings would not take place until early 2002. Such are the ways of Washington. Speaking Arabic is not a prerequisite for the job, but I thought it would be helpful. I made arrangements to take a course later in the fall.

Between July and September, I was briefed by former U.S. ambassadors to Saudi Arabia and other countries in the region, by experts at the National Security Council, and by career diplomats at the State

Department, including Karen Sasahara, a young foreign service officer who had served a tour in Jeddah, the Kingdom's second largest city;
assistant secretary of state for the Near East and former ambassador to
Jordan Bill Burns; and ambassador to Syria Ryan Crocker, who would
go on to ambassadorships in Pakistan, Iraq, and Afghanistan.

The briefings were not particularly comforting. Ryan told me that the
Saudi man on the street viewed Americans as decadent and immoral.

When I expressed my own reservations about the Saudi state's view
of women and Jews, Ray Mabus told me that I'd be dealing with good
family people in the government. He and others acknowledged that the
Saudis were moving too slowly on the human rights front but suggested
I should think of myself as an anthropologist in foreign territory. At the
same time others told me, "This is really an awful situation; sort of hold
your tongue from time to time and do the best you can."

Absorbing all this information as best I could, I was of two minds.
Sometimes I thought, *I'm not sure if I'm going to be able to tolerate it.
I'll do the best I can. I've committed to a year and if I can't stand it, I'll
get out.* But other times I thought, or at least hoped, *Maybe there's a way
I can make it better.*

I kept thinking of the biblical axiom, "Blessed are the peacemakers."
I had not been going to church regularly, but now I returned. Maybe
my role, perhaps by providence, was to somehow be a peacemaker, not
just between Israelis and Palestinians, but regarding the way in which
human beings were treated inside Saudi Arabia.

After I received my security clearance, the State Department sent
me over to the CIA. I've been there many times now, but my first visit
to headquarters in Langley, Virginia, was overwhelming. Entering, you
see a wall engraved with the names of agents who have lost their lives
in the line of duty. The operation is high tech; you are given little cards
and pass through several little gates, weaving through labyrinthine halls
to rooms that require special IDs. People speak in hushed tones.

On my visits I was briefed in detail on a number of subjects. Understandably, our country wants to know as much as possible about the leaders and potential leaders of all nations, especially nations as important
to our interests as Saudi Arabia. I quickly learned a great deal about
the royal family.

The first king of the modern Kingdom, Abdulaziz, ruled from 1932 to 1953. He was a direct descendant of the patriarch of the Saud family, Muhammad ibn Saud, who formed the "First Saudi State," which lasted from 1744 to 1818, when the Ottoman Empire interceded. According to the Quran, a Muslim can have four wives at any one time. He can also divorce and remarry as many times as he wants. Abdulaziz kept quite busy, as he was said to have married a daughter of every tribal chieftain in Saudi Arabia. The king had at least twenty-two wives (presumably within the Quranic stricture to have only four at a time), who bore him some forty-five legitimate sons.

All six kings following Abdulaziz have been his sons, but not all those sons shared the same mother. Rivalries abound, especially among half brothers whose mothers came from different tribes. Crown Prince Abdullah, who had assumed control of the country after his half brother King Fahd was incapacitated by a stroke in 1995, seemed to be Fahd's logical successor. But some of Abdullah's half brothers were said to oppose his ascension to the throne.[3]

Think tanks with an interest in the region also sought me out. The Washington-based Meridian International Center was particularly helpful. Center president Walter Cutler, who had served as ambassador to Saudi Arabia on two different occasions, arranged meetings with up to thirty Saudi experts at a time.

I tried to prepare for my new posting in the same way that I would prepare for complex litigation—by knowing my subject inside out and anticipating the unanticipated. I picked the brains of any expert willing to share his or her insights. My questions fell into two major areas—substantive and administrative.

On the substantive side: How do the senior people in the Saudi government think? What are their priorities? What are they going to be wanting from me, and what do I then want from them on behalf of the U.S. government? What are the issues that are bubbling up? What are the things that don't get covered in the press, that are perhaps secret, but are the really animating issues between the two countries and in their relationship?

On the administrative side: How do you run an embassy? What's expected? How much can I rely on the career people? What are the pitfalls? There was a second part to this: How do I also deal with Congress? With congressional oversight? With the media? With all of the other stakeholders that would have an interest in my success or failure?

Help with the administrative side came in August, when Ann and I attended the Ambassadorial Seminar, aka Charm School 101, in Washington. Over two weeks, ten of us nominees for postings in countries as different as Indonesia, Sweden, and Tanzania and our spouses were taught the ins and outs of running an embassy by former ambassadors, including Tony Motley, who had served in Brazil.

Based at the State Department, we were briefed by such luminaries as U.S. ambassador to the UN John Negroponte, who would go on to serve as our first ambassador to Iraq and our first director of national intelligence. He had previously been an ambassador to Mexico, the Philippines, and Honduras. His advice? *Remember, people are looking to you to be in charge. Act like you're in charge. Get to know the people in your embassy. Realize your first job is to protect American citizens in your country and to preserve classified material in your embassy. Understand why you're there.*

Secretary of State Colin Powell also spoke to us. In time, he and I would become strong allies, as I supported his approach and policies in most cases. We often had issues with the tone and policies of Defense Secretary Rumsfeld. One thing Powell told me informed my conduct once I became ambassador: *I put a lot of faith in my generals in the field, and I expect them to be the ones who come to me with suggestions rather than me telling them. I'll say either yes or no.*

I recall two other important pieces of advice from the seminar. Former ambassador Motley told us, "You have to come in and take charge of your mission, and you have to let people know you're taking charge." He said that when he first walked into our embassy in Brazil, he pulled the fire alarm switch. He explained that he wanted to see what people would do in the event of an emergency and that he also wanted to let people know that he was going to be proactive, that he was the type of leader who didn't mind getting in their grills.

I never did pull a fire alarm, but I followed to the letter the suggestion of another leader—I don't remember whom—who said, "You've always got to be ready to feed the beast." In other words, don't wait for Washington to send you instructions; you need to constantly send the players back home your views on what is going on and your positions on what the policies or tactics ought to be. Preemptively fill the vacuum yourself before it's filled for you.

I also took to heart the advice of Jim Baker. "Don't get clientitis," he counseled. This sounds like a dangerous disease, and in a sense it is. Diplomats, Jim told me, have a tendency to fall in love with their host countries. As they get to know the people, their history, and their culture, those in the foreign service understandably want the nation to succeed. This is fine as long as such success coincides with the goals and policies of the United States. The role of the ambassador, of the entire embassy staff, is to serve their own country, not their host.

The Ambassadorial Seminar included a trip to Fort Bragg, North Carolina, for a demonstration of the military's ability to thwart terrorism. Embassies, we knew, were a prime target of terrorists. Three years earlier hundreds had been killed in coordinated truck bombings in Dar es Salaam, Tanzania, and in Nairobi, Kenya.

Riding a bus to a firing range on the Fort Bragg base, my fellow ambassadorial appointees and I were rocked by an explosion. Suddenly two armed terrorists rushed in and took us hostage. Within seconds, we heard helicopters.

Looking out our windows, we saw U.S. commandos rappelling down from the choppers. They stormed the bus and quickly took out our captors. By this time we all realized that the event had been staged to demonstrate the skill of the Special Forces who might be called upon to rescue us in a real-life situation. Needless to say, however, our hearts were in our throats for a few frightful moments.

When we got to the rifle range, we were taken into a building with an area set up like a living room. There was a glass screen in the quarters, and we were told there was another room on the other side. "Okay," one of our handlers said, "now were going to show you an example of a hostage rescue within a room or building."

Bam! Another explosion. The commandos came into the room on the other side of the screen, where we now saw cardboard cutouts of terrorists and captives. In a live-fire exercise, the commandos blew out the brains of the cardboard terrorists and didn't harm the hostages. Comforting, I guess.

"Okay, now we're going to do this with the lights off, a night exercise," said our handler. "We need a couple of you guys to come in here and sit down as hostages." Two of my colleagues, far braver than I, volunteered.

Another *Bam!* Lights out. Commandos wearing night-vision goggles stormed in. Terrorists killed. Hostages again saved. When the details of the successful Navy Seal mission to get Osama bin Laden were revealed some ten years later, I had no trouble picturing the raid.

Speaking of bin Laden: he was on the radar of the State Department, CIA, National Security Council, and everybody else with whom I spoke about security issues *before September 11*. He was on the FBI's Ten Most Wanted list for his role in the embassy bombings and was even persona non grata within his native country. Saudi Arabia had banished him in 1994 after his repeated criticism of its decision to allow U.S. troops in the Kingdom during the first Gulf War in 1991.

I should add here that in all my briefings and discussions prior to my confirmation, there was no discussion of a potential attack on the U.S. homeland by bin Laden or anybody else. The focus was on potential attacks on the embassies. Saudi Arabia, as I recall, was considered to be a breeding ground for the ideological juice for terrorism, as well as home to a number of jihadis who were returning from Afghanistan with a taste for bloodshed.

Crawford, Texas, was also on my August itinerary. I decided, and the White House agreed, that it would be nice for me to meet with the president at his ranch and get some photos taken to display at the embassy, as well as have some private time with him and the First Lady. The people back in Washington thought the photos would heighten my credentials as an intimate of his, giving me a little more leverage with staff, visiting U.S. officials, the media, and foreign diplomats.

Harriet Miers, assistant to the president and staff secretary, made the arrangements. I had known Harriet, a highly respected fellow Dallas lawyer who would later make headlines as a (brief) Supreme Court nominee, for thirty years. Before driving to the ranch, I called to ask her if I could show up at the ranch in my foreign coupe or if I should switch to a U.S.-made car. I didn't want to create any waves with the media by being politically incorrect. She said a foreign car was fine; she was driving an aging red Mercedes.

Harriet told me that after I cleared the security roadblocks outside the ranch, I should come to the double-wide trailer with the pink flamingo in front. A pink flamingo in front of a double-wide? That's where she lived and worked when the president was in Crawford. Complete with young staffers, a laundry machine, and a well-stocked refrigerator, the trailer was like a college dorm. Harriet—presidential confidante and den mother—and I shot the breeze until I received word to join the Bushes for lunch.

Told to dress casual, I wore my khakis, a denim shirt, a cowboy belt, and boots. I carried a cowboy hat as well. My Howdy Doody or Hopalong Cassidy outfit looked formal compared to the president's garb. He was wearing a torn plaid shirt, ragged jeans, and sneakers with no socks. Laura Bush wore shorts and a t-shirt.

The new ranch house was relatively modest. It featured one wing with a kitchen and dining area and another wing with living quarters. In between was a screened-in porch with a poured concrete floor. We chatted there for a bit as the First Family dogs, Barney and Spot, vied with me for the commander in chief's attention. Barney, the famous black Scottie, was a little under the weather. A scorpion had apparently bitten him on the nose the previous day—a not-uncommon occurrence in the country. The president was not sympathetic. "Barney," he admonished, "you gotta suck it up! Act like a man, dog!"

After lunch we posed for some "candid" pictures in which my host can be seen pointing off in the distance in a very presidential way. Then we climbed into his Ford F250 pickup truck for a tour of the ranch. The Secret Service followed in an suv. Ever the joker, the president started fishtailing in the mud—it had been raining—throwing all sorts of slop at those charged with protecting him.

Tremendously proud of the ranch, Bush took me on tiny back roads, showing me some seventeen varieties of trees, a waterfall, and a stocked fishing pond. We passed a few cattle and a lot more Secret Service agents strategically arrayed across the property in kiosks. "Fortified" is perhaps too strong a word to describe the ranch, but no stones had been left unturned to assure the security of the First Family.

After lunch we moved to the porch for a discussion about the Middle East. The president was blunt. He acknowledged that he had little political capital this early in his term because he had lost the popular vote in 2000 and had been put into office by the Supreme Court. Whatever capital he did have was not going to be spent trying to do what his predecessors had tried and failed at: brokering peace between the Israelis and Palestinians.

They clearly didn't want to be partners for peace, he said. Israeli prime minister Ariel Sharon and Palestinian leader Yasser Arafat had shown no resolve to come to any kind of agreement, and until they did, he wasn't going to step in. He said he felt that President Clinton had wasted the last eighteen months of his second term trying to broker something.

I understood his logic. There had to be more than a modicum of will on the parties' part before sticking out the presidential neck. At this time, there wasn't. But support for this hands-off strategy was not universal.

On the day before my visit, the president had received a letter from the leader of the country where I'd soon be heading. Crown Prince Abdullah expressed his bitter disappointment with Bush on the Israeli-Palestinian issue. If the United States didn't start to show more leadership, Abdullah suggested, the Saudis would have to reevaluate their relationship with us, including their oil policy. This was not the best news for an ambassadorial appointee to hear.

"Just wanted to give you a heads up," the president said. He added that he hadn't yet decided how to respond to Abdullah.

As we finished our talk—I was there for about 2½ hours—the president said, "You know, my dad knows the Saudis a whole lot better than I do. You need to go down and see him in Houston when he comes back from vacation next week. He's in Kennebunkport right now. In fact, Prince Bandar is there with him."

Prince Bandar bin Sultan, a member of the royal family, was the longtime Saudi ambassador to the United States. He was so close to George H. W. Bush that he was nicknamed "Bandar Bush." I had yet to meet him.

A week or so later I went to see the elder President Bush in his office on Memorial Drive. After passing muster with the Secret Service and a bomb-sniffing dog, I took my meeting. We talked for about an hour about Saudi Arabia in general and some of its leaders in particular. He reserved his kindest words for Bandar. Gracious as usual, he posed for a few pictures with me.

As I started to leave, he stopped me. "Wait, Bob, come back," he said. He then pulled out a note card, wrote something on it, put it in an envelope unsealed, and said, "Here, give this to Bandar when you see him."

I said "all right" and "thank you" and left. Of course I had to sneak a look at the note (as I'm sure President Bush expected). It read,

Dear Bandar,

Great having you last week. Sorry the fish weren't biting.

PLEASE BE NICE TO THIS GUY OR BARBARA WILL GET YOU!

GHWB

This became my currency with Bandar. When we first met, I gave him the note. As he read it, he began to smile and then cackled out loud.

And then . . . Less than a month after my visits with Bush 41 and Bush 43, everything changed.

On September 11, 2001, I took my chair at the board meeting of the Dallas Foundation, a venerable Dallas charity that dispenses millions of dollars for worthy causes. This would be my final meeting, as my ambassadorial nomination was in process and I would soon be preparing for a late 2001 or early 2002 confirmation hearing, completing my indoctrination, briefings, and language school, and heading to Riyadh.

As I was nibbling on a roll and drinking my coffee, fellow board member Walter Humann hurried into the room. "A plane just hit the World Trade Center!" he exclaimed. I was seated next to Albert Black, a pal on the board and a distinguished leader in the Dallas business community. We looked at each other, unable to believe what we heard. As the events of that morning unfolded, our disbelief turned to shock.

Thinking ahead to the mission confronting me, I knew my life would never again be the same. Of course, the impact on me was neither as profound nor as tragic as the impact on the families who lost loved ones that day, but I knew my posting to Saudi Arabia had become a lot more important and a helluva lot scarier than it had been on September 10.

As the meeting disbanded I called Washington but could not get through to the State Department. I finally reached a duty officer and ultimately got word from Bill Burns to stand by and provide contact information. I went home and stayed glued to the television for hours as each sickening piece of news drilled into me an awareness of how immense this horror was.

Michael Hudson, a professor of Arab studies at Georgetown University, told the *Dallas Morning News*, "It [the ambassadorship to Saudi Arabia] absolutely is the most challenging post for an ambassador right now, excepting only maybe Pakistan, and for a lot of the same reasons."[4]

"Challenging" seemed like an understatement as I learned about all I'd be dealing with when I got to Riyadh. For starters there was the fact that the mastermind behind the attacks, Osama bin Laden, was a member of a prominent Saudi family and that fifteen of the nineteen hijackers were from the Kingdom. In denial, senior Saudi royals were advancing the preposterous argument that the attacks had been conducted by Israel, not Al Qaeda.

CIA director George Tenet and FBI director Bob Mueller each briefed me on the need to roll up the terrorist cells that we all suspected existed in Saudi Arabia. They also expressed their concerns that the operation may have been funded by well-to-do, well-connected Saudis. Never, however, was there an accusation that the king or any senior royals in the government had any involvement.

There was more. We had swiftly launched our own war on terror in Afghanistan, and our use of Prince Sultan Air Base in Saudi Arabia was essential. The Kingdom had given us permission to conduct operations from that base but was less than enthusiastic about the U.S. bombing of fellow Muslims. I'd be our nation's man on the ground talking to the Saudis about all of the above, not to mention their troubling record on human rights and their unhappiness over the Israeli-Palestinian conflict.

Then there was the question of safety, if not survival. If the U.S. embassy in Riyadh was considered a target before 9/11, now it had a bull's-eye on its front door. Friends and family were concerned about my safety, and many counseled me to bow out. Tempting as it was to find an excuse, I couldn't help thinking of my father, who had risked his life for his country by participating in the D-Day invasion of Normandy and working in Vietnam for the U.S. government during the height of the war there.

Briefings by the State Department persuaded me that security was a top priority. Still, while I never thought of telling the president that I'd changed my mind, I knew that I wouldn't bring any family members over until I was satisfied they'd be safe. As it was, Ann did not come to Riyadh until the summer of 2002.

Most people are surprised to learn that at the time of the deadliest attack on America in history, we had no ambassador to the country that was most closely associated with the action and was essential to prosecute the war on terror. The reality is, however, that ambassadorial positions often remain open for some months when administrations change. Career diplomats assigned to the embassies fill in until the nominees are confirmed.

The White House was scheduled to formally send my nomination to the Senate on September 4. Unfortunately, the White House counsel's office screwed up the paperwork. The new date? September 11. Obviously, the events of that day prevented submission. And so I was nominated on September 12.

There was some media hyperventilation to the effect of, *Gee, finally President Bush gets around to nominating an ambassador to Saudi Arabia one day after 9/11.* As if it had just occurred to him on 9/11 that we needed an ambassador there! Not so. It was just a bureaucratic mix-up.

Aware of the need to fill the vacuum, the White House and the Senate did put the nomination on the fast track. I hurriedly visited senators on the Foreign Relations Committee. My State Department handlers prepared me for tough questioning about my views on human rights, women's rights, religious freedom, terrorism, and the importance of the stability of the oil markets. I worried that some senators might ask about clients my law firm had represented.

Frankly, I didn't know the answers to everything that might be asked and didn't want to give some answers that I did know. For example, I had to walk a fine line between being sympathetic on human rights issues and not saying anything that would offend my soon-to-be-host country. I didn't want to arrive in Riyadh with a paper trail making the Saudis wary of me. My hearing was similar to that of a Supreme Court nominee who tries to give as many nonanswers as possible. There was a lot of, "I'll just have to deal with that when I get there."

Fortunately the senators were anxious to get a U.S. ambassador on the ground in the Kingdom. The questioning was short and noncontentious, and I was easily confirmed. Secretary of State Powell quickly swore me in at a small ceremony attended by my family, State Department officials, Saudi embassy representatives, and my former law partners. He reminded me how important it was to keep in touch, particularly with Bill Burns on the Near East desk. He also emphasized how important it was to take charge of the mission, to make sure that they understood that I was the boss.

By the second week in October, I was on my way to Riyadh, an accidental ambassador going to the country that had given us Osama bin Laden.

Well, almost on my way. I was to fly commercial out of Washington's Dulles International. Shut down on September 11, the airport had recently reopened. Security was tight. So tight that the new U.S. ambassador to Saudi Arabia was pulled out of line and his carry-on luggage clumsily searched. I had no idea what I'd done to arouse suspicion, but I didn't pull rank and tell anyone who I was.

2

FROM MY PLANE window the desert below was pitch black. As we headed toward Riyadh, I wondered how long it would be before I could see signs of civilization. And what would that civilization look like? Fighting off the exhaustion of last-minute briefings, the Senate confirmation hearing, the hurried swearing-in by Colin Powell, and an eighteen-hour trip, I felt both the adrenaline rush of a thrilling new adventure and an uneasy remorse that I had left a comfortable life, friends, and family to come to a place on earth completely unlike anything I had ever experienced.

The flight attendants began preparing the cabin for landing, yet I still saw no signs of life in the darkness below. Would there be an official greeting and press conference, as I had been warned might be the case? I had prepared some brief remarks in that event.

Four weeks after the attacks of September 11 and one week into the bombing of the Taliban in Afghanistan, I wondered if the Saudi streets would be teeming with terrorist sympathizers. Had there been any additional attacks while I had been in the air? Was my staff at the embassy up to the challenge of this new world?

Finally, as the landing gear was activated, I saw the lights of the city. They looked much like the lights of Charlotte or Oklahoma City. We eased onto the tarmac and taxied up to a large, modern terminal that would seem more comfortable in a major Western capital—except for the minaret peering out from the mosque next door.

I made my way into the brightly lit terminal and was relieved to be greeted by my deputy chief of mission (DCM), Margaret Scobey. A veteran of Middle East diplomacy, she had served in Yemen when the USS *Cole* was attacked and in Kuwait. She was a rising star in the State Department, where the "hall talk" was that she was smart, congenial, and tough when necessary. By chance, she'd taken her post in Riyadh on September 10. She would soon become my trusted right arm, then move on to ambassadorships in Syria and Egypt.

Margaret was surrounded by Saudis in white robes and checkered head scarves, some wearing shoulder holsters. They were my new best friends, my bodyguards. The embassy expediter took my baggage claim ticket and passport and attended to the formalities of retrieving my luggage and having my passport stamped.

The bodyguards rushed us through the terminal and into my waiting car. To my surprise, the car was an armored BMW, not the Ford or Cadillac so often used for government officials in the States. I later learned that no American car manufacturer made regular-sized cars with armor from the factory. *Armor is good*, I thought. So, too, was the button you could push to have an oil slick come out the back.

My driver pulled out and left the terminal quickly, entering a freeway ramp into the night. One bodyguard sat up front. Margaret accompanied me in the back. Another car full of bodyguards led the way.

In a few days I would acquire a second car full of bodyguards who would trail the lead car and my vehicle, cutting through traffic and heading off any car that approached us too closely. All of the men behind the wheel had been trained in special driving techniques. My trio of cars would weave in and out of traffic synchronized like tango dancers, one edging ahead of the other to fend off other cars, while the trail car protected our rear.

Saudi Arabia, which is about one-fifth the size of the United States, has a population of about 27 million people, including over 5 million nonnationals—mostly foreigners who have come to work there. Riyadh, population about 4.5 million at the time, is the Kingdom's largest city. It sits on a sizable plateau two thousand feet above sea level in the middle of the country, hundreds of miles from the bodies of water surrounding the Arabian Peninsula—the Persian Gulf (*always* called the Arabian Gulf in the Arab world), the Indian Ocean, and the Red Sea.

As we sped down the freeway, I noticed several rows of houses, dimly lit by street lighting, apparently stucco, with high stucco fences around them, punctuated by tall iron gates. We entered the edges of the central city, marked by taller buildings.

One building in the distance was taller than the rest, a modern skyscraper with a globe or a ball at the top. It was the Al Faisaliah Tower, a landmark that I would visit many times. Nearby was another skyscraper under construction, the Kingdom Tower, whose owner, Prince Alwaleed bin Talal, was one of the five richest men in the world.

Mosques were visible everywhere. The Kingdom is, after all, the birthplace of the Muslim religion. In 610, the prophet Mohammed was visited in Mecca by the angel Gabriel and instructed to proclaim God's (Allah's) message. Mecca, some five hundred miles southwest of Riyadh, remains the nation's holiest city, the destination of the annual hajj, or pilgrimage.

As we headed into the western part of the city, we entered an orderly neighborhood of boxy stucco buildings and homes, interspersed with square stucco apartment buildings and low-rise office buildings. Unlike the streets intermittently lined with rubble in the outlying areas, these streets were elaborately landscaped with palm trees and flowers. We had arrived in the Diplomatic Quarter and in a minute were entering the gate of my new residence, Quincy House.

Quincy House is named after the uss *Quincy*, the warship on which, in 1945, President Franklin Roosevelt and King Abdulaziz struck the deal that still animates the relationship between the two countries: in exchange for preferred access to a stable supply of Saudi oil, the United States would protect the Kingdom from foreign aggression. Why hadn't such an alliance been forged years earlier? Abdulaziz had established the modern Kingdom of Saudi Arabia only in 1932, after years of battle with warring tribes. And oil hadn't been discovered in Saudi Arabia until 1938. Until then, what is now one of the richest nations in the world was one of the poorest.

Motoring through the gate to Quincy House, I noticed the American flag flying on a tall pole in the courtyard. A private security guard gave me a quick salute as he let our car in. As Margaret and I stepped onto the marble and granite driveway and entry, we saw the house staff lined up to greet me.

Those who would take care of me so well during my posting came from all over the world. The butler, Rudy, was from the Philippines, as were the maids, Estella and Carlotta. The cook, Abdu, was Moroccan. Gopal, the assistant cook/assistant butler, was from southern India.

Rudy shook my hand with enthusiasm and led me on a tour of the house. The foyer faced a grand staircase with brass railing on each side. The floors were polished parquet covered with a hand-loomed round blue carpet with thirteen white stars around the edge. A baby grand piano rested just off the carpet. The look struck me as slightly nautical, somewhat like the ballroom of an elegant cruise ship.

The polished wood covered the walls of the living room and dining room, each with a high atrium ceiling revealing shuttered balconies on the second-floor family living quarters. Two months earlier a fire had damaged the upstairs quarters and new furniture had been brought in—a surprisingly casual array of comfortable white sofas and chairs reminiscent of a California living room. The dining table accommodated twenty-eight for a formal dinner, and the downstairs industrial kitchen would have done the Plaza Hotel proud.

Upstairs, the family quarters did not reflect the elegance of the public spaces downstairs. Due to the fire, however, all the furniture and carpeting were new. The atrium ceilings of the downstairs living and dining rooms cut the upstairs space into two long corridors, one containing the living and dining area, the other the bedrooms—a bit like two bowling alleys. At the top of the stairs was a guest suite for VIPs. The upstairs furniture was solid and functional in the manner of a mid-level hotel chain.

Rudy brought me some sandwiches and soup, and the expediter arrived with my baggage. I looked out at the backyard below and saw a nicely lighted swimming pool and tennis court surrounded by palm trees and crepe myrtles. A security guard patrolled in the shadows. I wondered how much time I would have for these amenities and how much privacy I could expect.

After the long flight and unpacking, I was ready to call it a night.

Riyadh time was eight hours later than Washington, nine later than Dallas. I wondered about friends and family back home, still in the middle of their day.

What was home now? I looked across the bedroom at the emergency lights and walkie-talkie radios. *Just in case of an emergency.* As I headed to bed, I adjusted the blackout curtains and turned out the lights. Time for sleep in a land so foreign it seemed like Mars. As I drifted off, I felt like mumbling, "Toto, we're not in Kansas anymore."

Sleep was fitful. Suddenly voices crackled over the walkie-talkie. I sat up straight. Back to sleep. More walkie-talkie chatter and static. I decided I did not need to monitor the chatter of Marine Corps security guards or motor pool dispatchers and turned the volume down.

Sooner than I expected, rays of light beamed through the cracks in the blackout curtains. Daylight comes early in Saudi Arabia, and before six o'clock the sun was out in full force. From my window I could see the top of the American flag by the front guard post. My room opened onto an outdoor balcony, but for security reasons the concrete and stucco balcony was about five feet tall, providing no chance at a view beyond the top of the flagpole and little reason to lounge on the outdoor furniture outside. This design had all the charm of a Soviet bunker, but I was grateful for the blast protection in the event of an attack.

After breakfast and a quick review of the Saudi English-language newspapers, I met my driver and bodyguards downstairs and headed to the embassy, about ten minutes away. Once there, we pulled past armored personnel carriers and machine guns manned by Saudi soldiers at the entrance, driving into the motor pool area where the third-country drivers and mechanics mingled with embassy staff. All snapped to an alert posture upon my arrival, flashing earnest smiles of recognition and respect.

Margaret met me at the entrance to the building, and we jumped into the elevator to go up to my new office. Secretaries and administrative assistants greeted me warmly as we went inside. The office was large but appeared remarkably cold. The concrete and glass embassy structure mirrored the Stalinesque exterior of Quincy House but was much less inviting inside. The black lacquer desk had a Chinese look to it, and the leather sofas faced a fireplace that seemed oddly out of place in a country where temperatures could exceed 120 degrees. Fax machines, along with secure and standard telephones, lined the credenza. Unfortunately, the encrypted telephone system was far from state of the art; it dated back to the 1950s.

Many Americans seem to believe that much of an embassy's staff is made up of undercover intelligence agents. Here's what I can tell you: almost every U.S. embassy has what's called a legal attaché. It's well known that this "legat" is the title used for the head FBI agent in that country. We had a legat and a couple of other FBI agents in the embassy, but in 2001 the FBI was not accustomed to operating overseas, especially in the Middle East. As a result, few of their agents spoke Arabic—a rather important skill when it comes to gathering information and conducting interrogations.

Our deputy legat spoke Arabic, but he was fired—for being too good a Muslim, apparently. He was accused—perhaps incorrectly—of having refused to tape-record an informant within the confines of a mosque. He was also viewed with suspicion for wearing native dress such as white robes. There was a real cultural witch hunt going on within the FBI at the time. Talk was, the FBI "liked to eat their own." And they were voracious in that appetite.

After the attacks on the World Trade Center and the Pentagon, many layers of embassy personnel were trying to learn as much as possible about the planners, the hijackers, their financiers, and the role any nation may have played. So, too, was Margaret, who had taken charge as the acting ambassador in my absence, directing and organizing the embassy's response, coordinating with Washington, and learning as much as possible from our Saudi hosts.

What we began to learn was alarming. First, a number of senior Saudi royals were in utter denial that fifteen of the nineteen hijackers were Saudis. Worse, a significant number of those hijackers had obtained their visas to enter the States legally, through our consular offices in Riyadh or Jeddah, a bustling trade center and port on the Red Sea. Loopholes in the visa regulations and legislation had created a system with virtually no screening for security risks.

Our officers reported that their Saudi counterparts would not cooperate in allowing us to interrogate terrorist suspects or even to inspect the "pocket litter"—the loose items such as cell phones, scraps of paper, and other clues—seized upon their arrests. Convincing the leaders of my host government that their sons had murdered over three thousand innocent Americans, and that we needed full Saudi cooperation immediately, was a massive challenge in my first days as ambassador.

There were other challenges as well. We had been launching air attacks on the Taliban in Afghanistan since October 7. Much of the support came from Prince Sultan Air Base (PSAB in government-speak), owned by the Saudis but occupied by the U.S. Air Force as the Saudis' "guests." Over five thousand personnel occupied the base, and the Combined Air Operations Command Center (CAOCC) was the hub of the entire operation.

The Saudis were nervous about the optics of our using their base to launch attacks on another Muslim nation, even if it was harboring the terrorists responsible for the deaths of over three thousand Americans on 9/11. To make matters worse in their view, the holy month of Ramadan was fast approaching, in mid-November. Launching attacks from PSAB on fellow Muslims in Afghanistan during this time would be particularly hard for the Saudis to swallow. Crown Prince Abdullah had been less than enthusiastic about allowing the United States onto Saudi soil to fight the first Gulf War after Saddam Hussein had invaded Kuwait in 1990, but King Fahd, who was healthy then, had overruled him. Now Abdullah was the one making decisions.

As sensitive as we were to the concerns of our host-ally, we did not want to suspend the air effort for a month. Momentum would undoubtedly be lost as the enemy regrouped and relocated. So along with General Tommy Franks, commander in chief of the Central Command, I was tasked with visiting the crown prince to try and secure his blessing for uninterrupted airstrikes that would be aided and abetted from a base in his country.

Allow me a brief detour here to explain some diplomatic protocol. Before an ambassador begins conducting official business, he or she is supposed to present credentials to the head of state. For all you foreign affairs buffs and Scrabble players: the formal term is *agrément*, which means agreement. The host country has to grant *agrément*, to accept credentials from all ambassadors. I had not yet presented my credentials to King Fahd because he was not well enough to receive me. Upon my arrival in the country, I had, however, presented a copy of them to the foreign minister, Prince Saud al Faisal. This allowed me to have meetings with the crown prince and other senior leadership.

There were about twenty other ambassadors to Saudi Arabia in the same position. One day, after I'd been in the country for several months, we all received calls instructing us to go to the airport in Riyadh. We were then flown to Jeddah to present our credentials to King Fahd at his palace there.

The ceremony was elaborate. We walked down a royal path outdoors and then went indoors where a military honor guard was waiting. The king was then wheeled in. Sadly, the monarch looked terribly feeble.

One by one we approached him. We nodded. He mumbled something that the interpreter chose to interpret as, "Thank you, I'm happy to accept your credentials," and off we went.

It was a sunny, hot day in October when Franks and I met Abdullah. I first rode from the embassy to Riyadh Air Base in my three-car motorcade to greet the general. Our trio of vehicles consisted of a lead Suburban, my armored BMW, and a trail Suburban shielding me from oncoming traffic, blasting a siren to clear cars away when necessary, moving at a brisk pace where possible in the daunting Riyadh traffic.

Riyadh Air Base, in the middle of town, was once the city's airport. It now is used for government and military aviation and is the preferred venue for official visits that do not command the royal terminal at King Khalid International Airport. When I arrived I was ushered into a waiting room and offered the customary thimbles of Arabic coffee laced with cardamom, followed by sweet tea in a glass demitasse.

The VIP waiting area looked slightly shopworn. Protocol officers and Saudi military milled about, mixing with my defense attaché, Colonel Bernie Dunn, and his staff. Embassy security officers eyed the tarmac and the horizon. "On approach," announced one of the staff, signaling General Franks's imminent arrival. Countless Suburbans appeared on the tarmac, forming a long procession as the heat radiated from the asphalt.

The noise of an approaching jet droned louder and louder. Then we heard the screech of tires as the plane made its landing. After taxiing to the far end of the runway, it turned around and headed back toward the terminal and the official greeting party. Soldiers took their places manning the ramp, and as the jet hit its parking spot, the ramp was positioned and the big plane's door opened. Several soldiers in full battle dress sped down, followed by General Tommy Franks, the top military official in the war on terror.

Franks descended the ramp stairs quickly, with an athletic gait. As I greeted him, he snapped a salute and said, "A pleasure to see you again, Sir." We had met for lunch at his residence in Tampa, the headquarters of Central Command, during my indoctrination and preparation to take my post earlier in the year—before the attacks of 9/11.

I never got used to four-star generals calling me "sir," but it was in their DNA. After a while I gave up asking them to call me Bob. Franks and I ultimately got onto a first-name basis, but even now he occasionally lapses into the military formality.

We were escorted back into the VIP terminal and offered another round of Arabic coffee and tea. Protocol welcomed the general and they exchanged pleasantries, but rather quickly we headed to the vehicles, which must have numbered over twenty. Franks and I shared the backseat of one of the Suburbans, while my car and driver followed the motorcade. And this was a serious motorcade—not just the three cars dodging trucks full of goats that I was used to, but a full-blown parade at high speed, with intersections blocked by local police cars with their lights flashing and sirens blaring from the Saudi escort cars ahead as well as the motorcycle officers behind.

As we made our way to the Royal Palace, we exchanged views on the task at hand. After a twenty-five-minute drive, we pulled through the majestic iron gates, guarded by soldiers and, since 9/11, by tanks flanking the entrance. The Royal Diwan, or Royal Palace, is divided into two sections. On one side is the king's court, and on the other side is the crown prince's court.

The Saudi deputy chief of protocol met us at the motor court entrance, shook our hands, and led us into the palace. The entry foyer is a vast space, several stories high, covered in gleaming white marble. The protocol officer quickly ushered us into a waiting room. The carpet featured an unusually bright, colorful design. The chairs were pure Louis XIV.

Our party included General Franks, his top two aides, and my political/military counselor, Martin Adams, as well as my political counselor, Matt Tueller. Franks and I sat down on one of the sofas and waited.

It was a considerable wait, and we eventually wondered why it was taking Crown Prince Abdullah so long to see us. We entertained all sorts of hypotheses. Was the crown prince trying to teach us a lesson, to show who's boss? Or were we waiting because the Saudis didn't have their act together? Perhaps Abdullah's protocol officer hadn't even informed him that we were there. It was impossible to draw any reliable conclusions, and it would have been impolite to press the point with our hosts.

The wait gave the general and me time to get better acquainted. He had lived in Oklahoma, my original home state, and then in Midland, Texas. He attended the same high school as Laura Bush, although they didn't know each other then.

As Muslims neither drink nor smoke—at least not in public—cigarettes were not allowed in the room. Franks was a heavy smoker, so the long wait was beginning to make him a bit cranky. Finally, after several hours, the protocol officer appeared at the door and motioned for us to head to the crown prince's inner office.

The huge space was also decorated in colorful carpeting, with a massive desk at the end of a long carpet leading in from the door. The crown prince was standing near the desk, and the right side of the room was lined with princes and military officials, who rose from their chairs to greet us. Two television camera operators photographed our every move as we approached Abdullah and his staff.

The crown prince was dressed in the traditional Saudi white flowing *thobe*, over which he wore a *bisht*, or outer cloak of brown cloth bordered with gold piping. He wore the usual red-checkered head cloth or *ghutra*, topped with a black *agal*, or rope cord, around his head. We shook his hand, and he greeted us warmly through an interpreter. He motioned for us to take the chairs and sofa on the opposite side of the room from the assembled princes and generals. Portraits of King Fahd and King Abdulaziz hung on the wall behind the desk.

Franks sat in a chair next to the crown prince, separated by a table with a telephone on it. (You always know where to sit in a dignitary's office; he sits next to the phone and the principal visitor sits on the other side.) I sat on the sofa next to Franks. Every horizontal surface, from Abdullah's desk to the coffee table at my knees, was covered with lavish floral arrangements of eye-popping color. On the coffee table I also noticed a large bowl full of Patchi chocolate pieces wrapped in gold foil. Over time I developed a great affection for these candies.

I had been briefed about Abdullah on numerous occasions. I knew that before becoming crown prince he had been mayor of Mecca, commander of the Saudi National Guard, deputy defense minister, and second deputy prime minister. His appointment to this last post by King Khalid in 1975 had put him next in line for succession to the throne after his half brother Fahd, who was then the crown prince.

Fahd was not happy with the appointment of Abdullah, as he preferred that his full brother Prince Sultan hold the position. Fahd, Sultan, and five other full brothers—known as the Sudairi Seven because they shared the same mother, who was a Sudairi—formed a power bloc in Saudi government that exists to this day.

Abdullah, like many of his half brothers, was one of the wealthiest people in the world. He'd had more than a dozen wives and fathered over three dozen children. He had numerous palaces and estates, though they were modest by Saudi royal standards. He was an accomplished horseman. And he appeared to have his health. Still, being crown prince in 2001 was not an easy job.

On the international front, Abdullah had to balance alliances with the pro-Palestinian/anti-Israeli Muslim world with his alliance with Israel's staunchest supporter, the United States. He had refused an invitation to the United States in the spring of 2001 as a protest against Israel's conduct that led to the Palestinians' violent eruptions in the Al-Aqsa Intifada.

At home, he had to balance the understanding that certain reforms were necessary, humane, and inevitable with the awareness that moving forward too fast would offend the Wahhabi, the influential Islamic fundamentalists who had enough power to undercut his regime.

The Wahhabi partnership with the ruling House of Saud dates back to the founding of the First Saudi State, when the clerics agreed to recognize the Sauds' political legitimacy in return for authority in religious matters. The Wahhabi enjoy strong support from the Saudi man on the street, and their doctrine is taught in the mosques and madrasas (Islamic schools). As that doctrine is extremely conservative with respect to the role of women and any other social issue you can think of, a ruler must think twice about pushing reform too quickly.

Before his assassination in 1975, King Faisal had instituted some reforms, such as schools for girls and the introduction of television. But two events in 1979 had a lasting impact on the royal family. In January the shah of Iran was deposed and fundamentalist clerics seized political power. And in November Muslim dissidents seized the Grand Mosque in Mecca. It took the Saudi military two weeks to regain control of the Kingdom's holiest shrine, with the help of French commandos,

In the aftermath, the Saudi leadership decided they needed to focus more publicly on their religious duties. After all, the shah had failed to do so and had lost power. Taking the fall of the shah as an object lesson and the seizure of the Grand Mosque as a potential existential threat, the government delegated to the religious establishment most of the domestic and religious affairs in the Kingdom. And so in an odd way, Saudi Arabia became more fundamentalist and conservative *after* 1979 than it had been before. (There was fallout to the United States as well from the ouster of the shah. We lost Iran, a major ally in the region, making our alliances with Saudi Arabia and Egypt all the more vital.)

In his last several years, Abdullah introduced many reforms. I'll outline some of them in future chapters. At the time of our first meeting, however, it's fair to say he was largely considered a traditionalist.

The crown prince seemed robust. Relatively tall, he wore glasses but looked younger than his age, partly because of the Arab habit of dyeing goatees to hide the gray. His color was good and he was in full command of the room. He was surrounded by several members of the royal family and advisors, including, if I recall correctly, his foreign policy advisor, Adel al-Jubeir. The Georgetown-educated Adel, who later became the Saudi ambassador to the United States, often served as interpreter at such meetings.

(I was never sure how much English Abdullah knew. In the many times I was with him after that first meeting, I only heard him say things like "thank you" or "have a good day" or other minor phrases.)

Franks got to the point quickly. His presentation on the need to continue bombing during Ramadan went something like this:

Your Royal Highness, let me explain it to you this way: Right now we're using precision-guided munitions and can shoot a missile into the second-floor window of an apartment building. But the targeting is done by a computer, and it takes a fairly long while to make these individual targeting decisions. And to continue to do it this way will take us well into and past Ramadan. But we're able to minimize civilian casualties this way. The alternative is carpet bombing, where we can just level a hillside or a village, but there would be many more civilian casualties if we did it that way. So, your Royal Highness, which of these options do you think you would favor?

The general had skillfully avoided the "none of the above" option.

Abdullah listened carefully and then said something to the effect of, *I understand. Well, do the best you can to minimize civilian casualties, because that's what we want to do. But you have my permission to continue doing what you're doing.*

Mission accomplished.

Throughout the meeting, which lasted less than an hour, the crown prince appeared serious minded, polite, and gracious. I got the impression that he had a lot on his mind. We were, after all, only about six weeks removed from September 11.

In subsequent meetings, Abdullah was always respectful. He obviously felt an obligation to listen to the personal representative of a U.S. president. I felt comfortable with him and took a chance early in our acquaintanceship by telling him that I was a man of faith, as was he, and we should be able to communicate well because of that commonality. He smiled and nodded.

Soon after I arrived in Riyadh, a fellow ambassador from a neighboring Arab state advised me that "a good ambassador has four ears and only half of a tongue."

I got it: *Keep your mouth shut and listen.* And listen I did for much of my early tenure. But as I got my sea legs after a few months as ambassador, I began to communicate more directly.

Often I would run my ideas by Adel al-Jubeir, with whom I developed a cordial friendship. I frequently expressed to the crown prince my support for his reform agenda and began to press further on issues of human rights, religious freedom, and women's rights. He was open to discussing these issues but clearly did not want to appear to be acceding to U.S. pressure to liberalize. This was a Saudi prerogative, carefully guarded. More about this later.

Our discussions would occasionally give me a glimpse of Abdullah's personality. Once, Assistant Secretary of State Burns (later deputy secretary under Hillary Clinton and then John Kerry) and I were invited to his "farm" outside of Riyadh, a lush, majestic farm if I ever saw one. When we arrived we were taken to a large tent outside the main buildings. As we turned the corner into the tent's opening, out shot a bocce ball at high speed, knocking aside the other balls on the lawn.

A roar of excitement burst from the tent, and we entered to find the crown prince and many other royals intensely engaged in their game of bowls. Naturally, the crown prince won the game. After he returned his custom bocce balls to their green-velvet case, we turned to conversation as he watched six soccer matches simultaneously on his bank of thirty-two television screens in the tent.

On another visit, he told me of his prowess at swimming. It seems that he was on a beach at the Red Sea training a baby falcon to hunt. This entailed sewing its eyelids shut with a needle and thread so that it would develop its other senses. On this occasion Abdullah lost his grip, and the blind falcon was washed out to sea. According to the crown prince, he chased after the falcon, diving into the surf and swimming through the waves to rescue the wayward creature.

Franks and I debriefed as the motorcade took us back from our meeting. From that day forward, we'd meet every three weeks or so. As our friendship grew, he opened up to me about how disgusted he was with Secretary of Defense Rumsfeld and how they didn't get along. At some point Rumsfeld instructed him to refrain from all communication with Secretary of State Powell. I later told Powell about this and he was none too happy. No doubt he brought it up with National Security Advisor Condi Rice at some point. This bizarre state of affairs just demonstrates the intensity and destructiveness of the cold war going on between the two departments that would later have to coordinate our effort in Iraq.

Early in 2002, Franks again confided how unhappy he was with having to deal with Rumsfeld. He said that from the Situation Room in the

Pentagon, Rumsfeld was making individual targeting decisions, saying, in effect, "Okay, I think we need to target this place, this place, and this place in Afghanistan."

Franks lamented that this was not the job of the secretary of defense. Rumsfeld was supposed to be a policy guy, not a bombardier. At some point he told me, "You know, I may just have to quit. I just don't know if I can take this any longer." The situation was obviously stressful.

One day as we were in my motorcade coming back from a meeting with Defense Minister Prince Sultan, Franks shared another tale of dysfunction. I wasn't in a good mood either, as the meeting—on a subject I no longer recall—had not gone well. I turned to Franks and said, "How'd you like to go get a drink at my place?"

"You betcha," he said.

I told my driver to make a quick right turn and go straight to my residence. The other cars in the motorcade weren't ready for that and kept driving ahead on our planned route. I knew they wouldn't be happy with me.

Back at the residence, I got out the bottle of Famous Grouse Scotch that Ambassador Fowler had left behind as a gift for me and poured us each a stiff drink. As we raised our glasses, I was summoned to the phone. At the same time my nineteen-year-old son, Andrew, who was taking a gap year in Riyadh before starting college at New York University, came into the room. I introduced him to the general and left for what turned out to be a thirty-minute phone call on my secure line.

While I was away, Franks and Andrew talked. The subject was leadership, I later learned. Franks told Andrew that he'd sometimes been in trouble as a kid and had dropped out of the University of Texas and joined the army to turn his life around. He said he felt really lucky because most people who get into trouble when they're young never live it down and are defined by their youthful indiscretions. Nowadays, Franks gets big bucks for that speech; Andrew got it free . . . or for the price of a Scotch.

When Franks complained about Rumsfeld—for whom I also had little patience—I tried to be as supportive as possible. "Look, we need you," I'd say. "I can understand how you feel. I feel the same way sometimes, but you're making a tremendous contribution to your country and

I hope you know that and I hope you understand how much many of us in the trenches appreciate it."

When I went back to the States for the first time in December 2001, I shared what Franks had told me during debriefings with my contacts at the State Department, including Rich Armitage, the deputy secretary of state. Armitage, a Powell loyalist, had little use for Rumsfeld and his crew. Later I heard someone describe meetings between Armitage and Rumsfeld's deputy Paul Wolfowitz as "bloodbaths."

My meeting with Armitage was memorable for another reason. Because the airline lost my suitcase containing all my suits, I showed up at Foggy Bottom wearing a blazer, khakis, and boat shoes. Armitage, a crusty Vietnam War gunboat captain with about a twenty-inch neck, dressed me down. "You should always carry a change of clothes in your carry-on, because your bag's gonna get lost," he said. "That's sort of a rookie mistake, pal."

Only two months into my ambassadorship, I was indeed a rookie. Still, in addition to my temporarily AWOL luggage, I'd brought a plan. And if I could persuade the vice president, the secretary of commerce, and the U.S. trade representative to buy into it, we might be able to accelerate the necessary reforms back in the Kingdom.

3

FOR A COMMANDER in chief whose homeland had been attacked just three months earlier, George W. Bush seemed unusually cheery. Then again, Christmas was approaching and with it the opportunity to escape, if only briefly, the pressures of the new age of terrorism.

"Hey, Bob, are you having a good time over there?" he asked as I entered the Oval Office.

Good time?

The president saw the look on my face and said, "Well, I guess it must be a fascinating experience."

Fascinating? That struck me as a little like describing the way someone looks as . . . *interesting.*

"Mr. President," I chuckled, "I thought you were my friend. What have you done by sending me over there?"

I think he knew that I was kidding. Well, half-kidding. Sometimes I did think, *If he was going to appoint me to an ambassadorship, why not New Zealand? Switzerland? The Bahamas!* Why Saudi Arabia? Home of Osama and the hijackers. Land of 120-degree heat. A place so dangerous that security dared not let me go out on the street. Other times, however, I was proud, even happy to be serving my country in such an important place. And a confession: sometimes I thought I was *the* person for the job.

After catching up on family matters, we turned to business. The president wanted the view from twenty thousand feet. What had I noticed about the Saudis during my first sixty days there, and what did I think he needed to know?

As I recall, I told him that we were beginning to get a more realistic response from the Saudis regarding September 11. While some members of the royal family still thought the hijackings must have been plotted by the Mossad, Israel's intelligence agency, we had made good progress in debunking that ridiculous theory. Our briefers had presented evidence demonstrating that the attacks were the work of Al Qaeda and that the vast majority of the hijackers had indeed been from the Kingdom.

That was the good news. The bad news was there was a major impediment to gaining Saudi cooperation in the fight against terrorism. The Al-Aqsa Intifada (or Second Intifada), the Palestinian uprising against the Israel defense forces and even some Israeli citizens, had been going strong since 2000. Each side was suffering casualties—469 Palestinians and 199 Israelis had died to date according to Amnesty International. A few days before my visit, a suicide bomber had attacked a bus in Haifa, killing fifteen and injuring forty. The militant Palestinian group Hamas was taking credit for the bombing.

Crown Prince Abdullah and others in the government had made it clear that Saudi assistance in our efforts inside the country and in Afghanistan might well be directly proportional to our ability to broker some kind of peace in the region, if not a permanent solution to the decades-old conflict between the Israelis and the Palestinians. The president was already well aware of how the Saudis viewed the Israeli-Palestinian issue, but I don't think he fully understood how much that colored their willingness to be cooperative in going after Al Qaeda and cooperating with us in our efforts against terrorism.

I know that President Bush has been portrayed as a disengaged, disinterested commander in chief. That was not the case on this day or on any other day I spent with him during my ambassadorship, including two summits. He was always engaged, lively, and interactive, asking many questions. On this day he asked me what the crown prince and the other senior Saudi officials were really like.

In keeping with the instruction to "feed the beast," I had been sending cables home on a regular basis since arriving at the embassy. By no means were all of these sent directly to the president; I knew he'd be briefed on those that the State Department or his national security staff thought worthy of his attention. Now he seemed attuned to the issues preoccupying much of our focus in the Kingdom: terrorist financing, support for Al Qaeda, and religious extremism.

On this visit, as well as others, I also saw National Security Advisor Condi Rice. She, like the president, was aware that we were dealing with two different factions in Saudi Arabia: one that was willing to support us in the war on terror and one that wasn't.

Rice, too, seemed to have a pretty good grasp of the Israeli-Palestinian issues and was interested in and curious about the Saudis' take on the matter. I wouldn't say she expressed skepticism, but she was interested in the theme that often creeps into analysis of the Muslim mind-set, which is: how much of the constant harangue about the Israeli-Palestinian situation is an attempt by the Arab royalty to deflect attention from their own problems? And how much do they truly care about the Palestinians?

In the short time I'd been on assignment, I'd become aware of and frustrated by the dysfunctional CIA-FBI relationship. The agencies didn't like each other any better than the Department of State and the Department of Defense liked one another. They didn't communicate well, if at all. And they were competitive at the expense of serving the country's interest. The president was aware of this. I didn't dwell so much on that with him because I thought I could personally get the message across to FBI director Bob Mueller and CIA director George Tenet.

What do I mean by dysfunction? Here's an example: there was still a huge friend-or-foe issue hanging over the Saudis, even though Crown Prince Abdullah and senior leadership seemed to be supporting us. We continued to get stories of terrorist financing emanating out of Saudi Arabia. I met a number of times with presidential advisor and terrorism expert Juan Zarate and Treasury Department general counsel David Aufhauser to discuss this subject.

Eventually we began to believe that a number of Saudi charities were funding the bad guys. At the same time we became concerned about the poor cooperation we were getting from the Kingdom on intelligence and law enforcement investigations. The FBI was complaining that the

Saudis were unresponsive to requests to provide records on people or to round them up.

Back in Saudi Arabia, I met with Mohammed bin Nayef, assistant minister of the interior and the Saudi point man in the war on terror, and pressed him impatiently for information requested some two months earlier. To my surprise, Prince Mohammed told me they had turned over the material to the FBI almost immediately. After getting the information from the Saudis, the FBI had never shared it.[1]

In one of my "feed the beast" cables, I chided the agencies about this embarrassing lack of communication, and on my next trip to Washington, I visited both Mueller and Tenet. To put it bluntly, I got in their faces. "Guys, we've got to have you people sharing and playing nice together." (That's one advantage a political appointee who's close to the president has: he or she doesn't have to worry about being knocked off a career path by pushing back against the CIA and FBI.)

The response? Tenet blamed the dysfunction on the FBI culture, which was secretive, harsh on its own people, and too compartmentalized. Like most others in government, he also blamed the FBI for not knowing how to operate in a foreign territory.

Mueller, who had taken his post only in July 2001, was not a career FBI guy. Most recently he'd been a well-regarded U.S. attorney. He acknowledged that he had a long way to go in transforming the FBI culture, but he assured me that he was working hard to do so. I got the impression that the director was sincere, but I wasn't so sure about the rest of the career guys in the bureau.

Most agents I met believed their job was to build cases and obtain evidence so that the U.S. attorney could secure the conviction of a bad guy. The mind-set before 9/11 was not "We have to go out and prevent a terrorist attack." It seemed that they would almost rather let a conspiracy unfold for a while and see how much evidence they could get for the biggest charge they could bring, as opposed to snuffing it out at the beginning. Equally upsetting was the fact that the FBI didn't appear to consider a posting in Saudi Arabia important enough to send us one of their top agents. We seemed to get agents who were in the twilight of their careers, not those on the fast track for advancement. A number of prospects for assignment to the Kingdom turned it down.

I don't want to let the CIA off the hook. The agency was also compartmentalized and didn't share information particularly well. It was
my impression that the agents cultivated and relished a cloak-and-dagger
mentality that was not always helpful in reaching desired goals.

Was the president to blame for these counterproductive intra-agency
rifts? To the extent that he was the nation's chief executive and the
buck stopped with him, I suppose some of the fault must be assigned
to the Oval Office. But during my tenure, I came to see that the vast
majority of dysfunction is hardwired into the government's DNA. It is
so ingrained that it transcends the officeholders, the bureaucrats, and
both political parties.

On that first trip home, FBI and CIA were not the only three-letter
acronyms to occupy my attention. During my first two months overseas, we had been so heavily involved in the Afghan campaign there
was little time to talk with the Saudis about economic, political, and
social reforms. My thought was that if we could dangle the carrot of
World Trade Organization (WTO) membership in front of the Saudis,
they might start making fundamental changes in their economy that
in turn would lead to reforms in human rights, women's rights, and
religious freedom. A country can't enjoy the economic advantages of
being part of the WTO—supervision of trade and an apparatus for dispute resolution—unless it undertakes significant economic and legisla-
tive reforms to accord with international standards.

This may sound sad or funny or both, but the truth is that during
my ambassadorship I was never exactly sure what the U.S. policy was
toward Saudi Arabia. While that may have held me back in some affairs,
it actually allowed me a great deal of freedom in others. Taking to heart
Colin Powell's instructions to be a proactive "general," I thought I might
be able to help bring the Kingdom into the twenty-first century through
WTO membership.

I concluded that the only way we were going to get reforms in human
rights, women's rights, and freedom of religion was if the Saudis saw it
in their own interest to do so. WTO membership was a place where their
interests and our interests were aligned because they would have the
incentive to pass the laws or the economic reforms necessary to qualify
for the WTO, and we would then help them get in.

Reforming their economy would have long-term social and political implications as well. That economy would have to be more competitive in a WTO-compliant world, with fewer subsidies for entrenched interests and more opportunities for women. Education and job training would improve. Over time the society would adapt to more international norms.

There was no question that this would be a long haul. Talks concerning Saudi accession to the WTO had been dormant since 2000. The Saudis had worked with the Clinton administration in trying to get into the WTO, and there had also been some work done by the U.S.-Arab Chamber of Commerce in Washington. But talks with the Office of the U.S. Trade Representative, the agency responsible for moving the ball forward, had apparently run out of steam.

Certain segments of Saudi society vigorously opposed membership. They had the impression that if they joined, they would be required to import pork and alcohol and would be forced to allow the establishment of cinemas that would show "pornographic" materials in their society. They were also worried that they would have to submit draft legislation to the WTO secretariat in order to have it approved before it was implemented, which was, in their view, a great incursion on their sovereignty.

Our Trade Representative Office has a small staff with a huge portfolio. If countries that are talking about joining the WTO are not that cooperative, the office has other fish to fry. My job now was to reinvigorate my own government's tepid view of Saudi membership and, at the same time, try to get better Saudi cooperation at the working level to make it happen. In other words: threading a needle. I took heart in the knowledge that Abdullah remained interested. After the 2000 election, the crown prince had sent letters to President Bush asking for our help in getting into the WTO.

Knowing that political buy-in from top government officials was necessary, I secured the blessings of Condi Rice and Colin Powell. Next stop: Vice President Cheney. He, too, was receptive to the argument that this was a political issue of consequence.

Before seeing our trade representative, Bob Zoellick, I visited my fellow Texan, Secretary of Commerce Don Evans. I had known Don largely on the margins of fundraising he had undertaken for George W. Bush's campaigns for governor and the presidency. Our hellos were warm but a little awkward, as he called me "Mr. Ambassador" and I called him "Mr. Secretary."

We lapsed into "Don" and "Bob" pretty quickly, and I joked that this was the first time I'd seen him when he wasn't asking me for money. He chuckled and we got down to business. I told him I had made the rounds, visiting the White House, Vice President Cheney, and Rice and Powell and now needed his concurrence in our efforts to get the Saudis into the World Trade Organization. Don readily understood the importance of the reforms this would require from the Saudis and the long-lasting impact they would have on the political and social fabric of the Kingdom. He was on board.

Now I was ready to take my "wto enthusiasm tour" to Zoellick, who had served in the administration of George H. W. Bush and had been a foreign policy advisor to George W. Bush during the 2000 presidential election. Jim Baker had told me Bob was one of the most brilliant and dedicated public servants he had ever worked with, high praise from the discerning and occasionally crusty former secretary of state.

The trade representative and his small staff (including his deputy, Jon Huntsman) were overworked and in no mood to help out a Saudi government that was, at best, inconsistent in its deliberations over wto accession. So I conveyed to Bob the reality: he was surrounded. I walked him step by step through the support I had enlisted from Rice, Powell, Cheney, and Evans. Then: "So what do you think, Bob? You think you can get behind this?" Realizing it was game, set, match, Bob wisely implored his skeptical staff to sign on for another round of wto roulette with the Saudis.

And so began a long and complicated set of negotiations that continued throughout my tenure and beyond, until 2005 when the Kingdom was admitted to the wto after making important reforms to its commercial and judicial legislation. Putting these reforms on the front burner, with the ultimate goal of enhancing broader human rights within international standards, is one of the things I am most proud of about my ambassadorship.

After taking care of business in Washington, I flew home to Dallas for Christmas. The welcome from my friends and colleagues was warm, though a bit awkward. When I had departed Dallas to take my post, the local bar association (of which I had once been president) had thrown a big farewell party for me. Both U.S. senators from Texas, several other public officials, and bar officials had attended. I'd given an emotional speech, remembering how in his fifties my father had gone far away to a dangerous place to serve his country in Vietnam and how fitting it was that I would have a chance to serve my country at about the same stage in my life. On this, my first return, the same people couldn't have been kinder. But many of them looked at me in what I can only describe as an "elevated way." I wasn't "Bob" anymore; I was "Mr. Ambassador."

Such ceremony makes me uncomfortable. I initially said, "Hey, I'm just Bob." But some people are just undeterred and persist. After a few tries I stopped correcting them. (I still have law partners who call me "Ambassador.")

Although my friends and colleagues were interested to know what I was thinking and learning and going through, they were most interested in my safety in a wartime environment. Many were shocked to learn that my bodyguards were actually Saudis and not U.S. Marine Corps. While I was initially surprised at this as well, I learned that no other ambassadors in Riyadh had such security, and our deal with the Saudis provided reciprocal U.S. security protection for their ambassador in Washington, Prince Bandar.

The Marine Corps security detachment numbered only twelve, working eight-hour shifts. Their job was not to protect me personally but rather to ensure that classified materials were properly protected and locked up at night, to monitor those coming to and going from the embassy, and to repel, as best they could, any attack on the embassy until reinforcements could arrive (if at all). I became quite comfortable with my Saudi security detail and knew they would stop a bullet for me if necessary.

In conversations during this holiday I sensed an overarching suspicion and resentment of the Saudis. One of the hardest things I had to do was persuade my friends that not all Saudis were terrorist sympathizers, that it was unfair to paint everyone in the Kingdom with the same brush.[2]

Less than a month after my return to the Kingdom, I was back in the States. To demonstrate post-9/11 solidarity with New York City, organizers of the 2002 World Economic Forum decided to hold the gathering in

Manhattan rather than its permanent home, Davos, Switzerland. The Saudis sent a seventy-person delegation and invited me to join them.

The agenda for this conference, held in what had been the shadows of the now-destroyed World Trade Center, featured the usual fare of panels on such topics as the global economic outlook, debt relief, and bridging business divides. But there were less traditional topics reflecting the new realities of the world: media and terrorism, new sources of vulnerability, and even a session titled "Thinking the Unthinkable, a Safer World: How Do We Get There?"

I attended many of these sessions, including one called "The Voice of Islam in Development." Here, as Reuters reported on February 6, 2002, Prince Turki al-Faisal, the Kingdom's former head of intelligence and future ambassador to Washington, anticipated questions about the country's record on women's rights and brought data to show it was reforming. "There are 198,967 women at Saudi universities. This is in a country where 30 years ago women were not allowed an education," he said, adding that 19,311 Saudi women had received advanced degrees. The prince also noted that women owned more than twenty-two thousand businesses in the country.

Those numbers may have indicated some progress, but here, sadly, is another statistic: *fifteen Saudi girls dead*. They perished in Mecca six weeks after the forum when the religious police refused to let them leave a burning school building because they were not wearing headscarves and *abayas* (black robes). As BBC News reported, "The *Saudi Gazette* quoted witnesses as saying that the religious police—known as the Commission for the Promotion of Virtue and Prevention of Vice—had stopped men who tried to help the girls and warned, 'It is a sinful [*sic*] to approach them.'"[3]

I don't recall that the WTO was on the agenda at the forum, but I was already starting to talk with Saudi businessmen about the idea. My primary contact was Abdullah Alireza, the head of the Jeddah Chamber of Commerce. Descended from an old-line family, kind of the Rockefellers of Saudi Arabia, he later served as the Saudi minister of commerce.

Merchant families like his would need coaxing because Saudi Arabia's accession to the WTO would end the monopoly those families had on being the exclusive distributors and agents for foreign businesses that wanted to invest and/or do business in the Kingdom. Under WTO principles it would no longer be required for those companies to have the same kind of agency relationships and they could be direct participants in the economy after a period of years. Perhaps contrary to his own economic interests, Abdullah Alireza was a steadfast advocate in favor of WTO accession and helped persuade many of his fellow merchant families to acquiesce to the idea.[4]

One evening during the conference, the Saudis invited me for a late dinner at Le Cirque, a fancy restaurant in midtown Manhattan. My hosts—all in finely tailored British suits—included the wealthy businessman Walid Juffali and Saudi adviser Hassan Yassin. There were about seven of us.

Shortly after we arrived, a woman who knew Hassan Yassin came up to our table. She said she was waiting for her party, and Hassan invited her to join us until they arrived. We soon learned she was Judith Miller, the *New York Times* reporter who in the coming months would write several articles alleging that Iraq had weapons of mass destruction.[5]

Soon Ms. Miller was joined by her party, which to the surprise if not shock of our table, included former Israeli prime minister and later president Shimon Peres and several of his countrymen. I assumed that they, too, were in town for the forum.

Our two parties were fascinated by each other. We moved our chairs together and had a remarkable roundtable discussion. The conversation was civil, thoughtful, and provocative. It was clear to me that these Israelis and Arabs had much in common, including a desire to solve the problems that divided their constituencies. The theme of the ad hoc discussion was, *Can't we find ways to peace?*

Peres was conciliatory, as were the Saudis. This was a kumbaya moment, and we ended up closing down the restaurant. I came away more hopeful about the future than I had been. I also wonder whether Hassan, a wily veteran of Middle East intrigue, may have actually set up this "chance" encounter surreptitiously.

After returning to the Kingdom, I was asked to participate in discussions about inviting Crown Prince Abdullah to a possible U.S.-Saudi summit in the United States. Bill Burns briefed me on some of the planning, including Abdullah's prior refusal of an invitation.

Soon I was jetting to the Royal Palace in Jeddah on Air Force One with Vice President Cheney. He and his staff peppered me with questions: What was the king's state of health and would we interact with him? What was the crown prince's temperature in light of the crisis in the Palestinian territories? What was their view on Iraq? How would the crown prince react to an invitation to meet President Bush?

4

On February 14, 1945, the United States of America and the Kingdom of Saudi Arabia held their first summit meeting. President Franklin D. Roosevelt, returning from his conference with Josef Stalin and Winston Churchill at Yalta in the southern Ukraine, met with King Abdulaziz on board the uss *Quincy* in the Great Bitter Lake between the north and south parts of the Suez Canal.

Another ship, the uss *Murphy*, carried the king, over forty countrymen, and the royal throne from Jeddah to the *Quincy*. Because the Bedouin Abdulaziz preferred the outdoors to an "iron cabin," the crew of the *Murphy* hurriedly sewed him a large tent made of canvas. And because the king would not step on the steel deck, his aides placed rugs in his path when he made his way around the destroyer.

The monarch brought several hundred-pound bags of rice, large supplies of tomatoes and watermelons, and eight sheep on the two-day voyage. The sheep were kept in a corral that the ship's crew built at the stern. After slaughter, the meat was hung on a two-by-six-foot plank set against the flagstaff. The lamb was cooked on deck in charcoal pots. Tasters ate from Abdulaziz's plate to make sure his food was safe.[1]

At Yalta the postwar reorganization of Europe was the main item on the agenda. At the Valentine's Day summit at Great Bitter Lake, FDR asked for Saudi help in settling displaced Jews in what was then Palestine. The president also sought assurances that the United States could locate military bases in the region and that his country could count on cheap oil from the Kingdom.

Roosevelt achieved two of these three goals—oil and the bases. The Saudis also benefited, as U.S. dollars, technology, and know-how poured into their country. But the president struck out on the Palestinian question. "Give [the Jews] and their descendants the choicest lands and homes of the Germans who had oppressed them," said Abdulaziz.[2] Not Palestine. Two months later, Roosevelt died.

In 1957 King Saud became the first Saudi monarch to visit the United States. New York City refused to extend the king an official welcome. Mayor Robert Wagner tartly explained that Saud represented a nation that was anti-Semitic and anti-Catholic and condoned slavery.

To counter this snub, President Dwight Eisenhower rolled out the red carpet. For the first time in his five years in office, Ike met a foreign leader at the airport. After a twenty-one-gun salute, the king joined the president in an open-air limousine for the drive to the White House. "Thousands of Washingtonians, given an extended lunch hour by the government, lined the route cheering and waving small Saudi Arabian flags," the *New York Times*' Russell Baker reported on January 31, 1957. Baker further noted, "The king is a tall, serene, olive-skinned figure whose gold-trimmed robes and regal carriage suggest a Caliph of Baghdad."

Five years later, President John F. Kennedy received Crown Prince Faisal in Washington. Said the man who would soon be king, "After Allah, we trust the United States."[3]

In 1974, trust was at issue when Richard Nixon became the first U.S. president to visit the Kingdom. The president's trip followed a tumultuous year in which the Arabs and Israelis had clashed in the Yom Kippur War. U.S. support of Israel during the conflict had triggered a six-month OPEC oil embargo, long gas lines, and a stock market crash.

Saudi Arabia is fiercely anticommunist—in large part because it abhors the atheism of communists. Fearful of inroads or a takeover by the Soviet Union, the Saudis have historically looked to the United States for protection—a wonderful example of the maxim "The enemy of my enemy is my friend." But Russia won its own friends in the Middle East by supporting the Arabs during the Yom Kippur War. In Jeddah, Nixon tried to repair any damage to U.S.-Saudi relations that might give America's

Cold War nemesis an opportunity to strengthen its hand. At their state dinner, King Faisal told the president there would never be peace in the region until Israel gave up Arab lands.

In the years that followed, the summits continued. The leaders of the two nations changed, but the issues they discussed remained the same—the Israeli-Palestinian conflict, cheap oil, and the continued presence of U.S. military bases.

Fast forward to April 25, 2002. Fifty-seven years after the first U.S.-Saudi summit, President George W. Bush and Crown Prince Abdullah were to meet at the president's ranch, the Western White House, in Crawford. I was privy to a great deal of intelligence about the royal family and government officials, but as I waited with Colin Powell for the crown prince's personal jet to land at an airstrip outside of Waco, I learned something new: the secretary of state told me that Abdullah did not think that helicopters were safe.

Because of the crown prince's fears, we would not be taking a short chopper flight from the airstrip to the summit at the president's ranch. Instead, we'd be traveling to and from Crawford for fifty minutes each way on a Saudi-chartered bus with the crown prince, Prince Bandar (the Saudi ambassador to the United States) and Prince Saud (the foreign minister). Powell then gave me another piece of news: He would not be returning to Waco after the meeting; the president wanted him to stay for a press conference. As a result, I'd be the lone American on the bus with the three Saudi leaders after what was shaping up to be a disastrous summit.

In my six months as ambassador, I had developed cordial relationships with all of the Saudi leaders. But on this day all signs pointed to a tense, if not acrimonious, summit that could worsen the increasingly shaky relationship between the United States and the Kingdom. I did not relish the notion of riding solo with a Saudi delegation that would, in all likelihood, be angry with the United States, the president, and me.

So how did I respond to Powell? Like a good diplomat should. "Okay," I said. "Thanks. I got it."

Why all the tension? The Saudis were upset over what they considered to be a tepid U.S. response to two ongoing Israeli sieges.

Number one: the Good Friday Siege of Ramallah, which (depending on your point of view) had left Palestinian National Authority leader Yasser Arafat confined or held hostage in a windowless two-room office in the Palestinian city located on the West Bank. Prime Minister Ariel Sharon's forces had acted following a Passover attack by a Hamas suicide bomber that killed twenty Israelis and one tourist in the seaside city of Netanya.

Number two: the siege of the Church of Nativity in Bethlehem in the West Bank. There, Palestinian militants on the run from Israeli forces had sought refuge inside the church. Claiming that the Palestinians were continuing their operations from within, the Israelis had signaled a willingness to fire upon those inside the holy place.

The escalation by both sides did not bode well for peace in the region or good relations between the United States and our Saudi friends. Nor did the Bush administration's refusal to condemn Israel to the degree the Arab world wanted. Indeed, a week before the Crawford meeting, the president surprisingly had called Sharon "a man of peace."[4]

The timing of the sieges was terrible. Israel began operations in Ramallah shortly after a peace proposal by Crown Prince Abdullah was approved at an Arab League summit. The terms: normal relations if Israel agreed to withdraw from the land it occupied after the Six-Day War in 1967 and allowed displaced Palestinians to return to their homes. A wary Israel responded, No thank you.

As I previously noted, after President Bush recruited me for the ambassadorship, he told me he felt he had "no political capital" to get involved in the peace process. By early 2002, circumstances had changed. Our eyes were already on Iraq. And if we were going to go to war with Saddam Hussein, we'd need Saudi Arabia's blessing and strategic support. Staging operations from Prince Sultan Air Base in the Kingdom and moving special ops forces and equipment across borders would be essential to the effort.

The Saudis did not like Saddam and would gladly have seen him vaporized. But they also didn't like the notion of our country invading a Muslim nation—at least not without getting something in return. Their blessing would be far more likely if we ratcheted up our efforts to bring about an end to the Israeli-Palestinian conflict. Thus the summit.

Dick Cheney had issued the formal invitation to Crown Prince Abdullah in Jeddah in mid-March. The vice president had been on the road for over a week, telling allies from London to Amman that because Saddam had weapons of mass destruction and ties to Al Qaeda, America would not allow him to remain a threat in a post-9/11 world. If a diplomatic solution could not be reached, the Bush administration was prepared to fight. (While most everyone believed Saddam did have those weapons, there was little, if any, evidence that Saddam had ties to Al Qaeda. I never saw any intelligence to support that assertion.)

I met the vice president on March 16, when he flew into Riyadh. We then flew to Jeddah, some six hundred miles to the southwest. We made the ninety-minute flight on Air Force One (although it is labeled Air Force Two when being used by the vice president). This was my first time on the plane, which I can only describe as an airborne version of the West Wing, complete with conference rooms, a word-processing section, an upstairs bedroom, and (far in the back) a section for the press corps.

I sat with senior White House and State Department officials in opposing captain's chairs separated by work tables. Cheney invited me up front into his airborne living room, where he and his staff peppered me with questions about Abdullah and the prospects for a summit. I had sent cables on most of these topics, but I repeated my estimation that the crown prince was livid at (in his view) the president's failure to bring Sharon and the Israelis to heel and at the catastrophic loss of civilian life among the Palestinians. Yet I was optimistic that the crown prince would want to meet personally with the president, if for no other reason than to personally express his horror at the carnage.

When we landed in Jeddah, we were met with full military honors, including a marching band and a greeting by several senior royals and cabinet ministers. We were then ushered into a reception room at the royal terminal, offered Arabic coffee and dates, and after a few pleasantries were ready to start the motorcade trek to the Royal Palace, not far from the airport.

When a president or vice president travels abroad, it's like Hannibal crossing the Alps. They bring several c-130s or c-17s full of gear, security, and even the ubiquitous presidential limousine—in this case a new, armor-plated Cadillac. Cheney and I sat in the back as numerous black suvs plowed through the sealed-off streets in front and in back of our limo. Saudi police sirens filled the air, and traffic police stood at intersections and saluted as we passed by.

As we neared the palace, we saw the King Fahd Fountain, the world's largest fountain, across the water. Reminiscent of the giant fountain on Lake Geneva, it shoots sprays of the Red Sea eight hundred feet in the air.

In Saudi Arabia, the palaces often have their own palaces. Set in the gardens a stone's throw from the royal residence, King Fahd's guest palace in Jeddah has several wings that are ornately decorated in the Arabic style with marble arches and columns.

The guest palace features rooms for dignitaries. Our traveling party, which included Cheney, his right-hand man Scooter Libby, his advisor John Hannah, and me, was to stay there. A foreign service officer was assigned to each senior visitor to escort us to our rooms. All names and room numbers were posted on an easel by the entrance . . . except mine.

"Where am I staying?" I asked. The junior officer assigned to me apologized. She explained that "Mr. Libby" had gone to my room, paced off the square footage, and decided to give it to one of his staff. I was relegated to another building of smaller rooms, where some of the junior staff and the interpreter were staying.

Hmmm. If it really happened this way, I was astounded that a senior U.S. official would have the arrogance to give my room to one of his traveling party—and even more astounded that he would take the time to size up the quarters. This game of musical rooms was a personal insult, but—and this is much more important—it also had the potential to undermine my relationship with the Saudis. Assuming any of the Saudis noticed this petty gambit, it sent a message that the United States did not value its representative to the Kingdom.

The next time I saw Powell I told him the story. He, of course, had his own problems with the Cheney-Libby crew. He shook his head in sympathy and said he'd already heard the story from his deputy, Rich Armitage. I wish I could say that antics like this are rare in Washington, but sadly they occur in all administrations of all political stripes.

Our U.S. delegation had dinner that evening in a vast dining room with a Saudi delegation that included Foreign Minister Prince Saud and many members of the royal court. Then the vice president and the crown prince, along with the United States' trusted interpreter, Egyptian American Gamal Halal, went off to a private room, where, I later learned, Cheney discussed the possibility of a war against Iraq. Prince Saud and I sat in a reception area outside the inner sanctum.

In his 2011 memoir, the vice president writes, "I assured the crown prince we would prevail. . . . The crown prince was concerned about Saddam, but skeptical about U.S. military action. He wanted more reassurance that we would in fact see it through." Cheney then offered to have Secretary of Defense Rumsfeld and General Richard Myers, chairman of the Joint Chiefs of Staff, meet Abdullah in Texas on the eve of the summit to brief him about U.S. military activity and planning in the region.

Abdullah told the vice president that at the summit he wanted to discuss the Arab initiative to advance the peace process. Writes Cheney, " I told him we would welcome his initiatives . . . but I cautioned we viewed Arafat as a serious problem. Abdullah was not naive about Arafat, but he saw him as the leader of the Palestinians, someone who should be treated as a partner."[5]

Three weeks later—four days before the Crawford summit—I met with Prince Sultan, the Saudi minister of defense and aviation (who would become crown prince in 2005 and serve in that capacity until his death in October 2011). Upon arrival with my security detail at Prince Sultan's palatial office at his ministry, we were met by an official and escorted into an anteroom where my political-military counselor and I were offered Arabic coffee, dates, and then sweet tea. When Prince Sultan was ready to see us, we were ushered down the hall and greeted by much of the general staff of the military.

As was the custom in the Kingdom, my host sat in an upholstered chair next to a telephone. I took the senior guest seat across from him. The topic immediately turned to the upcoming summit.

Through an interpreter Sultan expressed optimism at the prospects for the meeting but was concerned that the confinement of Arafat in Ramallah might continue past the crown prince's time of arrival. He worried about the optics of Abdullah visiting President Bush with the Palestinian leader still surrounded by hostile Israeli troops at his headquarters. I responded that our government was aware of the situation but did not control the Israelis.

Prince Sultan then sent an encouraging signal: he wanted to relaunch the Joint Planning Committee, which had been an effective Saudi-U.S. series of regularly scheduled meetings among senior defense and military officials. The committee had lain dormant since before 9/11, and we were missing an important chance to pursue joint military interests and build relationships. Sultan wanted Joint Chiefs chairman Myers to come to Riyadh to be present for the meeting, likely to occur between July and September (not an ideal time to visit Riyadh, but Dick Myers was committed to doing whatever was necessary).

I emphasized the importance of our bilateral relationship and supported Sultan's suggestion. Sultan then turned to me and, referring to an old Arab proverb, observed that our relationship had been affected by a "slight wind," which cleared the land and made it ready for the rain to come and bring forth the land's bounty. I decided this was a good sign.

Returning to the topic of the Crawford summit, Prince Sultan expressed the crown prince's difficulty in understanding why he had not been invited to the White House instead of Crawford. Again, optics are so important in summits. I explained that this was an even more prestigious invitation, as it was the president's private home. Very few heads of state had been invited there. It was a rare, personal gesture.

Sultan seemed satisfied on this point but then ominously disclosed that the crown prince was under severe pressure from within the royal court to decline the invitation in light of the desperate situation in the Palestinian territories. He added that President Bush's recent characterization of Prime Minister Sharon as a "man of peace" had almost been the last straw.

I had little ammunition with which to counter this and in fact later told the president that the "man of peace" reference was not well received in the region. (I suspect that the president was trying to pacify Sharon and encourage less aggressive behavior, but the statement appeared to condone conduct that I knew the president found objectionable.) By the end of the meeting, Prince Sultan indicated that despite these reservations, the crown prince would go forward with the summit meeting. He added that Abdullah wanted to personally show President Bush evidence of the killing of innocent Palestinian women and children by the Israelis—perhaps in the form of a videotape. Most important, the

Saudis wanted an important deliverable: the release of Arafat from his confinement in Ramallah.

As our conversation was ending, Sultan asked me about the rumors that the United States wanted to remove its Air Force personnel from Prince Sultan Air Base. Indeed, numerous press reports darkly observed that we were about to be asked to leave PSAB due to the Saudis' discomfort at our footprint in the Kingdom. I countered that I was unaware of any U.S. effort to withdraw but acknowledged that our military was a guest of the Kingdom and respected Saudi sovereignty. (The press continued to publish dire predictions from their government sources that we were on the verge of eviction, but we remained in active operation at PSAB through the 2003 invasion of Iraq. We finally reached a decision to shut down our operations in mid-2003, after the fall of Saddam.)

Ambassadors are discouraged from accepting free transportation from their host countries. I flew to Houston as I flew almost everywhere while I was ambassador—commercial (business class only on flights longer than six hours). Vice President Cheney was to host a dinner for the principal members of the U.S. and Saudi delegations in a private dining room at the Intercontinental Hotel near Bush Airport on the night before the summit, April 24. Some of us would then leave the next morning and meet the president, who was already in Crawford.

As I recall, our dinner party delegation included the vice president, Deputy National Security Advisor Steve Hadley, Libby, Cheney aide John Hannah, and myself. Powell was flying in early the next morning, and Condi Rice was already with the president. In addition to the crown prince, the Saudi group included Prince Saud and Adel al-Jubeir. Bandar had another commitment, I believe. As promised by Cheney in Jeddah, Rumsfeld and Myers were also in Houston to meet privately with the crown prince. I do not recall them attending the dinner.

About an hour before the event, I went down to the dining room to see if the hotel had set the tables properly and if there were place cards. Seating arrangements were up to the vice president. As I stood alone, the door to the kitchen burst open and Cheney roared into the room on a scooter like a bat out of hell. That's scooter as in a motorized transportation device, not as in Libby.

Hobbled by a torn Achilles tendon, Cheney was using crutches and the scooter to get around—quite aggressively, I might add. He came close to popping a wheelie as he stopped in front of me. He had lunched with the crown prince earlier in the day. Now he had come to the dining room for the same reason I had. We exchanged pleasantries, checked out the arrangements, and left.

There were not a lot of pleasantries at the dinner, and in contrast to similar gatherings, there were no warm speeches or toasts. The theme of the evening was, *Let's get this over so we can start the summit tomorrow.* Prince Saud looked uncomfortable. Crown Prince Abdullah was testy. I imagined he was anticipating an unpleasant confrontation with the president over the Israeli-Palestinian issue.

I didn't know then, but believe now, that he was also uneasy because of his earlier meeting with Rumsfeld and Myers. On April 25, 2002, the *New York Times'* Elisabeth Bumiller quoted a "senior Washington official" who explained that the secretary and the general had been sent to brief Abdullah "on the American accomplishments in Afghanistan and in the broader war on terrorism." Yes, but I think there was more: a request to cooperate if and when we broadened that war to Iraq. (This may account for the absence of Powell, who at this time was pressing for a diplomatic solution to whatever problems we had with Saddam's regime.)

Early the next morning, I flew to a remote airstrip at Texas Technical College outside of Waco to receive the crown prince. Before Abdullah landed, I met Powell and briefed him on the previous night's dinner, and he explained the day's unfortunate traveling arrangements to me. We also lamented another article that appeared that same day in the *Times* under the less-than-encouraging headline "Mideast Turmoil: Arab Politics; Saudis to Warn Bush of Rupture over Israel Policy." Reporter Patrick Tyler's piece described the mood before the summit and demonstrated how parties to such an event can use the media to send out a warning and advance their own agendas . . . anonymously.

> Crown Prince Abdullah of Saudi Arabia is expected to tell President Bush in stark terms at their meeting on Thursday that the strategic relationship between their two countries will be threatened if Mr. Bush does not moderate his support for Israel's military policies, a person familiar with the Saudi's thinking said today. . . .

"This is not a mistake or a policy gaffe," the person close to Abdullah said, referring to Mr. Bush's approach. "He made a strategic, conscious decision to go with Sharon, so your national interest is no longer our national interest; now we don't have joint national interests. What it means is that you go your way and we will go ours, economically, militarily and politically—and the antiterror coalition would collapse in the process."

I still suspect Prince Bandar was the "person familiar" in the article, although the common practice is to deny such things leaked to journalists. Powell and I waited in an airplane hangar that doubled as a reception area. When the crown prince landed, he was met by a delegation of bouquet-bearing retired secretaries. Not secretaries of state or defense, but elderly American women who had worked as secretaries for Aramco, the national oil company of Saudi Arabia that has strong ties to the United States, particularly in Texas. I suspect they had been solicited by Qorvis, the Saudis' public relations firm, which would have had to clear the event with U.S. chief of protocol Don Ensenat. These women clearly had enormous affection for Abdullah and fond memories of their times in the eastern province at the Aramco compound.

The crown prince had rented an exceptionally well-appointed tour bus for the trip to Crawford. Gold filigree. Leather seats. Striking decals and decoration on the exterior. From its over-the-top appearance, I could think of only one thing: this bus would look good on tour with Dolly Parton.

The chain-smoking Abdullah rode shotgun in the captain's chair next to the driver so that he could look at the Texas countryside. In his *thobe*, *bisht*, *ghutra*, and *agal*, he looked every bit the part of an Arab potentate. He was fascinated at the rural scenery that we drove through on the way to the Western White House.

Powell, Prince Saud, Prince Bandar, and I sat on captain's chairs in the rear of the bus. Don Ensenat sat farther back. Apprehensive about the summit, we chatted politely. By this time Bandar knew we knew about the *New York Times* article and that we likely thought he was the source. He was quick to deny this.

Bandar is a gregarious, talkative former fighter pilot, the kind of fellow with whom you'd like to have dinner or a drink. With a graying beard and handsome looks weathered by the passage of time and circumstance, he was the dean of the Washington diplomatic corps, having served twenty-two years. We had many candid conversations and developed quite a friendly relationship, to the benefit of both of our countries.

Likewise, I felt an increasing respect for Prince Saud. Suffering back ailments and rumored to have Parkinson's disease, he had soldiered for many years as the Saudi foreign minister. By 2002 he was the longest-serving foreign minister in the world. A graduate of the Hun prep school in New Jersey and then Princeton, he spoke better English than I did.

Central Texas is always beautiful in the springtime. Wildflowers bloom and the hills are colorful. There aren't many towns on the two-lane road between the airstrip outside Waco and the ranch outside Crawford. As our bus made its way, Saud looked out the window and saw a hillside full of flowers. He turned to Powell, with whom he had been friends for years, and asked, "What are those flowers?"

"I think that's alfalfa," said the secretary of state.

Saud looked surprised. Smiling, he retorted, "Colin, what do you know about alfalfa? You grew up in New York!" It broke the tension, and we all had a good laugh at the secretary's attempt at interpreting Texas horticulture. As the lone Texan in our party, I was left to explain that the flowers were not alfalfa, but bluebonnets.

We arrived at the ranch around 10:30 and were met by the president. He welcomed the crown prince and the delegation warmly, but a chill remained in the air as the meetings started.

At summits like this, there are one-on-one meetings of the heads of state, meetings of the other diplomats, meetings of everyone, and meetings that ambassadors aren't always invited to. I retreated to the same double-wide trailer with pink flamingos I'd visited the previous August and waited. About an hour later, I was called back to the main house. By then the president and the crown prince had met privately. I believe that during their talk Abdullah showed Bush the videotape about the plight of the Palestinians.

As I arrived, the president and the crown prince were coming outside from the ranch house. The two men climbed into the president's beige Ford F250 pickup truck along with the interpreter Gamal Halal. Off the trio went for a tour of the ranch, just as I had eight months earlier. Two Suburbans full of Secret Service agents scrambled to keep up.

While the leaders were out, Powell and Rice told me the meetings were not going well. I later learned that Gamal had been talking with the Saudis in Arabic during breaks. He reported back to Powell or Rice that they were about to walk out and that somebody needed to do something or this summit was going to be over quickly. This sorry state of affairs may have been the genesis of the offer to take a time-out with the pickup ride.

A walkout would be catastrophic. What was the problem? Here's a secret. Most summits are fixed. Before the meetings begin, the parties have reached agreement on most or all of the issues at the staff level. The leaders then fine-tune that agreement and issue a joint statement that in all likelihood was written days earlier. But Crawford 2002 was different.

Unbeknownst to many of us at the ranch—*including the president of the United States*—the Saudis had sent the White House a list of eight demands four or five days before the summit. Prince Bandar later told me that he had personally delivered the list.

It's my understanding that the Saudis threatened to walk out at Crawford because the president didn't have a prepared response to those demands. How could he? He didn't even know they had been presented. Staff had let him down—either negligently or, worse, intentionally.

It very well may have been intentional. I was later told that "the vice president's office" had intercepted Bandar's delivery, explaining that they would be handling "the staffing," or response. But to my knowledge there had never been any staff workup of a response to those demands. There was also no joint statement that had been agreed upon.

When the president and the crown prince returned from their forty-five-minute ride, we could see they had bonded. They weren't holding hands, as they would so famously the next time at Crawford in 2005, but they were on good terms. Five or six of us then joined the two new friends on the ranch's screened-in porch for a lunch of beef tenderloin, potato salad, brownies, and vanilla ice cream.

As we pulled up our chairs, the president turned to the crown prince and said through Gamal, "Do you mind if I ask a blessing?" The crown prince smiled, nodded, and replied through Gamal, "Of course, thank you." The president prayed for the health of his guests and for the success of our meetings. I don't know how many Christian heads of state have asked Crown Prince (now King) Abdullah to pray with them, but the Saudi leader clearly was moved by the president's sincerity.

After lunch we Americans stayed in the room to work, while the Saudis moved to work in the nearby living room. At this point the president turned to Rice and said something to the effect of, *What are these eight demands? I don't know what they're talking about.*

Rice said something like, *Well, they were sent in, and we don't know much about it either.* She seemed fuzzy about it as well.

I think the president was shocked. I know I was. The leader of the free world hadn't been briefed on these critical demands, and the United States of America did not have a position on all of them. For all practical purposes, there had been no staff work done to prepare for this summit. Unbelievable.

Now we were finally seeing the eight demands. One: get Arafat released from his confinement in Ramallah. Two: end the siege of the Church of the Nativity.

The Saudi paper, which might have formed the basis of a joint statement by Bush and Abdullah, listed six other points related to Abdullah's peace plan, which had recently been approved at the Arab League summit. These included immediate political talks between Israel and the Palestinians, an armed multinational peacekeeping force, and an end to Israeli settlements in Palestinian areas.

This was important information to have been kept from the president. My guess was that someone in the vice president's office had made a conscious decision to conceal the list because the vice president and his ideological cohorts, fiercely pro-Israel, did not want to give other "enemy" camps within the administration the chance to do something about the demands. This is not the way to run a government.

It's fair to ask whether President Bush was aware of such palace intrigue and if he wanted to get down to the bottom of such skullduggery. Did he know that he was being ill-served by the rivalry or factionalism in his administration? Did he understand that having a secretary of state marginalized by a vice president and staff and secretary of defense was neither productive nor in the national interest?

The president was not usually that open with me on these issues.

But he clearly was perturbed at Crawford when he learned he hadn't been briefed. Then he did what he was supposed to do: he took charge.

"What are the sticking points here?" Bush asked Rice as we went through the list demand by demand. After we discussed the two sieges, he ordered her to call the Israelis. She quickly rang up (and woke up) Danny Ayalon, Ariel Sharon's foreign policy advisor (who would become ambassador to the United States later in 2002). Ayalon tentatively agreed to release Arafat from his confinement in Ramallah and end the hostilities at the Church of the Nativity. (Three days later the siege of Ramallah was lifted. On April 29, 2002, Tony Karon of *Time* magazine reported that the Israeli cabinet agreed to do so "in the face of what an Israel official called 'brutal' pressure from President Bush." Soon the siege in Bethlehem also ended.)

After Rice got on the phone, the president asked me whether the Saudis were bluffing with their threat to walk out if all eight demands were not met. Here's where an ambassador earns his pay by understanding the culture and the personalities of his host country's leaders. I said I didn't think they were bluffing but that they would likely take less than the full eight. My suspicion was that there was room to negotiate and keep them from walking out without delivering the entire package. I explained that in the Arab world, you always ask for more than you expect to get. That may be true in many countries, but it is particularly pronounced in the Middle East.

Talk now moved to whether the president would have to overtly approve Abdullah's peace plan, something he was loath to do. The president asked if we could "park the issue." Translation: could we find a way to just defer discussion and hope it went away?

"Maybe you can park it today," I said. "But you can't park it much longer. At some point you're going to have to address it."

One thing that would be parked today for certain was a joint post-summit statement. Each country would issue its own communiqué.

Rice presented a draft. It included language something like, *We reminded the Saudis of how important it is to speak out against terrorism and to do everything possible to counter the threat of terrorism.*

I spoke up. "You can't possibly want to use this word 'reminded.'" I thought it condescending and so inappropriate here that it would be a huge mistake to use it. Fortunately, it was removed.

(I am truly fond of Condi Rice, a smart and savvy diplomat, but at press conferences and in written statements, she was, in my opinion, too taken with "reminding" other nations. I don't like the word. Rare is the occasion when the leaders of other nations need to be reminded of something. In all likelihood, they haven't forgotten.)

Although our delegation and the Saudis would not be issuing a joint statement, we gave each other the courtesy of seeing our respective communiqués. And so by the end of the day, we had some progress, enough agreement so that the Saudis didn't walk out.

Press Secretary Ari Fleischer told reporters that our talks with the Saudis on their eight points would continue.

The president said that he had created a "strong personal bond" with Abdullah. But as the *Times'* Tyler reported on April 27, Bush added, "I told the crown prince that we've got a unique relationship with Israel, and that one thing that the world can count on is that we will not allow Israel to be crushed."

In the April 26 *New York Times*, Bumiller reported on the Saudi perspective, noting that Abdullah had "bluntly told President Bush today that the United States must temper its support for Israel or face serious consequences throughout the Arab world." Bumiller noted that Adel al-Jubeir had said that leaving Sharon "to his own devices" did not serve the interests of the United States or the Kingdom. Still, as al-Jubeir said, Abdullah had not threatened to use Saudi oil policy as "a weapon" against the United States.

Because the meeting had not blown up as feared, the crown prince, Prince Saud, Prince Bandar, and I were more than relieved as we climbed back on the bus to Waco. Again, Abdullah sat up front, smoking. Again, the princes and I sat in the back. Saud and Bandar were so relieved that they started humming something musical.

What was the tune? It sounded familiar. Then, in a giddy moment of exhaustion and relief, they broke into song. Now I recognized the melody. "The rain in Spain falls mainly on the plain." They were performing Rex Harrison's Professor Henry Higgins from *My Fair Lady*.

Their next offering from the show was laden with irony: "Why can't a woman be more like a man?" they sang.

The next day President Bush publicly called on Israel to end the siege of Ramallah. Said Adel al-Jubeir, "It speaks to the commitment of the president and the United States to see a peaceful solution and an end of the violence so work can be begun to implement the vision the president and the crown prince share."[6]

We had avoided a crisis.

5

IT'S JANUARY 2002. We're attending a USO show at the Eskan Village American military compound outside Riyadh. The comedian Drew Carey spots me in the front row and pulls me up onstage to join the Improv All-Stars from the popular television show *Whose Line Is It Anyway?* As I reluctantly climb onto the stage, the hundreds of servicemen and servicewomen at the show go wild.

"What do you like to do, Mr. Ambassador?" Carey asks.

"Watch NFL football and go out to dinner," I say.

"What else?"

"I like to play golf when I can."

The comedian turns to the audience. "Ladies and gentlemen, meet your golfing *Badassador.*"

The nickname would stick. Over a year later, just before the beginning of Operation Iraqi Freedom, General Buzz Moseley invited me to go on a twelve-hour A-WACS mission to the Iraq border (more about this in chapter 9). When I arrived at the air base, the brass presented me with an Air Force flight suit. My name had been stitched on: BADASSADOR JORDAN.

Flying on an A-WACS mission was not a typical day at the office. Then again, there really is no "typical" day in the life of an ambassador, especially a U.S. ambassador in Saudi Arabia in 2002. There were, however, certain recurring daily themes.

I'd rise in the morning, hit my Schwinn Airdyne stationary bike for twenty minutes most days, then head in to breakfast in the family quarters on the second floor of the residence, Quincy House. Rudy the butler or Carlotta the housemaid would serve eggs, toast, coffee, and juice along with a copy of the *Arab News*, the largest English-language newspaper in the Kingdom. Then a shower and dressing, then the drive from Quincy House to the embassy, accompanied by my trusty bodyguards.

The embassy lies in the Diplomatic Quarter of Riyadh, where most embassies and ambassadors' homes are located. It's in a residential area west of the central business district, near a number of royal palaces. The quarter includes a number of Saudi government agencies, like the Supreme Commission on Tourism, as well as apartment blocks. Most of our embassy personnel lived there, either in villas or apartments. It's lavishly landscaped with towering palm trees and vegetation. It was intended to be a place where local Saudis and expatriate diplomats and families could mix and at one time had a community center where women could—perish the thought—actually swim openly in a swimming pool. That didn't last long.

Because of the circuitous street layout, it takes a bit longer than one would expect to drive there, about eight to ten minutes. The route, which we occasionally varied, usually took me past an attractive park, the British Embassy, and the United Nations building.

We would usually enter through the motor pool entrance, which is one of the largest of its kind in any U.S. embassy. Because women are not allowed to drive and thus don't own vehicles, we needed more cars and drivers to chauffeur female staff or guests than the average U.S. embassy.

An aside: until recently females were not allowed to ride bicycles or motorbikes in public. That restriction has been lifted, but only like many restrictions in the Kingdom—slowly and incrementally. As *Time* magazine's Kristene Quan reported on April 3, 2013, "The Saudi newspaper the *Al-Yawm* cited an unnamed official from the Kingdom's religious police saying that women are allowed to ride bikes in parks and recreational areas, but they have to be accompanied by a male relative and dressed in the full Islamic head-to-toe abaya. . . . The official reportedly specified that women aren't allowed to use bicycles for transportation purposes, 'only for entertainment,' and they are being advised to avoid places where young men may congregate 'to avoid harassment.'"

Upon arriving at the motor pool, I'd greet the other drivers, enter the embassy, and proceed to the elevator, which took me to the executive suite. I'd say hello to Donna, my secretary (OMS, or office management specialist, in government-speak), grab a cup of coffee, and check the email and briefing books. Email would be my first stop, as we did not have BlackBerries or iPhones for email in those days, and I would not have seen the overnight traffic. The email would be a mix of correspondence about new regulations, personnel transfer orders, budget issues, and social invitations. Occasionally I'd also receive personal emails in addition to those that came to my separate personal email address. I made sure to keep all official emails on the state.gov server.

When I first arrived, classified information would have to be sent through pouches, teletypes, or other primitive means. Ultimately classified email was installed, truly a step into a new century. "Classified" is a broad category and could include emails about upcoming travel by Secretary Powell, talking points to present at my next meeting with a government official, or analysis of political or security trends in the region.

Next I'd tackle the briefing books, binders of classified and unclassified cables and briefing papers digesting the overnight reports, with analysis pieces occasionally attached. In my short career as an officer with the U.S. Naval Security Group in Washington thirty years earlier, my "classified" reading even included newspaper clippings from the *New York Times* and *Washington Post* describing Vietnam war protests and civil rights incidents, all labeled "CONFIDENTIAL." At least my current reading hadn't overclassified such mundane public records. Overnight intelligence assessments could include threats asserted in conversations, evaluations of the reliability of the reporting, and reports of meetings with local religious or political activists. Often the contents were ambiguous, with vague references using names either in code or with unclear meaning.

Usually within thirty minutes of my morning arrival I'd be joined by Margaret, who was not only my DCM but my TRA (trusted right arm). I've already described how her experience and intelligence made her the perfect deputy and how she deservedly would go on to become an ambassador in her own right.

We had the usual staff meetings, sometimes in my office, which was fairly large. Beyond my desk sat several sofas, arranged in front of the wood-burning fireplace. Needless to say I never lit it up in the blazing heat of Saudi Arabia. My senior staff attending these meetings included the heads of the various key departments, such as political, consular, administrative, political/military, defense, public affairs, and security. Some meetings covered material so sensitive that we took extra security precautions, which I am not at liberty to reveal.

Fridays were particularly special. Some background for the non-Arabist reader: In the Muslim world, the official weekend is Friday and Saturday. Saudi Arabia was the last of the Arab countries in the Middle East to declare this—in 2013. Prior to that the Kingdom's official weekend was Thursday and Friday. Thursday was the equivalent of the Western Saturday—not an official work day, but many of us would go in to the office to catch up on paperwork for a few hours. Some government offices were open Thursday mornings, but we rarely sought a government meeting on such days. At first it seemed odd to me to be working on Saturday as the beginning of the workweek, and I found myself talking about taking "Sunday" off when I really meant Friday.

There was no more consideration of Jewish traditions of taking Saturday off than there was of Christians taking Sunday off. Both were workdays. The Saudis never showed me any antipathy toward American Jews working in the embassy or in the private sector. A number of our embassy officials over the years were Jewish, including one very senior official who served after I departed. The Saudis reserved their antipathy mostly for "Zionists," generally meaning the Israelis.

Friday will continue to be the most important day of the week for Muslims—a holy day of prayer. As for non-Muslims, we held morning services in the embassy for the community at large. Protestant services at 8:30 brought a group of forty to fifty. The Catholic services that followed attracted overflow crowds, upward of two hundred, including many from the large Filipino population of house servants in Riyadh. This was followed by a Mormon service. The Saudi police would take down the license numbers of those who came for all of these services, as it is a capital offense to proselytize a Muslim to change religion.

There was no Jewish service because there were hardly any Jews at the mission then. If such services had been requested, however, we would have had them. While some Jews had trepidations about visiting Saudi

Arabia, they encountered little difficulty. The visa application requires a disclosure of the applicant's religion, but I never heard of any rejection based on disclosing one's Jewish faith. We had no special warnings for Jews or members of any other faith, apart from the inconvenience of a death penalty if they were caught proselytizing. I occasionally heard stories about religious symbols like crosses or Stars of David bringing enhanced scrutiny. Perhaps for that reason I wore a ring with a cross on it to show my Christian faith. I was never challenged.

I attended the Protestant services—in part to set an example, but more importantly because I found them very comforting. As I've previously mentioned, my appointment as ambassador and my experience on the ground caused me to rekindle a Christian faith that had been in the background for many years. Perhaps it came from living in a culture that was intolerant of competing religions and where Christians who gathered together shared a bond in resisting the authoritarian anti-Christian environment.

Unlike their Gulf neighbors, the Saudis didn't allow the sale of Christmas trees or ornaments. If red and green decorations showed up on store shelves, they would be swept away by the religious police. And there were no valentines allowed on Valentine's Day, let alone any hope of egg decorations or religious symbols at Easter.

At a farewell party in Dallas hosted by the Dallas Bar Association, I had shared my view, with a lump in my throat, that "blessed are the peacemakers." Maybe the appointment was God's mission for me to try to find a way toward peace, even though it might be at some personal risk.

After services, I would be joined at my residence by the ambassadors from Belgium and France and occasionally Denmark, a Canadian doctor and nurse couple, the manager of the Rosewood Faisaliah Hotel and his wife, one of my embassy colleagues and his wife, and an IT executive. We would use the pool and tennis courts at the residence, have a few drinks, and talk about life and work.

The Friday Group, as we called ourselves, became a coveted sanctuary from the stress of war, governmental dysfunction, and local resentment of American policy. We would alternate the venue with Franz Michils, the Belgian ambassador. His wife, Jacqueline, was a talented jewelry maker and outstanding cook. Her meals were always a highlight of the week. Their residence was attached to their embassy and was an older building than my residence.

One form of stress did invade the Friday Group: tennis. When I arrived in Riyadh, I was an average to below average tennis player, and most of the other guys in the group were about the same level. Soon, however, a couple of them began taking it seriously, especially Franz and the Rosewood Faisaliah's manager, a Belgian American Alphy Johnson. After about a year they started beating me routinely.

I grew weary of being beaten so I asked around and learned there was a fellow in the embassy cafeteria named Noli who was a great tennis player. I started taking lessons from him . . . but to no avail. Alphy and Franz continued to maintain the upper hand.

Ambassadorial residences were not the only places at which I dined out. I was frequently invited to dinner parties at the homes of Saudis. They had their reasons for putting me on the guest list: For some, I was a convenient ornament, a means of showing that they were important enough to warrant the attendance of the U.S. ambassador. Others desired my presence so they could get a particular message across. And some, believe it or not, just wanted to be friends.

There were plenty of evenings when I would have preferred to stay in my residence reading a nice book by John Grisham or Tom Clancy. The social circuit could be exhausting, especially because the parties usually ended late. I didn't accept every invitation. But I had my reasons for attending, and more often than not I went.

I viewed going as part of my job description. I was able to associate with a group of people that my younger and more junior officers rarely met. Among the guests at these functions were Saudi business and government elites (cabinet and subcabinet), ministers of state, members of the Majlis Al Shura (the Kingdom's consultative council), journalists, and educators. I was on the clock—listening, probing, mining for useful information.

Typically, I would brief my staff the morning after. Often I would send a cable to Washington, feeding the beast, noting something I had learned. Occasionally, I might even recommend a policy change based on what I heard or discussed.

While the food and drink were usually superb, the conversation didn't always go down well. The guests were opinionated folks. There was no "polite" in their politics. At many of these gatherings, we ended up engaging in an unpleasant exercise I called "pin the tail on the ambassador." There are only so many nights a week that one can tolerate being verbally accosted by angry Saudis. Frankly, this was a contributing factor in my decision to quit after two years.

The Palestinian situation was a recurring theme and source of Saudi anger directed at me. *America should be able to resolve this,* they told me. After all, the United States was omnipotent. All Washington had to do was snap its fingers and Israel would come to heel, do whatever we commanded it to do.

I also endured a healthy dose of anger at American visa policy post-9/11. As much as the Saudi elites criticized our policy on Palestine, they expressed even more anger at the enhanced scrutiny given to their visa applications. They were no longer kissin' cousins of the United States and often suffered great indignities upon arriving at an American port of entry. I made a point of urging officials in Washington to promote a more humane attitude toward Saudis entering the States, even though we could not relax the necessary security procedures. Ultimately, sufficient resources were provided to reduce the waiting times, and the officers on the front line improved their manners in dealing with visitors to our country.

I was able to slip away from Riyadh on occasion and relished periodic weekend visits with Hassan Alkabbani and his family in Jeddah. Hassan was in his mid-thirties and was both a successful businessman and the honorary consul of Belgium. I met him through Franz, and we immediately hit it off. Hassan, a graduate of Pepperdine University in California, is a fun-loving, happy soul who lights up all those around him. Active in the Young Presidents Organization—a global network connecting chief executives—and the ultimate successor to his father's business empire, Hassan was the consummate host. His extended family's beach house was often my weekend retreat. His cousin Khairy had a sailboat, and I especially enjoyed venturing out into the Red Sea for an afternoon of sailing and snorkeling.

The only drawback was my Saudi security detail. As they insisted on accompanying me, we hired a motorboat so they could follow—with the proviso that they had to stay five hundred meters away from our sailboat. The bodyguards had only one problem: even though they were tough as nails, they were not used to being on the water. Several of them got seasick from the choppy waters. I can still visualize them in the distance behind us, bobbing up and down like a cork, throwing up over the sides of the small motorboat.

After one weekend in Jeddah, Hassan offered to drive me to the airport in his new Mercedes sports car. My bodyguards and driver had anxious looks on their faces as I walked over to the car and my friend handed me the keys. We jumped in and I gunned it. We raced down the highway toward the airport, my entourage struggling to keep up behind us. A rare, exhilarating, independent moment—reminiscent of home, where I had been known to take my antique 1965 Corvette well into triple digits on deserted roads.

My friendship with Hassan was, quite frankly, a lifesaver for me because my existence was often a lonely one. There weren't many people I could call friends other than the Friday Group. Although our relationship was almost exclusively social, I would rely on Hassan for occasional interpretations of what I thought I was seeing, for cultural translations. One example: I was curious to learn how he and those in his circle felt about the fundamentalist Wahhabi.

My visits to Jeddah were the exception to the rule. Due to prevailing conditions in Saudi Arabia after the attacks of 9/11, my regional security officer discouraged me from visiting many other Saudi cities. I went into the souk, the old public market in downtown Riyadh, a few times but was often advised against mingling with crowds, where security could be an issue.

On my rare visits to the souk, I thoroughly enjoyed the chance to roam through the aisles and pathways. The hustle and bustle, the smells of spices, the ancient rugs and furniture combined with stalls full of silks, vcrs, and knickknacks all were a delight to experience. In one tiny, cramped stall I bargained with the shopkeeper over a modestly priced rug. I opened the bidding at around one-third of the asking price and ended up paying just under half the "retail" price. The seller feigned grave disappointment and appeared near tears at the end of our session, but I suspect he was more than satisfied with our deal. Not a great negotiating triumph for me, but an entertaining way to spend some time.

I would have enjoyed more time on the street in the Kingdom, but it was important that my activities outside the embassy be as safe as possible. U.S. ambassadors, particularly those in hotspots, are prized targets for the bad guys. As is well known, the United States suffered a terrible loss on September 11, 2012, when Chris Stevens, our ambassador to Libya, was killed during an attack on the U.S. special mission compound and annex in Benghazi. (The embassy is in the capital, Tripoli.). Ambassador Stevens was a highly regarded career diplomat with a special love for the people of Libya, who had only recently emerged from years under the thumb of the brutal dictator Muammar Gaddafi. While I did not know him, our mutual colleagues held him in high esteem and considered him a model of what a career diplomat in the Middle East should be.

I heard the terrible news of his death following an overnight flight to New York for a speaking engagement at a conference. A number of Middle East experts and former ambassadors were assembled for the event, and we all were deeply affected by the loss of Ambassador Stevens and the three other U.S. officials. It brought home to me once again how our diplomats serve in dangerous places, often with little or no real physical security in the face of real threats. My good friend Deborah Jones, the former ambassador to Kuwait, went on to replace Chris Stevens as our ambassador to Libya, a gutsy move by a very brave woman.

Chris's death raised many questions. When can or should an ambassador be out among the people in the country in which he or she serves? How safe are our embassies and consulates from attack? Did I feel I was safe and received the proper support and intelligence from the State Department? What else had I learned about the attack from my contacts in the diplomatic world? And finally, what should Congress do in the wake of such a tragedy—investigate, demand heads roll, turn into a political football? Let me address these.

As the president's personal representative, an ambassador needs to connect not only with the leadership of his or her host country but also as much as possible with the people. American culture, entrepreneurship, individualism, and ideals are better communicated in personal settings than in slogans or brochures. I never agreed with some of the State Department honchos who wanted to sell America like cornflakes. The best way to know America is to visit there, and the next best way is to know an American. America's "soft power" lies in the examples of the spirit of America each of us can project.

I was frustrated that one of the aftereffects of 9/11 was that threats to my own security kept me from traveling widely around Saudi Arabia and meeting many of the people. Because of the need to get to my post, my language school sessions were cancelled. In the best of all worlds, I would have had that training so I would have been able to better understand what I was hearing. Instead, I usually relied on my political officers, who would mix with the people anonymously. They would go out into the coffeehouses, back alleys, and rural towns, including hotbeds of Al Qaeda activity. They would speak Arabic with the people and then come back and report to me on what they were finding. Several of our officers reminded me of Peace Corps volunteers who so easily assimilate into a culture like this, who can gain the confidence of the people they're talking to and then can come back and provide good information.

My family's security was as important to me as the safety of my staff. As noted earlier, Ann did not accompany me to the Kingdom when I began my posting. She came in the summer of 2002, after I had persuaded myself that she would not be in danger and she had arranged a leave of absence from her university teaching job.

As a woman, she had access to a slice of Saudi life that I never saw. She could travel in the female segment of society and made many friends. Unlike a male in the Kingdom, she had a 360-degree view of the culture. Although initially she was quite skeptical about living in a world that seems so misogynistic, she ultimately viewed the Saudis with great affection, at least individually. She undertook a research fellowship at the King Faisal Center for Research and Islamic Studies. She also got to know a number of accomplished Saudi women professionals and wrote an excellent book about her experiences and research, *The Making of a Modern Kingdom: Modernization and Globalization in Saudi Arabia.*

The spouse of an ambassador lives in an atmosphere almost as rarefied as the ambassador. In Saudi Arabia, that means frequent social events and invitations and a constant stream of new acquaintances, mostly in the female half of the society. In Ann's case, she was able to meet people of both genders from many walks of life. Her training as an anthropologist likely aided her in getting to know and understand much of the new life she had thrust upon her. This included an eclectic group of friends, some of whom performed in the satirical television show *Tash ma Tash,* or "No Big Deal" in English. The show, broadcast for nearly twenty years during Ramadan, is a kind of Monty Python look at Saudi society, poking fun at elements of the male-dominated culture in a way that came close to crossing certain lines in the sand.

Ann also was able to travel anonymously and made several side trips to places like Yemen, where my regional security officer said I could not venture for security reasons. She did not travel with security, although she had to have a driver, given the Saudi view on women driving. Two of our sons joined us for part of the time. Andrew, mentioned earlier, was studying Arabic. Peter, who had graduated from Duke and was working on documentary films in Kenya, spent four months in Riyadh during a break, instructing the male students at the King Faisal preparatory school on documentary film techniques. My boys and their mother were able to take a number of adventurous trips to Egypt and surrounding countries.

As noted earlier a fellow ambassador had provided wise counsel: pay attention and keep your mouth shut. During my first few months I followed that advice. I am not impressed with government officials who pontificate and pretend to be know-it-alls, especially in as opaque and complex a society as Saudi Arabia. But as I listened and learned, I also realized it was time to begin to assert my position, to advocate for U.S. policy with increasing energy and firmness.

In the chaos following 9/11, it was difficult to set a mid- or long-range agenda or to settle into a routine. By the time I returned to the Kingdom from a trip to Washington in early 2002, I had my bearings. I was now comfortable enough in the job to take it to the next level.

An important audience for my outreach efforts was the American Business Group of Riyadh. It holds monthly breakfasts (attended by twenty to forty), quarterly luncheons (attended by up to two hundred) and occasional social events, with speakers on topics of interest to the

American expat community. My law partner, former secretary of state Baker, has addressed them several times, as have CEOs of major international corporations and, occasionally, Saudi government officials.

Membership includes most of the top-level executives of corporations doing business in the Kingdom—ExxonMobil, Procter and Gamble, Raytheon, and Marsh McLennan. They were eager to learn of the latest developments in our relationship with the Saudis, and I shared with them what I could. A large part of my mission was to promote American business and to hear the views and concerns of those trying to do business there.

As the Israeli-Palestinian conflict was raging and the anti-Saudi reaction to 9/11 in the United States was increasingly bitter, anti-American sentiment in Saudi Arabia was a real problem. Local groups began to encourage a boycott of American goods. Schoolteachers would give their students lists of products and brands to be boycotted: Coca-Cola, Chevrolet, Tide, Fritos, Crest, Charmin, Duracell, etc.

Because many of these brands were owned by Procter and Gamble, the company's president for the Middle East came to see me, complaining about the serious damage P&G was suffering from the boycott. I sympathized with him and made a case to the ministries of foreign affairs and commerce that this was unfair. The boycott ultimately petered out, likely more the result of Saudi demand for American-quality goods than a change in political views.

(It amused me that one of the automobiles on the boycott list was Porsche. I'm sure the Porsche executives in Stuttgart were surprised to learn that their high-priced supercars were actually American!)

My outreach included frequent contact with the Saudi press and writing occasional op-ed pieces in Saudi publications. It did not extend, however, to American media. I was welcome to meet with American journalists, but only on background and not for attribution. The White House and State Department wanted to control the message for the American audience and didn't want an ambassador going off script.

This policy did not stop me from meeting off the record with the constant stream of Western reporters flocking to Saudi Arabia for a story or photo op. Most of those who came to visit were sincere and well prepared. In these critical times, they were anxious to learn something about Saudi Arabia.

Leslie Stahl of 60 *Minutes* shared with me that her husband, Aaron Latham, was from Ranger, Texas, a town of two thousand not far from Dallas. He had cowritten the movie *Urban Cowboy.*

Katie Couric spent an hour drinking coffee in my living room, asking excellent questions reflecting extensive preparation. Her professionalism ran counter to the "cutesy" image she showed on television. She did, however, enjoy kidding me that, as a University of Virginia graduate, she assumed that my son, an honor graduate of Duke, could not get into her alma mater as an out-of-state applicant. The next day she returned to cutesy, swinging her legs on the wing of an F-15 fighter jet as she reported for the *Today Show.*

CNN's Christiane Amanpour also spent an hour with me in my living room. I remember her smoking cigarettes and giving me her opinion on the world. She knew her stuff, but I couldn't get a word in edgewise.

My daily life also included a media lifeline to the United States. We subscribed to the Armed Forces Network, so I was able to view a few American television shows and sports broadcasts. Weekly NFL games were not to be missed. CNN was on my regular diet.

Beginning in 2003 MSNBC featured a young former congressman from Pensacola named Joe Scarborough on a show called *Scarborough Country.* Pretty conservative stuff, but not as rabid as Bill O'Reilly and some of the others on Fox and other outlets. Scarborough seems to have moderated his views over the years, and now I quite enjoy his popular MSNBC show *Morning Joe.* I didn't have access to some of today's faux news shows like *The Daily Show with Jon Stewart,*" which would have been a welcome relief from the harsh reality reflected in my television news in Riyadh. Apparently a number of high-ranking Saudis also were glued to the Armed Forces Network, as I learned when it was temporarily disconnected and several princes called me personally to restore their television subscriptions. I guess this was an example of America's "soft power."

My visitors were not confined to the American media. I felt that it was critically important for as many of our lawmakers as possible to visit the Kingdom. Very few in Congress seemed to understand what was going on in the Middle East, and Saudi representatives visiting America had not been effective in communicating their efforts to fight terrorism and preserve their relationship with us.

All too rarely, we hosted congressional delegations (this, too, has an acronym: CODEL). In chapter 6 I address at length a rather infamous visit by a CODEL led by Representative Dan Burton in the late summer of 2002. And in chapter 8 I detail a remarkable visit by Senator Joe Lieberman on Christmas Day 2002. At the time Lieberman was considering a run for the presidency. John Kerry, then the U.S. senator from Massachusetts, also visited in advance of his successful bid for the Democratic Party nomination in 2004.

Another CODEL did not even get off the ground. Michigan's Carl Levin and Virginia's John Warner, both grizzled veterans of the Senate, had scheduled a trip to Riyadh. When their plane was set to take off from Bahrain at 8:00 a.m., they had not yet received clearance to land in Riyadh, a mere forty-five minutes away.

We often had air clearance problems, partly the result of Saudi administrative incompetence and partly the result of occasional reminders by the Saudis that they were a sovereign nation that could jerk us around from time to time. I wasn't sure which it was here, but I called the foreign minister, Prince Saud, and told him we urgently needed the air clearance. He acquiesced, but I then received word that Levin had scrubbed the visit. Why? Because if the delegation landed on the delayed schedule, its crew would require a mandatory rest overnight in Riyadh and could not continue on to what was viewed as a more pleasant place for a layover.

Spending the night in Riyadh was a fate worse than death for many congressional visits. It was far more attractive to overnight in Crete, the next stop. I called Levin, still cooling his heels on the tarmac in Bahrain, and urged him to soldier on to Riyadh. He was not amused. I pleaded further. He said something like, *Goddammit, we're not coming!* and hung up on me. Such is the way of the imperial Senate.

One senator whom I saw more often than others when I was in Washington was Chuck Hagel of Nebraska. A Vietnam combat veteran, he understood the brutality of war and the often-unintended consequences. He always asked probing questions and challenged conventional wisdom. He demonstrated a seasoned understanding of the dynamics of the Middle East and the importance of the Saudi relationship. In 2013 I was disappointed that so many of his fellow senators failed to support his nomination to be President Obama's secretary of defense. I was heartened that he was eventually confirmed, even though he really never became a member of Team Obama.

On the House side, I made it a point during one trip to Washington to see the chairman of the International Relations Committee, Henry Hyde. He was not particularly interested in the U.S.-Saudi relationship, and especially not interested in visiting Saudi Arabia. I remarked that many more Democrats than Republicans had visited us and that I hoped more Republican congressmen would visit the region. Hyde dismissed these comments, saying something to the effect of, *Democrats are always interested in spending the taxpayers' money on junkets.* I guess I hadn't realized that Riyadh was such a tourist attraction for Democratic representatives![1]

My diplomatic efforts extended beyond dealing with the Saudis. As the representative of the most powerful nation on earth, I had access to the Saudi leadership that far surpassed that of any other ambassador in the Kingdom. As a result the rest of the diplomatic corps maintained an intense curiosity over my comings and goings. Each time my picture would appear in the newspaper or on television in the midst of a meeting with the king, the crown prince, or a cabinet member, I would receive a round of calls from the diplomatic corps. I was willing to share with them what I could, but handling all the calls became time consuming.[2]

The Council of the European Union has a presidency that rotates every six months, and the ambassador whose country holds the presidency hosts meetings of the EU ambassadors. It occurred to me that I could meet with all the EU ambassadors or brief the ambassador whose country held the presidency and save time. This evolved into periodic briefings of the group and led to healthy and friendly exchanges with those present. These meetings intensified in early 2003 when the impending invasion of Iraq held everyone's attention.

The buildup to the invasion began to occupy most of my time. I had numerous meetings with Saudi officials. They detested Saddam Hussein and suggested we pursue everything from assassination to bribing him into a well-heeled exile.

Doing something under the radar was the preferred method. Foreign Minister Prince Saud told me in August 2002, "With covert action there is deniability; with war there is no way out." Even though Prince Saud also maintained that "the best war is the one you win without fighting," apart from covert action his only suggestion was to wait for Saddam to make a mistake that would allow us to gain widespread support for an attack. He even threatened to deny us use of air bases and flyover permission for an attack. However, I wasn't convinced that when push came to shove the Saudis would deny us the cooperation we needed.

In November 2002 Assistant Minister of Defense Prince Khalid bin Sultan provided the first words from a Saudi official encouraging military action. He told me that if the chips were down, the United States could count on Saudi support in Iraq. He also suggested that we wait until March to launch an attack, both to show patience and to enjoy better weather.

In December the crown prince's foreign policy adviser, Adel al-Jubeir, told me that the Saudis would provide all the United States needed, though perhaps not all we wanted. Based upon these and similar statements, I continued to believe that if the weapons inspectors made no progress, and if all else failed, the Saudis would give us the necessary assistance to undertake the invasion. I conveyed this to President Bush on my visit.

My views were reinforced in January by the Saudi reaction to our requests for basing and logistical assistance in the invasion. Prince Saud, hopeful that Saddam's less culpable lieutenants could be kept in place to assist in running a post-Saddam Iraq, urged us to give assurances that only the "top tier" of Iraqi leadership would be removed. Ever the fervent believer in multilateral action through the United Nations, he also advised me that he was urging the French to cooperate with us on the second Security Council resolution (an unsuccessful gambit).

Countering this optimism was the fact that the Saudi leaders were deeply concerned that their own people would react angrily to an American invasion. They were also concerned that we did not know what we were doing. The invasion would be the easy part, they said. Providing governance and security and a path forward for self-governance, would be nearly impossible. And any power vacuum created by Saddam's fall would potentially be occupied by the Saudis' archrival, Iran.

Both the foreign minister and the assistant defense minister implored me, "Mr. Ambassador, please do not win the war but lose the peace." Their concerns turned out to be well founded. Prince Saud will be remembered for declaring after the invasion, "You have given Iraq to Iran on a silver platter."

6

In Riyadh the average temperature in August is 96 degrees, with the average daily high 108 degrees in the shade. If you have to visit, why not come in the spring, when the temperature is between 70 and 80 degrees? So the fact that six members of the House Committee on Oversight and Government Reform, Congress's primary investigative body, were journeying to the Kingdom during the last week of August 2002 sent an unmistakable message: *We're coming on important business that can't wait.*

The fact that the committee chair and delegation leader, Congressman Dan Burton (r-in), was trying to bring along the iconic reporter Mike Wallace and a *60 Minutes* film crew suggested something more: *Maybe we can get a little publicity for ourselves as well.*

The delegation came to investigate State Department policy on two hot-button subjects. One: the issuance of visas to Saudis seeking to come to the United States. And two: child custody and abduction. These were important subjects, and I'd spent much of my own time addressing them. But the manner in which Burton and his minions conducted themselves over their four days in Saudi Arabia was, in my opinion, less than professional.

Let's start with the visas. As one would expect, after the 9/11 attacks, Congress wanted to know how the hijackers from Saudi Arabia had entered the United States. It soon became clear that some of them had obtained legitimate visas from our consulate in Jeddah. Early in 2002 reporter Joel Mowbray broke a disturbing story. Three of the Saudi hijackers had obtained their visas through Visa Express, a program instituted by the State Department's Bureau of Consular Affairs (BCA) in June 2001.

As Mowbray explained it in a later column, under this program, "a Saudi national, or someone just living in the country, was *expected* to submit a visa application to a *private Saudi travel agent*. Sure, the application was then passed on to the consulate or embassy, but the result was that most Saudi applicants could avoid contact with any U.S. citizens until stepping foot off an airplane on American soil."[1]

Mowbray's use of the word "expected" may be questioned. But the bottom line is that Saudis no longer had to go to a consulate to start— and usually complete—the visa process. Less than 30 percent of those issued visas were actually interviewed by our people.

How could this be? Visa Express began before I was even nominated for my ambassadorship, and I am not here to defend what was clearly a shockingly lax system. But I can explain it. In the pre-9/11 world, we weren't as worried about terrorists entering the country on visas as we should have been. Our consular workers focused on whether a Saudi was likely to overstay his visa and take a job from an American, and the legislation in place did not require a security screening.

With large numbers of Saudis applying for visas, BCA wanted to help speed what was then an overwhelming tide of applications, wrote the *New York Times* reporter Douglas Jehl on December 7, 2001: "By allowing applicants to submit their paperwork at travel agencies in major Saudi cites instead of visiting American missions, the embassy promised that applicants would 'no longer have to take time off from work, no longer have to wait in long lines under the hot sun and in crowded waiting rooms, and no longer be limited by any time constraints.'"

Before 9/11, there was such a crush of applicants at our consular visa windows that our staff would stand on their feet for eight or ten hours and would have only about ten minutes to interrogate each applicant. Based on the applicant's body language and other answers to questions given rapid-fire, the officer would make a decision on the spot: *You're in*, or *You're out*. That was the culture under existing law.

Post-9/11 newspaper reports made it sound as if, by implementing

Visa Express, the consulate was simply abdicating its responsibility to screen these applicants before they were given a visa. The reality of it was that Saudi Arabia had among the lowest rates of overstaying visas in the world. The Saudis didn't need or want jobs in America, and they had families—usually wealthy families—to return to. Records showed that the people who were the most likely to overstay were Filipinos or Chinese or various other nationalities, but not Saudis. The only part of the process where Visa Express provided a shortcut was the completion and delivery of the application forms.

Still, the revelation that three of the hijackers had taken advantage of Visa Express in Jeddah moved Burton's committee to hold hearings in Washington in late June 2002. Following that, more hearings were scheduled to determine whether responsibility for the issuance of visas should be transferred from the State Department to the newly created Department of Homeland Security.

Very few government agencies or departments like to see their turf threatened. In a move that seemed designed to appease Congress as much as it was to hold a bureaucrat responsible for misfeasance, the State Department ousted BCA head Mary Ryan, a highly regarded veteran of some thirty-six years at Foggy Bottom. Our career foreign service community was most unhappy with her "resignation." Some claimed that our boss, Colin Powell, had caved in to pressure and made Ryan the scapegoat.

Meanwhile, back in the Kingdom . . . I had launched my own investigation of our visa operations and had sent a cable to Washington with my conclusions: we needed to institute security procedures that had not been in place prior to 9/11. Even though there was no legislation requiring it, I insisted that we start interviewing applicants to screen for security risks in addition to the traditional risk of overstaying the visa. I asked the FBI and CIA people to give us some guidelines on what to look for and how to do that. Regardless of its intended efficiency, I was done with Visa Express.

In July 2002 Mowbray wrote, "Bowing to a month's worth of criticism of the program in Saudi Arabia that let in three of the Sept. 11th hijackers in the *three* months it was in operation before 9/11, the officials in charge of the U.S. Embassy in Riyadh have requested permission to shut down Visa Express." He reported that our embassy and our consulate in Jeddah would, in the words of a confidential memo, "move toward interviewing all adult applicants and toward eliminating the role of travel agencies in forwarding visa applications to the Embassy and Consulate."[2]

In the days ahead, the State Department began to tighten up the background check requirements and other security requirements related to getting a visa. Also, ambassadors no longer had the authority to waive an interview or to otherwise get a visa issued. This relieved me of responsibility for answering a lot of Saudi royal family questions like, "Can't you get me a visa right away?"

I remember one unpleasant telephone conversation with the king's son, Mohammed bin Fahd, who was governor of the eastern province. When he asked me to waive the requirement for an interview, I said, "I can't. I don't have the authority." Outraged, he hung up on me. This was an extraordinary act of rudeness, as in most instances senior royals displayed impeccable manners to the U.S. ambassador. (The Department of Homeland Security was eventually given the final say on the issuance of visas in certain countries, namely Muslim ones.)

It was essential to tighten security, but in late summer 2002 there was some fallout from the new policy requiring interviews. Our consulate and embassy simply did not have the capability to process all applicants—mostly businesspersons and students—in timely fashion. We also had to integrate databases listing potential threats into embassy computer systems.

As a result of the delays, many Saudis studying in America couldn't get appointments for interviews in time to make the opening of fall classes at their universities. Deciding not to apply to universities in the United States or to withdraw, they started going to study in the United Kingdom or Australia or elsewhere. Over the next years, we lost a generation of Saudi students because we couldn't accommodate the interview process and because the background checks had also become much more rigorous. Moreover, Saudis needing critical medical treatment in the United States were unable to obtain visas in time to see their doctors, leading to allegations that some lives were placed in jeopardy by the delays.

In December 2001, even after the lines had thinned out, the *Times* reporter Jehl spoke in Riyadh with Sahim al-Shalaan, a twenty-four-year-old Saudi who had studied in the United States. "[The young man] said he could not help but think that he and other Saudis were being blamed for others' crimes. 'We like Americans, we love Americans, we want to be like Americans,' Mr. Shalaan said, shaking his head as he left the United States Embassy here, still undecided about whether to request that his visa be renewed. 'But after what happened, we don't want to be there, because of the way they treat us, the government and the people.'"[3]

The tragic consequence of the Visa Express system vis-à-vis the hijackers was not the fault of our consular employees in Jeddah, who had dutifully been following government procedures that were set back home in Washington. Nevertheless, Congressman Burton seemed bent on carrying out a witch hunt to impugn their competency instead of correcting the gap in legislation that failed to take security sufficiently into account in the visa review process.

On that late-August trip to the Kingdom, Burton went to Jeddah along with Committee Chief Counsel Jim Wilson and other committee members. I went along, too. I could smell trouble and was not going to leave loyal consular officers to twist in the wind alone.

Having gathered several of our consular officers in a room, Wilson started interrogating them in a manner reminiscent of the McCarthy hearings of the 1950s. *How could they possibly have allowed these scumbag hijackers to get visas?* he wanted to know. *Didn't they care anything about their country?*

I was stunned when Wilson started browbeating some of the female consular officers, one of whom was almost in tears. He seemed to enjoy his prosecutorial role, as if he were performing in front of an audience.

Enough. I slammed my hand down on the conference table, making an even louder noise than I had intended, stood up, and said, "All right, that's it. You're going to treat these people with courtesy or we're done. You understand me?' That pretty much broke up the discussion. (Burton's committee later subpoenaed some of these officers. They went to Washington and had to hire their own attorneys—I think at their own expense. After the hearings, none of them were ever charged or, to my knowledge, disciplined—and for good reason, as they'd done nothing wrong.)

While the committee's investigation of the visas caused some internal stress within our mission, its investigation of child abduction and custody almost caused an international incident. For years, there had been a problem with foreign-born fathers (and, on rare occasions, mothers) who were divorced or estranged from their American spouses taking—some would say kidnapping—their children and returning to their homeland. Some of these parents were from the Middle East.

In the mid-1990s the BCA had issued an eight-page primer titled "Marriage to Saudis." As the Middle East Forum's *Middle East Quarterly* noted, "The document is an advisory to American women contemplating marriage to Saudi men, based on the long experience of U.S. consular personnel in the Kingdom. It is remarkable for its undiplomatic and anecdotal tone, so distant from the department's standard bureaucratic style."[4]

This brochure offers a fascinating view of life in the Kingdom for a U.S. woman married to a Saudi around the time I arrived in 2001, including these observations:

- The American citizen wives . . . have virtually no knowledge of Saudi Arabia other than what their fiancés have told them, and do not speak Arabic. When they arrive in the Kingdom, they take up residence in the family's home where family members greet them with varying degrees of enthusiasm and little English.
- For many women, the Saudi airport is the first time they see their husband in Arab dress.

As for custody rights under Sharia law:

- Theoretically, a mother should maintain custody of the children until the ages of 7–9, when their primary care would be transferred to their father. However, the ultimate objective of a Sharia court in the settlement of custody issues is that the child be raised a good Muslim. And leaving the Kingdom with dual-national children:
- It is impossible to legally leave the Kingdom without the express permission of the Saudi husband. A woman who wishes to leave her husband but is pregnant at the time, can be required to wait until after the birth of the child.

Finally, with respect to visitation rights of American women:

- A Saudi husband must give explicit permission for a divorced wife to visit her children in the Kingdom.[5]

According to the *Middle East Quarterly*: "The Saudis themselves were not perturbed by the document. But when the brochure went up on the department's website, the American Muslim Council demanded its removal, calling it 'hurtful,' 'derogatory and biased.' In February 2000, the department removed the document from its website for 'revision,' but it was never replaced."[6]

At hearings in June 2002, Congress heard of the plight of Alia and Aisha Roush. Sixteen years earlier, when they were seven and three, respectively, Alia and Aisha had been abducted by their Saudi father in Chicago and taken to the Kingdom. A criminal warrant had been issued in the United States, but the father had escaped prosecution.

According to the girls' mother, Patricia Roush, they wanted to return to the United States, but the Saudis were not permitting them to do so and the State Department was not doing enough to help. As Joe Dougherty of *World News Daily* reported on April 13, 2002, prior to the hearings, Patricia Roush had said, "The State Department will be asked to account for what they have done not only in my case, but in several other most egregious cases of Americans in jeopardy in Saudi Arabia. I am hopeful that the truth will be revealed about how the U.S. State Department has sacrificed the lives of my daughters for the sake of this 'special relationship' with the Saudi princes—for economic, military and political gain."

Within days of those hearings, on July 11, 2002, the *Wall Street Journal*'s William McGurn had reported on one of those egregious cases. Amjad Radwan had been born in Houston in 1983 to an American woman, Monica Stowers, and a Saudi man, Nizar Radwan. Soon the family moved back to the Kingdom, where Stowers was shocked to learn that Nizar already had a wife and family. When Stowers decided she wanted to return to the United States, her husband took Amjad and another child (a son) from her. Eventually an Islamic court gave Nizar custody of the children because Stowers was a Christian. "Miss Stowers returned to America believing her government would help her—a big mistake," wrote McGurn.

Stowers returned to the Kingdom in 1990. Once there she picked Amjad up at school and headed to our embassy. "There, she believed, she would find refuge," McGurn reported. "But as she later told the House Government Reform Committee, a State Department officer, told her that the American Embassy was 'not a hotel.'"

Amjad was taken from Stowers, who was eventually arrested and imprisoned for attempting to spirit her daughter out of the country. Meanwhile, Amjad was married off by her father at age twelve. Eventually she ran away. "There is no future for me in Saudi Arabia," she told McGurn from inside the Kingdom. "I can't go to school, I can't get a good job, and my father wants to marry me off [again] to a man in his 40s."

McGurn concluded, "Though State Department officials say they have raised this and other cases with Saudi officials right up to Crown Prince Abdullah, they make clear that they have done so only in the context of a custody dispute and not as what it really is: a thumb in America's eye."

The column was representative of growing anti-Saudi sentiment in the U.S. media and general population. Not surprisingly, the Kingdom responded. "Worried Saudis Pay Millions to Improve Image in the U.S.," ran a *New York Times* headline on August 29, 2002. The article by Christopher Marquis that followed chronicled how the Kingdom had spent over $5 million on lobbyists and public relations firms to combat the fallout from 9/11. Among other things, a commercial produced by the Washington-based Qorvis Communications showed the U.S. and Saudi flags being raised together with the commentary, "In the war on terrorism we all have a part to play. Our country has been an ally for over 60 years."

I could have used my own PR firm on the eve of Burton's visit. On August 24, 2002, correspondent Matt Welch of the unabashedly pro-Israel *National Post* of Canada castigated Americans' "shilling for the House of Saud," opining, "But the most obnoxious recent response may well have come from the new ambassador to Saudi Arabia: Robert Jordan, a Texas lawyer who has represented the Bush family in Middle Eastern oil deals. On the same day (June 25) that Dubya unveiled his Mideast peace plan calling for sweeping democratic reforms of the Palestinian

Authority (the likes of which have never been contemplated in Riyadh), Jordan penned a condescending op-ed in the *Dallas Morning News* admonishing Americans for criticizing the House of Saud so harshly."

In that June 25, 2002, piece, I had written, "If we strike out blindly against perceived enemies and undermine the ability of our friends to work with us against the scourge of global terrorism, we will have a lot to answer for. Do we agree with the Saudis on every issue? No, of course not. If that were the criterion for friendship with the United States, we wouldn't have a friend in the world."

I dispute the characterization of my op-ed as "condescending." I note that, contrary to the allegations in the article, I never "represented the Bush family in Middle Eastern oil deals." And I stand by my commentary, which the *Post* termed as "realpolitik."

Our critics in the press may not have known it, but even before the congressional hearings we were working behind the scenes to develop a protocol for resolving Amjad's case and all the other custody and abduction battles. The White House itself was involved. When Prince Bandar visited Crawford that summer, President Bush brought up Amjad Radwan by name.

As I recall, before Burton arrived he announced that he was going to come over and bring Amjad home. The *60 Minutes* crew had been invited to capture the rescue of the girl and her return to the United States on Burton's plane. Unfortunately for the congressman, the Saudis got wind of this and refused Wallace a visa.

I didn't care for what appeared to be congressional grandstanding. At the same time, I felt for Burton. Shortly after he and his delegation arrived in Riyadh, we were invited to dinner at the home of Osama al-Kurdi, secretary general of the Saudi Council of Chambers of Commerce. Kurdi, who was focused on business development, enjoyed meeting a lot of our delegations; he was very pro-American. His home was modest compared to those of many members of the Saudi elite, and we ate at several round folding tables assembled in his basement recreation room.

The attendees joining the delegation included a few Saudi business and media figures, along with some of our embassy leadership. The meal was traditional Saudi fare: *mezze*; *fatoush* salad; lamb, chicken, and beef shish kebobs; and dessert, including a creamy specialty called *um ali*.

Without being asked, Burton took out a picture of his recently deceased wife and began to show it to people. Explaining she had died a few months earlier, he broke into tears. He was clearly wired tightly and probably emotionally overwrought. Maybe that's why he was a loose cannon for most of his visit.

Burton had arranged a meeting with Amjad. But before he arrived in the Kingdom, we found out that she had married. She was now the second wife of a Saudi airline pilot, a devout Islamist with a long beard. I believe we later learned she was pregnant.

I insisted on going to the meeting, which was scheduled to take place at a middle-of-the-road kind of hotel in an older part of Riyadh. As I recall, a representative of the Saudi government was also present. We walked through the dark, fraying lobby and went upstairs to a floor with several meeting rooms. We had been told that Amjad had agreed to meet with one of our female consular officers, but that was one of several twists and turns that never seemed to pan out. Our group sat on sofas in the central area of the space; conference rooms surrounding us were available for private caucuses. Amjad was behind one of the closed doors.

There was just one problem: Amjad did not want to meet with Burton. She said she would talk only to the Saudi official. He moved back and forth between our respective rooms and finally told us, "She doesn't want to leave. She's not going with you, Congressman. She doesn't want to leave."

Finally, Amjad emerged from the meeting room, covered in the traditional black *abaya*, looking down and not making eye contact with us. She seemed nervous and clearly did not want to be there. One of our consular officers gently inquired whether she really wanted to stay in Saudi Arabia or to return to America. She mumbled something quietly and lapsed into Arabic, seeming uncertain of how to answer.

"Mixed signals" is the best way to describe the message. Amjad said she was considering the possibility of returning to the United States but that her husband was opposed. His consent was required, she said. The door, however, was not completely shut. Amjad said that she would continue to think about this.

As Burton and I drove back to his hotel, the Conference Palace, my mobile phone rang. Foreign Minister Prince Saud was on the line. He told me that Amjad said that Burton had offered her a million dollars to get on the plane with him. Saud was incredulous that Burton would have pulled such a stunt and clearly was taking it very seriously. Saud said Amjad was free to leave if she wanted to, but he clearly resented this kind of manipulation on Burton's part. I listened carefully, calculating how I would deal with such a shocking allegation. The more we talked, the more my blood began to boil.

I didn't share the particulars with Burton at this point, but as the car neared his hotel, I said, "We need to talk." Once in his suite with him and Chief Counsel Wilson, I told him what Saud had said. "What's this all about?" I asked, barely containing my anger.

Burton adamantly denied Saud's allegations. He said he had never done such a thing and then glibly pointed the finger the other way. He charged that, in fact, *the Saudis* were the ones who had offered Amjad $1 million to stay. As he had never raised this blockbuster claim with me before, I found it a little too convenient that he would now have such an explanation. I wasn't buying it.

This was a classic "he said, he said" situation. Or, more accurately, a "she said, he said" situation. We were never able to confirm who said or did what. Burton returned to the States without Amjad.

On September 4, 2002, Al Bernstein of the *Houston Chronicle*, in Amjad's hometown, wrote, "Burton reported that the negotiations were in limbo partly because Radwan apparently married a Saudi a few weeks ago but has no intention of living with him. Burton reported that Radwan's latest marriage means her husband's word, not her father's, may now be required for her to leave."

Burton also issued a press release, which read in part, "The Saudi Foreign Minister pledged that no adult American woman will ever be held in Saudi Arabia against her will. This is an important step forward."

Although Amjad's status remained up in the air, we used her case and several others to ramp up our advocacy with the Saudis for some long-term solutions to the problem of children whose parents were divorced and who needed to go back to the mother in the United States, either permanently or on visits. Negotiations over the next year or so finally resulted in a new protocol. Any Saudi female who formerly needed the consent of her male relative to return to the United States could make her own decision after she reached the age of eighteen. This was quite a concession by the Saudis, as it flew in the face of their traditional culture, in which even a wife would have to have her husband's consent to leave the country.[7]

The Burton visit raises a question: How should an ambassador walk the fine line between the wishes of an elected official from his or her own country (especially if that official is a loose cannon) and those of the government of the host country?

I can only answer for myself. My obligation was to my country and not to any particular congressman or agenda that grandstanding politicians might have. My obligation was also to the truth. And my further obligation was to American citizens who needed their government's help.

In this instance, Burton was doing no one any service by his theatrical display and was likely going to be doing violence to the cooperative efforts that I already had underway to try to solve this problem by agreement with the Saudis. Luckily, I think the Saudis saw that as well, and so Prince Saud was still cooperative, even after the Burton episode, as we moved forward on this.

There's a cautionary addendum to this story. A few days after Burton returned to the United States, he called me at three or four in the morning Saudi time. He was frantic. During his visit, he had met with a number of American women—married or formerly married to Saudi husbands—living in the Kingdom. Some of these women offered graphic accounts of being beaten by their husbands, of not being able to see their children, or of otherwise being abused by the mother-in-law or other family members.

Now he told me something to the effect of, *I think I may have inadvertently done something to endanger the life of one of those American women. I was giving an interview and I gave enough information about this woman that I think she could be identified, and so I want you to take whatever precautions are necessary to protect her.* Whatever that meant.

A congressman should know better. Especially one whose well-publicized mission was to protect women, not put them in harm's way. Fortunately, this time there was no harm done. We checked out the woman and she was fine.

I received another call in Riyadh on the subject of child abductions. "Mr. Ambassador," the voice at the other end of the line said, "this is Ross Perot. I want to talk to you about some important matters." Unless it was Dana Carvey reprising his famous *Saturday Night Live* impersonation, the fellow on the other end was definitely my fellow Texan.

Although I had previously seen Perot around town and we had attended many of the same social and charity events, I did not know him. To be honest, before meeting him I was not a big fan. I held his third-party run for the presidency in 1992 responsible for George H. W. Bush's loss to Bill Clinton. Through his earnest efforts for these families, however, I soon developed a new respect for him.

Perot proceeded to tell me that he had been providing financial assistance to various American women whose children had been kidnapped by their Saudi husbands. There was a particular woman in Indiana who had divorced a Saudi and secured a federal court order prohibiting her ex from taking the children out of the country. Somehow, ostensibly with Saudi embassy assistance, the husband had obtained extra passports for the kids and spirited them away to his homeland in violation of the court order.

Thus began a relationship with Perot focused on helping these women. Whenever I returned home to Dallas, I would meet with him at La Madeleine, a French coffee bistro, and discuss the progress we were making, or the lack thereof. He had a kind of military bearing and was crusty and impatient, but he was always cordial, always respectful of me; he always called me "Ambassador."

He never played the blame game. Perot was very supportive of the effort I was making on this front. He wouldn't unload on me and say, "Can't you do better than this?" even though neither of us was satisfied with the progress that was being made.

Perot asked me to keep him in the loop and to stay in touch with his right-hand man, Harry McKillop, a former Green Beret colonel who came out of retirement in 1979 to rescue two employees of Perot's company EDS being held in Iran after the revolution—a gambit that the author Ken Follett turned into a bestselling book, *On Wings of Eagles*. "You call Harry night or day, whatever you need," Perot told me.

McKillop, who was about eighty at this time, had been rescuing or trying to rescue folks since the Vietnam War. In 1995 he had rescued a woman held in China for some fifty years because she was suspected of being a CIA spy. My purpose was not to provide information to abet a rescue in Saudi Arabia. Rather, I was interested in learning as much as I could about the tragic cases out there in order to help us understand who needed help and in finding out what the Perot camp was hearing from the Saudi government about the plight of the victims.

Perot was providing funding for some of these women to visit Saudi Arabia to see their children and to negotiate with their ex-husbands over visitation or even custody. And Perot was interested in learning about U.S. government efforts to reach an accord on visas and exit permission for children who wanted to return to America. Unfortunately, we made little progress on the cases.

Occasionally I would hear of efforts by American mothers to spirit their children out of Saudi Arabia. One was rumored to have taken a family "vacation" to Bahrain and then hopped a flight to Indonesia or Malaysia with the children as an escape. I wondered what I would do if asked to participate in such an attempt, which would be blatantly illegal under Saudi law. It would be the end of my service to my country and would wipe out any efforts I was making to get a more balanced policy for these families from the Saudis. I also thought of the allegations that American girls and their mothers seeking refuge were turned away from the U.S. embassy. I made a clear public statement that such an episode would never happen on my watch.

I also learned of one mother with an infant who went on a vacation to Morocco. The Saudi husband allegedly drugged her and ran off to Saudi Arabia with the child. The mother was heroic in her efforts to regain custody. She moved to Saudi Arabia, and Steve Matthews, one of the partners in the Riyadh office of my former law firm, Baker Botts, took on her case pro bono. She never gained custody but instead joined the army, went to language school to learn Arabic, and returned to Saudi Arabia to be close to her child, who was being raised as a Saudi. Remembering the claims about turning Americans away from the embassy, I allowed the mother to stay at our consulate in Jeddah for quite a while, and she was able to occasionally visit with her child there.

To make matters marginally better, our government worked with the Saudis to create an "advance warning" document. Moving forward, the Saudi embassy in the United States would have to approve any marriage undertaken by a Saudi citizen in the United States. If it was to be with a non-Muslim woman, the new wife had to sign a document acknowledging (1) the cultural differences between the two; (2) that she would be subject to her husband's restrictions; and (3) that any child of the marriage would be a Saudi citizen. (Children born of such a union have dual citizenship, but the Saudis don't recognize dual citizenship; they consider the offspring to be solely Saudi citizens because they were born to a Saudi father.)

This "advance warning" document was intended to let these couples know what they were getting into. But it was only a Band-Aid. The real issue remained what to do about the deeply embedded cultural tradition in Saudi Arabia that gives so few rights to mothers and their children and leaves the male relative with unfettered discretion in domestic matters.

How do we as Americans deal with the effective abandonment of the protection of American laws for the children of Americans who live on Saudi soil? I initiated many discussions of these issues with my Saudi counterparts, largely to no avail. My successors have continued to press the issue, receiving the same promises that foreign spouses and their children would be granted permission to come and go freely. And modest gains have been made.

According to information posted by the Bureau of Consular Affairs, this is the situation today:

A Saudi man who wishes to marry a foreign woman is required by law to seek the permission of Saudi authorities. A regulation, enacted February 20, 2008, requires Saudi men to sign a document giving irrevocable permission to their foreign wives and the children born of their union to travel in and out of the country without restrictions. In practice, however, authorities rarely require this document and it is not retroactive when signed. Even with such documentation, foreign spouses and their children may still have difficulty leaving Saudi Arabia freely. Also, if a couple consisting of a foreigner and a Saudi living in Saudi Arabia divorce, the foreign parent cannot under any circumstances leave the country with the children born of their union even if he or she is granted custody rights. . . .

99

A married woman should be aware that she must have her husband's permission for her and their children to depart Saudi Arabia. This is true even if the woman and/or her children are U.S. citizens and even if her husband does not have Saudi nationality. The U.S. Embassy can intercede with the Saudi government to request exit visas for adult U.S. women, but there is no guarantee that visas will be issued, and obtaining an exit visa without the male guardian's consent takes many months, if it can be obtained at all. The U.S. Embassy cannot obtain exit visas for the departure of minor children without their father's permission.[8]

The child custody and visitation dilemma was one of the most frustrating issues I dealt with as ambassador. While we cannot expect to overturn thousands of years of male-dominated tradition overnight, we certainly cannot condone the minimal progress that has been made. Is the situation better now than it was twelve years ago? In modest ways, yes. But the women who fell in love with rich, handsome Saudi men in U.S. colleges, only to lose their children after they returned to the husband's home and extended family, will never recover from the grief and the injustice. We owe them more.

1. While my nomination as ambassador was pend-
ing, I met with President and Mrs. Bush at their
ranch in Crawford, Texas, in August 2001. It was a
casual, friendly meeting to discuss the president's
vision of my mission.

To Bob Jordan, With very best wishes,
Laura Bush

2. (*Opposite top*) A warm welcome in Crawford from the First Lady, totally unpretentious in shorts and a t-shirt.

3. (*Opposite bottom*) My kind of lunch with the Bushes, far better than a White House state dinner.

4. (*Above*) I've known Jim Baker since 1978 and have valued his advice and friendship immensely. He encouraged me to accept the appointment as ambassador. We met in Houston in August 2001 before my confirmation. (*Gittings*)

5. After an expedited Senate confirmation, Secretary Powell swore me in at the State Department. I was on a plane to Riyadh within twenty-four hours.

6. (*Opposite top*) I met periodically with the president when I was in Washington. When we met in December 2002 he told me he was "fixin' to do a regime change in Iraq."

7. (*Opposite bottom*) On my first return visit to Washington as ambassador, I lobbied Vice President Cheney to support Saudi membership in the World Trade Organization. Saudi accession helped liberalize their economy and open them up to international competition.

to Bob —
Thanks for the Best
advice — wkp   George Bush

8. The Friday Group was an informal, small weekly gathering of Western diplomats and their wives for tennis, swimming, and an occasional beverage. My Saudi buddy Hassan Alkabbani (*right*) joined us for this weekend. (*Jacqueline Visser*)

9. (*Opposite top*) Prince Alwaleed asked me to help cut the ribbon for the grand opening of the new Saks Fifth Avenue in his shopping mall. This high-end store, for women only, featured designer dresses and became a landmark shopping destination. (*HRH Prince Alwaleed bin Talal*)

10. (*Opposite bottom*) Prince Alwaleed often shared his views on international affairs with me. He hosted the U.S.-Arab presidential summit at his Four Seasons Hotel in Sharm el-Sheikh, Egypt, in 2003. (*HRH Prince Alwaleed bin Talal*)

11. (*Opposite top*) My consul general, Richard Baltimore, organized an off-road trip through the Hejaz desert of western Saudi Arabia. One of the desert emirs invited us to join his encampment for tea and a sword dance by his entourage.

12. (*Opposite bottom*) From 1916 to 1918 T. E. Lawrence (Lawrence of Arabia) led an Arab guerrilla campaign against the Ottoman Turks in the Hejaz area of western Saudi Arabia. Lawrence's raiders regularly blew up parts of the Hejaz railway. On our off-road trip, we encountered several railcars blown up by Lawrence nearly one hundred years ago.

13. (*Above*) Our Friday Group enjoyed occasional camping trips in the desert. On this trip my Saudi bodyguard jumped aboard a passing camel and promptly was stampeded by the miniature schnauzer belonging to one of our group.

14. Some portions of old Riyadh's walls date back to the fifteenth century. (*Jacqueline Visser*)

15. (*Opposite top*) With Secretary Rumsfeld on the tarmac in Riyadh.

16. (*Opposite bottom*) Flying with Secretary Rumsfeld to Jeddah, I was able to discuss with him and Torie Clarke the status of Saudi prisoners at Guantanamo Bay.

17. (*Opposite top*) Meeting in the Royal Palace with Secretary Rumsfeld, General Tommy Franks, and a Saudi
general.

18. (*Opposite bottom*) With Rumsfeld, Franks, and Clarke
in the Royal Palace to meet with Crown Prince Abdullah and Defense Minister Prince Sultan.

19. (*Above*) The aftermath of the May 12, 2003, terrorist
bombing of the Al Hamra compound in Riyadh. (*Jacqueline Visser*)

20. The terrorists blew up their car near the pool area of the Al Hamra compound. (*Jacqueline Visser*)

21. The remnants of the terrorists' car after the suicide attack on Al Hamra. (*Jacqueline Visser*)

7

WITH THE EXCEPTION of "I love you" and "Congratulations, you're a father," I can't think of anything I'd rather hear than "You saved my life." So when Pastor Michael Baba Yemba said he's alive only because of me, a shiver went up my spine.

We were lunching safely on chicken-fried steak in Dallas several years after my ambassadorship had ended, sharing memories of a harrowing time in 2002 when Michael appeared to be facing certain death. I include that story here because it demonstrates what an ambassador is sometimes—not always, to be sure—able to achieve working behind the scenes and because it offers the opportunity to discuss the practice of religion in the Kingdom.

As previously noted, we held religious services every Friday—the holy day—at the embassy. Spending part of my Fridays at the services, I got to know many in Riyadh's Christian community. One day a regular attendee came to see me and said something to the effect of, *"I've got a real problem. There's a fellow named Michael Baba Yemba. He's the head of security at the Al Faisaliah Hotel. He's a Sudanese Christian and his life is in danger."*

My friend told me that Michael's stepfather was a Christian leader in Sudan, a Muslim country. Christians were not looked upon charitably in that nation either. Militant Muslims pulled the stepfather and

Michael's mother from their home in Khartoum and shot them to death. Michael escaped to Saudi Arabia.

A man of deep Christian faith himself, Michael had been holding religious services for thirty or so people in his home in Riyadh. The Saudis had told him that they would not bother him as long as these gatherings remained private. Again, the private/public distinction is subject to interpretation . . . by the government.

One Friday the *mutawa*, the Saudi religious police working under the Commission for the Promotion of Virtue and Prevention of Vice, burst in and spirited Michael away to prison. Two weeks passed before his wife finally found out where he had been taken. He was in solitary confinement for several months, never charged with a specific crime.

My Christian visitor told me that the Saudis now planned to release Michael. That was the good news. The bad news was they were going to deport him back to Sudan, where, thanks to his legacy, certain death awaited him for his Christian beliefs and practices. Could I help? I said I would try.

When Michael was released he found his home in Riyadh destroyed and his wife gone. Fearful for her own life, she had relocated to a friend's home. My visitor was able to put me in touch with Michael, whom I invited to the embassy.

Michael and his wife met with me and explained his ordeal and his fear for his life. A large man, he was direct, soft-spoken, and gentle. Despite the danger he faced, he was calm and had put his faith in God. His wife was understandably nervous, more nervous than Michael. They both pleaded with me to intercede with the Saudi authorities.

Normally an American ambassador would not spend much time dealing with the plight of Sudanese or other non-American citizens. But Michael touched my heart. No one from Sudan, or anywhere else, was going to save him. I knew it was up to me to find a solution to avoid sending him back to a death sentence. I told them I had been praying for them and promised I'd go to bat with the Saudis.

Shortly after seeing Michael, I went to a previously scheduled meeting with Prince Nayef, the Kingdom's interior minister (who later became crown prince after Abdullah became king). While many Saudis begin work late in the day and continue into the early hours of the morning,

Prince Nayef worked particularly late hours. The ministry of the interior's agents and security forces report back at the end of the day and into the night. Our meetings usually took place at midnight.

The ministry's headquarters is across from the Intercontinental Hotel in an inverted-pyramid building that looks like an angular flying saucer. It closely resembles the city hall in Dallas, of all places. There is some irony in the fact that a ministry dedicated to maintaining order with a centuries-old iron fist is housed in a building with such a modern, cutting-edge design. Gaining entry to the building is roughly the equivalent of entering the Pentagon, but without much English-language capacity.

Prince Nayef was always the most stern and conservative of the senior princes, one of the Sudairi Seven brothers who had been rivals of the Al Faisal liberal wing of the royal family and, to a degree, rivals of Crown Prince Abdullah as well. Abdullah's reform agenda reportedly had not gone over well with Prince Nayef, and many believed Nayef was one of those seeking to frustrate the Kingdom's march into the twenty-first century. He had strong personal relationships with a number of the desert tribes.

Nayef's son, Prince Mohammed bin Nayef, effectively ran the counterterrorism portfolio of the ministry, and we spent many hours together. He would occasionally joke that his father did not deserve the Darth Vader image he had and would argue that Nayef senior was considerably more liberal under his harsh veneer. (Mohammed later became minister of the interior and deputy crown prince and is regarded as one of the up-and-coming "younger" princes, who are only in their fifties. I have a lot of respect for him and consider him a friend.)

When Prince Nayef and I finished our scheduled meeting, I asked if I could have a conversation of a personal nature with him for a minute or two. Through his interpreter, he said yes.

"I'd like to ask you a favor," I said. Then I told him the Michael Yemba story. When finished, I asked, "Can you give me thirty days to find someplace to send him so that he doesn't have to go back to Sudan? I'd be very grateful, Your Royal Highness, if you'd give me this favor."

Asking a Saudi cabinet member and senior prince for a favor was unusual. Personal requests don't have much role in official diplomacy.

But, as Jim Baker says, diplomacy is largely politics, and personal relationships count. I was about to find out.

"Yes, you can have thirty days," the elderly prince said.

Back at the embassy, I called Washington and spoke with John Hanford, the State Department's ambassador at large in the Office of Religious Freedom. John happened to be the nephew of former Reagan and Bush 41 cabinet member Elizabeth Hanford Dole, soon to become North Carolina's first female senator. Years earlier, under the name "Liddy" Hanford, she was a recently graduated campus celebrity at Duke University when I was in college there.

John and I brainstormed ways in which we might save Michael from deportation and its consequences. John told me there was a program that offered refugees a temporary religious worker visa (or "R visa"). To qualify, an applicant had to prove he or she was coming to the United States to work in a religious capacity with a legitimate institution or organization. Michael had no such work awaiting him. Thankfully, John and his office were able to find an Episcopal seminary outside of Pittsburgh that would take Michael and his wife. The Christian Rescue Committee, a not-for-profit organization that helps people who have been persecuted for religion reasons, then purchased Michael an airplane ticket to the States. (The Christian Rescue Committee was founded in 1998 by Dean Jones, an actor best known for his roles in several Disney films in the 1960s and '70s. You may remember him from the classic movie *The Love Bug.*)

Eventually Michael received a divinity degree from this seminary. By coincidence, he wound up as the pastor of a church in the Dallas area. We are still in touch, sharing stories of our faith as well as good ol' chicken-fried steak.

I would go on to thank Prince Nayef for his indulgence in granting me a favor. And in one of my periodic meetings with his son in 2012, we reminisced about this episode. He finished our conversation by saying that my intervention on Michael's behalf with his father was one of the most important moments of my time as ambassador, which he still remembers with respect.

In recent years, Saudi Arabia has slowly—*painstakingly* slowly— instituted human rights reforms. Unfortunately, religious persecution persists. In February 2013 the *mutawa* arrested and jailed fifty-three Ethiopian Christians involved in a private religious service in the city of Dammam.

These arrests were the latest in a series of such actions—including discrimination against the country's Shi'a minority—that led our Department of State in 2012 to re-designate Saudi Arabia "as a Country of Particular Concern (CPC) under the International Religious Freedom Act for having engaged in or tolerated particularly severe violations of religious freedom."

Why? A lengthy quotation from the State Department's *2011 Report on International Religious Freedom* provides a snapshot of life in the Kingdom:

> Freedom of religion is neither recognized nor protected under the law and is severely restricted in practice. According to the 1992 Basic Law, Sunni Islam is the official religion and the country's constitution is the Qur'an and the Sunna (traditions and sayings of the Prophet Muhammad).
>
> The legal system is based on the government's application of the Hanbali School of Sunni Islamic jurisprudence. The public practice of any religion other than Islam is prohibited, and there is no separation between state and religion.
>
> The government generally permitted Shia religious gatherings and non-Muslim private religious practices. Some Muslims who did not adhere to the government's interpretation of Islam faced significant political, economic, legal, social, and religious discrimination, including limited employment and educational opportunities, underrepresentation in official institutions, restrictions on religious practice, and restrictions on places of worship and community centers.
>
> The government executed individuals sentenced on charges of "witchcraft and sorcery" during the year. The Commission for the Promotion of Virtue and Prevention of Vice (CPVPV) and security forces of the Ministry of Interior (MOI) conducted some raids on private non-Muslim religious gatherings and sometimes confiscated the personal religious materials of non-Muslims. There were fewer reported charges of harassment and abuse for religious reasons at the hands of the CPVPV compared with the previous year, although online criticism of the organization increased.

Efforts to revise school textbooks were ongoing at year's end. The government reported completing revisions in half the grades, but Arabic and religion textbooks continued to contain overtly intolerant statements against Jews and Christians as well as intolerant references by allusion against Shia and Sufi Muslims and other religious groups.

The report explains the historical reasons for refusing to accept the separation of state and religion:

The government considers its legitimacy to rest in part on its custodianship of the two Holy Mosques in Mecca and Medina and its promotion of Islam. The official interpretation of Islam is derived from the writings and teachings of 18th-century Sunni religious scholar Muhammad ibn Abd Al-Wahhab, who advocated a return to what he considered to be the practices of the first three generations of the Muslim era and urged Muslims to be stricter in their obedience to Islam. The country's religious teaching opposes attempts by the Muslim reform movements of the 19th, 20th, and 21st centuries to reinterpret aspects of Islamic law in light of economic and social developments, particularly in areas such as gender relations, personal autonomy, family law, and participatory democracy. Outside the country this variant of Islamic practice is often referred to as "Wahhabi," a term the Saudis do not use.

On a somewhat more positive note, the report points out,

The 24-member Human Rights Commission was established in 2005 by the Council of Ministers to address human rights abuses and promote human rights within the country. The board does not include women, but each regional branch includes a women's branch operated and staffed by women. The board previously did not have Shia members, but now includes at least one. The HRC regularly follows up on citizen complaints, including complaints of favoritism or unfair court decisions, but has not specifically addressed issues of religious freedom and tolerance and does not issue a report on its actions.

The report outlines the policy of the United States with respect to religious persecution in the Kingdom: "(To) press the government to respect religious freedom and honor its public commitment to permit private religious worship by non-Muslims, eliminate discrimination against minorities, promote respect for non-Muslim religious belief, and combat violent extremism."[1]

By law the president of the United States is obliged to impose sanctions upon those receiving Country of Particular Concern status. These sanctions, which have the potential to be quite devastating, include public condemnation; delay or cancellation of scientific and/or cultural exchanges; denial or delay of working, official, or state visits; withdrawal, limitation, or suspension of U.S. development and/or security assistance; cancellation of trade guarantees and credits; votes against World Bank and International Monetary Fund loans; prohibitions on U.S. financial institution loans to the country; and prohibition of the U.S. government procuring, or entering into any contract for the procurement of, any goods or services from the foreign government.

In its report, the State Department announced it was waiving sanctions against Saudi Arabia in order "to further the purposes of the act." Translation: sometimes the carrot is preferable to the stick. I am not a great believer in sanctions, so I generally supported less public efforts to bring the Saudis around to a more tolerant position, realizing that, given their culture, reform cannot occur overnight. "Naming and shaming" the Saudis might feel good, but it does not move the ball. Bringing them into compliance with international commercial norms and opening their borders to foreign investment and skilled jobs will do more in the long run to modernize their society. (In addition to Saudi Arabia, the following countries received CPC designation in 2011: Myanmar [Burma], China, Eritrea, Iran, North Korea, Sudan, and Uzbekistan.)

While I was ambassador, my family and embassy staff had their own runins with the *mutawa*, as did a prominent visitor, the often-provocative columnist Maureen Dowd. None of these brushes with the religious police compare to the life-threatening persecution of Michael Yemba and others. But the fact that an ambassador's son, a U.S. consul general, and a *New York Times* columnist all experienced the wrath of these frequently unchecked fundamentalists demonstrates the length to which they will go to enforce the state's standards for social intercourse.

I've mentioned the *mutawa* earlier. Some more background about these so-called pious men who enforce Sharia, or Islamic law, is in order. They're not hard to recognize. They wear short robes instead of the longer, ankle-length *thobes*; they do not wear the black band around their checkered red-and-white headdress; they have scraggly beards; and, to be honest, to a Westerner they usually look deranged.

By Western standards their behavior is certainly deranged. When not breaking up religious gatherings, they might be, as *Time* magazine's Scott MacLeod so vividly explained on July 26, 2007, "patrolling streets and shopping malls, caning shopkeepers who fail to shutter their doors at prayer time, scolding women who allow flesh to show from under their mandatory black gowns, and lecturing adolescent boys caught following or talking to girls. . . . Frequently, however, the mutawa have gone further: from barring shops from selling roses and teddy bears on Valentine's Day to verbally abusing, physically assaulting or effectively abducting women deemed to be committing sins."

Under Saudi law, unless in the company of a police officer, the *mutawa* are not permitted to detain anyone. But during my tenure in the Kingdom, these moral arbiters were notorious for beating up people or throwing them into cars and taking them for detainment and questioning—without the presence of a single police officer. They were out of control.

In discussions with Foreign Minister Prince Saud and Prince Nayef and his son the assistant interior minister, I registered concern about the *mutawa*. The princes assured me that they were aware of the situation and were taking steps to improve it. Crown Prince Abdullah was also supportive of curbing the *mutawa*, but he couldn't effect change unilaterally. Even though the Saudi Arabian monarchy theoretically has absolute powers, the society is really consensus driven. Because the leaders must get buy-in from various constituencies, including the retrograde ultra-Wahhabi religious establishment, the government is always juggling the tension between modernization and adherence to tradition.

I think we made some progress in tamping down religious persecution. Today the state does exercise greater control over the *mutawa*; there's actually a training program for them. King Abdullah installed a more progressive head. The "pious men" are receiving explicit instructions on what they can and cannot do, and finally those instructions are being enforced.

My nineteen-year-old son Andrew's dust-up with the *mutawa* in

November 2002 occurred in one of the favorite hunting grounds of young Saudi men: that hotbed of forbidden activity, the mall attached to the Al Faisaliah Hotel. The five-star hotel was, at the time, part of the Dallas-based Rosewood Hotels and Resorts worldwide chain of luxury hotels. It catered to a wealthy international business clientele and featured butlers for every room, a Kenyan meat and game restaurant transported from Nairobi, and the Globe restaurant and cigar bar at the top of its office tower. The lobby was a bit like the Plaza Hotel in New York—*the* place to meet and greet.

Andrew, as I've noted, had taken a gap year after high school to live in Riyadh with Ann and me and began to study Arabic. He was enrolled in a hotel and restaurant management training program at the Faisaliah, affording him a rare glimpse of the underbelly of the service industry in Saudi Arabia. He spent his days underneath the hotel, moving between gargantuan hidden kitchens and housekeeping areas run by the immigrant labor force made up of Bangladeshi, Indian, Pakistani, and Filipino workers, some of whom became Andrew's closest friends in Riyadh. The underground areas, as well as the bunk-style dormitories housing the predominately male labor force, were hidden from the delicate sensibilities of some of the world's wealthiest and at times most entitled guests.

Unlike me, Andrew was able to move around the city freely without bodyguards. Spending most of his days serving Saudi elites at the Faisaliah, he spent his nights avoiding the upscale malls and over-the-top hot spots of Riyadh and instead visited friends' homes, the open-aired souks, and shisha bars. But one night, in search of a good restaurant that reminded him of home, he met up with a friend who had invited along two young Saudi women for dinner at one of the Faisaliah's Western restaurants.

Girls aren't supposed to mix with boys in the Kingdom, but young people have found a way to circumvent the taboo. Their strategy reminds me of Tulsa, Oklahoma, circa 1961 or '62. Back then, we'd spend our weekends on Peoria Avenue circling in and out of Pennington's Drive-In—bunches of girls in their cars and bunches of boys in our cars. Cruising. Occasionally we drag raced up and down Forty-First Street in front of Edison High School.

In Saudi Arabia, women are forbidden to drive (though some do in remote places, out of sight from the powers that be). But the well-to-do girls of Riyadh—and there are many of them—don't sit at home. They cruise in their luxe Mercedeses and BMWs driven by family chauffeurs.[2] At the same time, young Saudi men are also on the road.

Here's how the mating dance usually works: The boys would pull up next to the girls at an intersection and the girls would roll down their windows about an inch. The boys would then expertly fling their business cards into the narrow window openings. If the boys were successful, one of the many ladies they had approached would call the number on their card and they'd arrange to meet for coffee or a meal.

Andrew and three friends (two of them female) arranged to get together for lunch in the restaurant of the posh Harvey Nichols department store in the Faisaliah mall. When the foursome sat down for lunch together, they knew that they were breaking the law. Tired of the limited food options available to them when they wanted to dine with members of the opposite sex and fairly confident that Andrew's diplomatic status would likely shield them from any punishment that might otherwise be inflicted by the *mutawa*, they ordered their meals. Before the waiter was able to bring their drinks, the music in the restaurant stopped suddenly, a cue that the management had devised to warn staff and clients to prepare themselves for a likely unsettling encounter with the religious police. The boys scrambled to another table, but when the *mutawa* arrived they put two and two together. There were four plates at the girls' table.

Andrew and his friend, looking nervous at an adjacent table, were the obvious culprits. The *mutawa* took the boys outside, started interrogating them about whether they had been with the girls, and asked for their ID cards. Much to the boys' relief, the *mutawa* noticed Andrew's relationship to the U.S. ambassador and allowed the group to resume their meals. Not exactly proud of having to use his diplomatic status in order to have dinner with friends, Andrew was quite relieved that his friends were safe.

There's a second part to this story. A couple of days later I was in the Al Faisaliah for a meeting with Adel al-Jubeir. He had columnist Maureen Dowd in tow.

As we stood in the lobby, they discussed what they were going to do next. It was late, but the mall was still open. As Maureen wrote in a column on November 10, 2002, "This Kingdom is a thicket of unfathomable extremes. Frederick's of Hollywood–style lingerie shops abound, even though female sexuality is considered so threatening that the mere sight of a woman's ankle will cause civilization to crumble." She wanted to go to the mall to "verify that there is a 'women only' lingerie section in Harvey Nichols."

She also wrote that she "had been wanting to catch a glimpse of the mutawa, the bully boys from the Commission for the Promotion of Virtue and Prevention of Vice who go around harassing and arresting Saudis in the name of Islam." She got her wish. As we chatted, I told the story of Andrew's recent confrontation in Harvey Nichols. Maureen became interested. As I recall, she said something like, *So how does one find the* mutawa *and how do you get busted by them?*

Dressed in a snug black turtleneck with her flaming red hair flowing, she then went into the mall, walking toward Harvey Nichols with Adel. There she was indeed confronted by the *mutawa*. "They pointed to my neck and hips, and the embarrassed diplomat explained that I had been busted," Dowd wrote in the same column. Adel told her, "'They say they welcome you to the mall, which is a sign of our modernity, but that we are also proud of our tradition and faith, and you must respect that."

Released after about fifteen minutes, Dowd couldn't help noticing that the vice squad had been "oblivious to the irony of detaining me in front of the window of [a] lingerie shop displaying a short lacy red slip."

A final incident also bears telling. In 2003 Gina Abercrombie-Winstanley, our consul general in Jeddah, went to a meeting in a Japanese restaurant in Riyadh. Our standing policy for female staff was that they should dress with respect for the culture but should not wear *abayas* when on official U.S. business, as no diplomat, male or female, should be required to wear a costume dictated by local conditions. In the old days, even Western male diplomats were expected to wear the white *thobe* and *ghutra*. That era had passed for men, and Americans would not stand for unequal treatment of our female diplomats. How anyone dressed on their own time was up to them. As Gina was on business, she was not wearing an *abaya*.

Again the *mutawa* materialized. They began to berate Gina because she was not wearing an *abaya*. Let's just say Gina can give it back as well as she can take it. The confrontation grew heated.

Gina apparently flashed her diplomatic identity card. Then, as MacLeod reported in his *Time* magazine article of July 26, 2007, "The mutawa's response was to throw it on the ground and grind it into the pavement with the sole of his shoe, a gesture considered a grave insult in Arab custom."

This treatment of an American diplomat was inexcusable. We filed a complaint with the Saudi government. As usual, informally the Foreign Ministry expressed embarrassment, but I don't recall receiving a formal response.

Some people call me an apologist when I say the Saudis are making reforms. No doubt they think I came down with a case of clientitis during my time in the Kingdom. Clearly, the State Department's designation of Saudi Arabia as a Country of Particular Concern shows that religious persecution continues. Such persecution is unacceptable.

After reading Maureen Dowd's November 10, 2002, column, few would call her an apologist. She concluded by writing, "I was left to ponder a country at a turning point, a society engaged in a momentous struggle for its future, torn between secret police and secret undergarments."

Eight years later she returned, and on March 2, 2010, she wrote in the *New York Times*, "After spending 10 days here, I can confirm that, at their own galactically glacial pace, they are chipping away at gender apartheid and cultural repression." She cited new laws that permitted female lawyers to appear in court for female clients, the opening of the Kingdom's first coeducational university, and the appointment of a woman to the Council of Ministers.

And what of her one-time antagonists? "Young Saudi women whom I interviewed said that the popular king has relaxed the grip of the bullying mutawa, the bearded religious police officers who patrol the streets ready to throw you in the clink at the first sign of fun or skin."

Dowd concluded, "The attempts at more tolerance are belated baby steps to the outside world but in this veiled, curtained and obscured fortress, they are '60s-style cataclysmic social changes."

I agree.

8

WHAT'S MORE IMPROBABLE? Watching a Jewish U.S. senator and the crown prince of Saudi Arabia share verses from the Old Testament and Quran on Christmas Day? Or watching the director of the Central Intelligence Agency jump across a sofa and get into the face of a Saudi prince? Or threatening to resign one's position as ambassador because your government won't share important information with you? During my tenure, I was a party to all three of these head-scratchers—each of which had important implications in the Kingdom.

Let's start with Joe Lieberman's give-and-take with Crown Prince Abdullah during the senator's ten-day tour of the Middle East. Although the next presidential election was more than twenty-two months away, the then-senator from Connecticut who had run for vice president in 2000 was a likely candidate for the Democratic Party nomination. And as we all know, likely candidates like to show their presidential chops by visiting Israel and the Arab states.

I confess I wasn't terribly happy to learn that Lieberman would be coming to Riyadh on December 25. My first thought was, *This means sixty of my people are going to have to give up their Christmas Day to host a guy who's politically grandstanding?* They would have to coordinate meetings, provide security and logistics, including transportation, and maintain full office capability in case of unexpected developments.

My next thought was more diplomatic: *Okay, this goes with the territory, so suck it up and do it.*

Lieberman was coming to the Kingdom from Israel, where he had met with Prime Minister Ariel Sharon. According to news reports, he expressed support for Israel in its war on terrorism and in its right to self-defense. No surprise there, nor that he chose not to talk with PLO leader Yasser Arafat. He did, however, meet with Saeb Erekat, who had previously been the Palestinians' chief negotiator.

Lieberman and I spent much of Christmas Day with the crown prince. The senator told the *Arab News* the next day that he considered Abdullah's March 2002 peace initiative a "missed opportunity." He added that he had "made an appeal to the crown prince . . . to find a way to restate it."[1]

The Arab Peace Initiative, aka the Abdullah Plan, unanimously ratified by twenty-two Arab states, bears restating here, particularly because an influential Jewish senator/would-be president appeared to be endorsing it. It read,

> Emanating from the conviction of the Arab countries that a military solution to the conflict will not achieve peace or provide security for the parties, the council:
>
> 1. Requests Israel to reconsider its policies and declare that a just peace is its strategic option as well.
>
> 2. Further calls upon Israel to affirm:
>
>> I-Full Israeli withdrawal from all the territories occupied since 1967, including the Syrian Golan Heights, to the June 4, 1967 lines as well as the remaining occupied Lebanese territories in the south of Lebanon.
>>
>> II-Achievement of a just solution to the Palestinian refugee problem to be agreed upon in accordance with U.N. General Assembly Resolution 194.
>>
>> III-The acceptance of the establishment of a sovereign independent Palestinian state on the Palestinian territories occupied since June 4, 1967 in the West Bank and Gaza Strip, with East Jerusalem as its capital.

3. Consequently, the Arab countries affirm the following:

> I-Consider the Arab-Israeli conflict ended, and enter into a peace agreement with Israel, and provide security for all the states of the region.

> II-Establish normal relations with Israel in the context of this comprehensive peace.

4. Assures the rejection of all forms of Palestinian patriation which conflict with the special circumstances of the Arab host countries.

5. Calls upon the government of Israel and all Israelis to accept this initiative in order to safeguard the prospects for peace and stop the further shedding of blood, enabling the Arab countries and Israel to live in peace and good neighbourliness and provide future generations with security, stability and prosperity.[2]

I agreed with the senator that restating the accord would be advantageous. Crown Prince Abdullah had taken risks by advancing his plan and had done so in an unusually public way. Our government had been lukewarm in its response at a time when we could have been more helpful. The plan has continued to have life and efforts to implement it have continued.

Describing his meeting with the crown prince as "very productive and enjoyable," Lieberman explained, "My message here is that it has been a difficult year for U.S.-Saudi relations and I wanted to say personally that I remain committed to this relationship. So the first message was a message of reassurance, and the second was that while there has been expressions of anger and distrust from the American side these should be seen as disagreements among family and friends."

He added that there was a small group of Islamic extremists who, if given their way, would begin "a civilizational struggle" between Islam and the rest of the world. "In that sense I see this conflict not just as Al Qaeda against everyone else, but as a civil war within the Muslim world between a minority who are extreme and a majority that is ethical, moderate and non-violent. It's important to the Muslim world that the mainstream majority emerges victorious, and that's why Saudi Arabia—with its place at the center of the Muslim world—has such a critical role to play."[3]

I agreed with that, too. Lieberman hit the same themes that I had been advancing. Despite our frustrations with such a conservative, insular society, the Saudi leadership was key to heading off the truly radical elements that wanted to bring down the Western world.

By the time we arrived at the Royal Palace for dinner, the senator and the crown prince had bonded. Abdullah led Lieberman through the buffet line, pointing out all the halal dishes, which are essentially kosher. The crown prince selected a plate for Lieberman, then for me, and we followed him through the line.

Abdullah heaped servings of hummus, baba ghanoush, stuffed grape leaves, *fatoush* salad, couscous, tabouleh, various kebobs, lamb, hammour (a grouper-like fish), and a few slabs of pita bread. He took obvious pride in selecting delicacies for Lieberman and explained to him through the interpreter what he was adding to the senator's overflowing plate.

We sat down at the head table in a gargantuan dining hall that looked like it might have hosted Henry VIII and his two hundred best friends. As we were beginning to eat, the rest of the entourage lined up and made their way through the buffet as we had. There was no formal introduction or speech, just a lot of chowing down.

Over dinner the crown prince and Lieberman chatted through an interpreter. There was a noticeable rhythm to their exchange, a respectful back and forth, with each man speaking a few sentences at a time. Familiar sentences. I soon realized that they were riffing passages from the Old Testament and Quran—not to point out any differences but rather to note the similarities between their respective holy books.

I was mesmerized by this sweet, revealing exchange. The passages were almost identical. And the two leaders were always respectful (and at times amused). I can't remember the exact words, but I remember their eyes lit up when one said something like, *He who saves an olive tree saves all of humanity,* and the other riffed, *He who kills an olive tree kills all of mankind.* All the passages they chose were surprisingly similar, and their ability to respond so quickly to one another was quite impressive.

Most of us in the States have been led to believe that the Jews are the archenemies of the Arabs. But the truth is more nuanced, and it was evident on this evening. The Arabs consider themselves, Christians, and Jews all to be "people of the book" and Jesus to be one of the true prophets (though not the son of God). The Arabs' real hatred is reserved for the "Zionists," whom they say advance an Israeli political agenda and displace Palestinians who have occupied their homes for centuries. Among Sunni Muslims, Jews are often ranked higher than Shi'a Muslims.

After over a year of war, struggles between the Israelis and Palestinians, and the fight against a very real terrorist threat in my midst, I let myself enjoy this moment of genuine friendship between two men of goodwill whose backgrounds seemed so different but who in fact had much in common.

We finished dinner at the relatively early hour of 9:30, but our night was far from over. The senator and I had been invited to a second dinner, one ostensibly beginning at 10:30. Our host would be Prince Abdul Aziz bin Fahd, one of the sons of the incapacitated king.

Just twenty-nine years old, Abdul Aziz was head of the Office of Council Minister. Translation: he was secretary of the cabinet. In this capacity he saw every piece of paper that came through the royal court. It's fair to say that he did not achieve this important position at such a young age based on merit. He was considered a playboy and a big spender and according to Robert Baer, who worked for the CIA in the Middle East for over twenty years, "craven [and] a bit slow." He appeared to have some physical problems, as well.

Baer explained in an article in the *Atlantic*, "Apparently . . . he was regarded as the king's good-luck charm. Fahd's favorite soothsayer had once told him that as long as Abdul Aziz was by his side, the king would have a long, fulfilling life. So Fahd did not complain when Abdul Aziz spent $4.6 billion on a sprawling palace and theme park outside Riyadh, because Abdul Aziz was 'interested' in history. The property includes a scale model of old Mecca, with actors attending mosque and chanting prayers twenty-four hours a day, and also replicas of the Alhambra, Medina, and half a dozen other Islamic landmarks."[4]

This palace/theme park about thirty miles outside Riyadh was the site of our late Christmas night dinner. Unfortunately "late" turned out to be an understatement. As our motorcade drove to the palace, we received word that the prince was "not quite ready" to receive us. Indeed, the prince was not ready until 12:30 a.m. For two hours we circled around in the pitch-black desert.

During our wait, Lieberman and I got to know each other better. I liked him. He was genuinely interested in understanding what was going on in the Middle East. He had a keen desire to promote peace between the Arabs and Israelis and showed considerable respect for Crown Prince Abdullah and the other Saudi leaders. We talked about people we knew in common. We also talked a little bit about Iraq, but because our driver could hear us we didn't want to say anything sensitive.

We were becoming impatient and tired, and at one point I turned to him and said, "How do you manage this? It's just astounding that you can do this with so little sleep." He'd already been on the road for several days and was scheduled to depart at 5:30 a.m.

He said that having run a national campaign for vice president, he was prepared. *This is just what you do, you catnap, you do what you can*, he explained.

There is a great deal of wealth and showmanship in the Kingdom, but I never experienced anything approximating the reception that we finally received. As we drove up to the palace entrance, we were greeted by a virtual army of Saudis dressed in native costume, armed with swords and bandoliers, on majestic Arabian horses. The riders, perhaps twenty deep, formed a cordon, and we entered the floodlit grounds. Now we saw camels. Dozens of them. Arabian nights meets Disneyland meets . . .

. . . Colonial Williamsburg. Artisans and craftsmen worked in cubby-like spaces lining the massive interior courtyard. Glassblowers. Saddle makers. Silversmiths. All on duty well past midnight.

Why the show? I think the young prince wanted to impress a dignitary of Lieberman's stature. After all, the senator had run for vice president and might one day be president. Abdul Aziz wanted to be noticed by senior officials from the United States.

As we stood outside thanking the prince for this over-the-top welcome, he couldn't help but notice that we were shivering. Riyadh, as previously noted, sits two thousand feet above sea level. Winter nights can become quite chilly. Lieberman and I wore only our suit coats.

Abdul Aziz snapped his fingers. Servants appeared carrying robes for each of us. Mine was a sheepskin-lined *bisht*, or cloak, which immediately kept my teeth from chattering. Lieberman, the guest of honor, got a black one lined with mink.

By the time we sat down to eat, it was 1:00 a.m. At dinner the talk soon turned to Iraq. President Bush already had told me of his plan to remove Saddam Hussein. I was working the Saudis to support us if we went forward, and I was optimistic that we'd have their backing. But I was shocked to hear Prince Abdul Aziz tell us, "As a representative of the Saudi government and of my father the king, I can promise you that you have our full support for an invasion of Iraq."

Although he was the secretary of the royal court, he had never played any role in diplomacy or our bilateral relationship. I was pretty sure this was a case of freelancing, perhaps with the inside knowledge that the royal court intended to support us despite their negative public rhetoric. I don't think Senator Lieberman took it as a real commitment of the Saudi government any more than I did.

After further conversation, we thanked the prince for a pleasant evening and for his show of support and returned to the city. Abdul Aziz refused to let us return the *bishts* so we wore them home. Mine was relatively modest in value, and I was permitted to keep it as a token; Lieberman's mink was over the U.S. limit for gifts, so it now hangs today in the coat closet of Quincy House as an "official" wrap for guests.

Despite my doubts about the young prince's assertions about Iraq, as ambassador I had to follow up. Later that morning, I cabled Washington with the news. Everyone was as skeptical as I was, but we agreed that in all likelihood the Saudis would give us what we needed if and when we invaded Iraq. Rumsfeld and the Pentagon were still claiming that we wouldn't receive such support.

A final word about the evening. It wasn't the first time that I had to attend two dinners in one night in the line of duty. There's no need to pace one's alcohol intake, because it's not served on such occasions. Mocktails, not cocktails, are served. These are fruit drinks, often a combination of flavors like mint and mango, heavily laden with sugar. Very tasty, but a lot more calories than a Diet Pepsi. Some prefer "Saudi champagne," basically a mixture of apple and lemon juice, sparkling water, and sugar. Not my favorite.

Food, however, is a different matter. At most of these dinners, the host followed me through the buffet line piling food on my plate because I was a respected guest—the U.S. ambassador. It's difficult to manage your intake, because if you don't have three helpings, if you don't go back to refill your plate three times, it's considered an insult. Then again, if you do clean your plate, it's assumed you want more.

I learned to ask for or take relatively small portions and to leave a few remnants on my plate. This balancing act didn't work very well. In my two years in the Kingdom, I gained twenty pounds. And, unlike the Saudis, I couldn't hide my weight gain with a robe.

Although relatively confident that the Saudis would cooperate when we invaded Iraq, I was less sanguine that they would, or could, help us track down any from their country who had funded the 9/11 hijackers, Al Qaeda, and other terrorist operations. Frustrated as I was, however, I never reached a boiling point. The same cannot be said of my friend then–CIA director George Tenet. As 2002 drew to a close, he made his displeasure with the Saudi government quite clear.

Tenet's behavior is best understood after reviewing a brief history of the effort by the Treasury Department, the CIA, and the FBI to determine how the sophisticated attacks on New York City and Washington had been financed and to stanch any further bankrolling of terrorist activity. That effort began immediately after the hijackings. Soon there were questions about the involvement of particular Saudi individuals and charitable organizations. Some of these individuals were prominent, and some of the charities were associated with those close to or part of the royal family.

Two weeks after the attacks, the government froze the U.S. assets of more than two dozen organizations believed to be linked to Al Qaeda and other terrorist groups, including al-Wafa Humanitarian Organization. And in October, NATO found before-and-after photos of the Twin Towers, maps of government buildings in Washington, material on crop duster aircraft, and other incriminating evidence when it raided the Saudi High Commission for Aid to Bosnia. This charity had been founded by Prince Salman bin Abdul-Aziz (now the king) and supported by King Fahd.

Saudi connections to the financing of previous terrorist acts such as the Kenyan embassy bombing had already been explored. New information related to 9/11 was, therefore, taken very seriously. The leads had to be followed even if they led to Riyadh. As the Washington Institute for Near East Policy noted in 2002, "Saudi-sponsored humanitarian organizations such as the Mercy International Relief Organization (Mercy) played central roles in the 1998 U.S. embassy bombings. At the New York trial of four men convicted of involvement in the embassy attacks, a former Al Qaeda member named several charities as fronts for the terrorist group, including Mercy."[5]

This was tricky terrain. We would need Saudi support if we invaded Iraq. We were to some extent dependent on Saudi oil. The Kingdom was a longtime friend and stabilizing force in the region. We couldn't turn a blind eye to any official links to the terrorists, but we certainly hoped, and believed, the royals and the government were not involved.

We expected of Saudi Arabia what we would expect of any other ally: cooperation in following the money trail; in shutting down any funding of terrorism by individuals, businesses, and charities; and in changing procedures and laws to prevent future funding. In March 2002 Secretary of the Treasury Paul O'Neill came to the Middle East to make sure that the Kingdom and three of its neighbors—Bahrain, Kuwait, and the United Arab Emirates—were on board with our antiterrorist financing initiatives.

This would be no slam-dunk. The Washington Institute for Near East Policy contended, "Saudi officials have at minimum a clear pattern of looking the other way when funds are known to support extremist purposes. According to former State Department official Jonathan Winer, 'a number of Saudi charities either provided funds to terrorists or failed to prevent their funds from being diverted to terrorist use.'"[6]

The tricky part was determining whether any high-ranking member of the royal family or the government knowingly participated in funding the extremist activities of these charities or whether the charities misused the funds given to them in good faith. After more than a dozen years of seeking answers, there still has been no evidence directly linking high-level royals or officials to intentional funding of terrorists.

On the positive side, however, the Kingdom had made strides to control money laundering and to encourage charitably minded Saudis to contribute "only through established groups operating under the direct patronage of a member of the royal family" (some of which, it must be noted, were themselves suspect at the time). The Saudi government also took the extraordinary step of prohibiting the deposit of cash into the collection boxes in the mosques. This would be tantamount to refusing to allow passing the collection plate in American churches.

Before visits such as O'Neill's my staff would brief me extensively on the agenda, in this case conferring with Secretary O'Neill's staff and State Department liaison officers. As he was en route, I learned that O'Neill was prepared to, as the jargon of the day would say, "name and shame" some of the Saudis who were thought to be terrorist financiers. We had received a list of about a dozen alleged culprits.

"Look at the list and tell me what you know about each person," I asked my FBI and political officers who knew these people from having studied and lived in this arena.

The conclusion? Some of these people were very unlikely to be terrorist financiers and a lot of them were just unknown to us. Others could have names similar to a suspect's, but it was far from certain they had the right "Mohammed" or "Abdul." False accusations could spell trouble and hurt our credibility.

I got O'Neill on the phone on his plane as he was flying to the Kingdom. "Mr. Secretary," I said, "it's extremely important that our government not be embarrassed by revealing a list of names that we cannot then successfully prosecute. I think you need to be absolutely certain of every single name on that list before you publicize it. Are you that certain?"

He paused and said that they weren't certain.

"Well, my recommendation is that you keep that list to yourself until you are," I said.

He agreed.

While in the Kingdom, O'Neill met with Crown Prince Abdullah, Interior Minister Prince Nayef, Finance Minister Ibrahim bin Abdulaziz bin Abdullah al-Assaf, and Saudi businessmen. As James Dorsey of the *Wall Street Journal* wrote on March 7, 2002, "O'Neill told Saudi officials and business leaders here he understands their concern that freezing the assets of charities and individuals based in the Kingdom could damage their reputations."

Dorsey further reported, "At the same time, Mr. O'Neill defended the need to act against those suspected of funding terrorism even before all evidence against them had been collected. 'If we wait until we have 100% evidence, it may be difficult to incriminate them. However, we have become much more sensitive to the problem of damaging reputations,' a participant quoted Mr. O'Neill as saying."

The Saudis were particularly concerned about the reputation of a Jeddah businessman named Yassin al-Qadi, whose assets had been frozen in the United States and several other countries after 9/11. His Muwafaq Foundation was thought to have given funds to Osama bin Laden.[7]

By all accounts O'Neill's visit went well. Dorsey reported, "The Saudis, who since the Sept. 11 attacks have worried that the Kingdom's businessmen were being singled out as suspects, said they walked away from their meeting with the secretary reassured."

O'Neill was trying to balance the need to aggressively go after terrorist financiers in the Middle East against a blunderbuss approach that would destroy the reputations of local businessmen against whom we had very little evidence, if any. He later was fired by President Bush over policy disagreements, including his criticism of the invasion of Iraq. His story of dissent within the administration is chronicled by Ron Suskind in *The Price of Loyalty.*

O'Neill was not the only administration official concerned with terrorism to visit. I've previously mentioned presidential adviser Juan Zarate and Treasury general counsel David Aufhauser. In 2003 National Security Council counterterrorism expert Frances Townsend also met with me in the Kingdom. She would go on to become our homeland security advisor from 2004 to 2007.[8]

December 20, 2002, saw the filing of *The Report of the Joint Inquiry into the Terrorist Attacks of September 11, 2001—by the House Permanent Select Committee on Intelligence and the Senate Select Committee on Intelligence.* The report, well over four hundred pages, included testimony given by George Tenet on October 17. Among the CIA director's recommendations and pledges was the following: "We must disrupt and destroy the terrorists' operational chain of command and momentum, deny them sanctuary anywhere and eliminate their sources of financial and logistical support."[9]

Several pages of the report detailed what the CIA, the FBI, and other investigative agencies had learned about those "sources of financial support." But twenty-eight of those pages were redacted. They would remain blank when the report was issued to the general public on July 24, 2003. More about this later.

As with so many classified documents, information related to the inquiry was leaked before the report was filed in December and released to the public six months later. On November 24, 2002, Julian Borger of the *Guardian* reported, "Two mysterious Saudi citizens living in California before the September 11 attacks may link the Al Qaeda hijackers to Saudi intelligence, according to reports yesterday which are likely to provoke a new row between the US and Riyadh." The article noted that two of the hijackers may have been linked "indirectly" to a bank account in the name of Prince Bandar's Saudi wife, Princess Haifa.

Borger noted that the Saudi embassy called the report, "untrue and irresponsible." If indeed sent, the checks might have been meant to help a needy Saudi living in the States, explained Saudi officials. Adel al-Jubeir described Princess Haifa as "a very generous woman" who gave to many charities.[10]

When Tenet visited the Kingdom, he was armed with all the intelligence gathered over the previous several years about Saudi ties to acts of terror from Kenya to New York City. His mission, simply put, was to get in the face of Prince Mohammed bin Nayef and the Ministry of the Interior and demand a greater crackdown on those financing terrorism.

This wouldn't be the first time he'd be nose to nose with a Saudi prince. In his autobiography, *At the Center of the Storm*, Tenet tells of a 1998 visit to Riyadh after foiling a plot to assassinate then-vice president Al Gore on a trip to the Kingdom. The director didn't think the ministry had shared information in the necessary timely fashion. And so, after moving toward Interior Minister Prince Nayef and putting his hand on his knee, he said something to the effect of, *Your Royal Highness, what do you think it will look like if someday I have to tell the* Washington Post *that you held out data that might have helped us track down Al Qaeda murderers, perhaps even plotters who want to assassinate our vice president?*[11]

Let me set the scene: As I recall, Tenet, Prince Mohammed, myself, one of my aides, Prince Bandar, and Bandar's aide Rihab Massoud had gathered in the living room of Bandar's beachfront house in Jeddah. We were to have our discussion and then spend the night at this spectacular mansion, which sits on the Red Sea. Imagine Dr. No's hideout, complete with its own marina entrance on a cove blocked off from public access. Bandar's yachts and water toys line the cove, which is patrolled by Saudi gunboats. Brits staff the house.

We all knew the Saudis weren't getting very far at ferreting out the bad-guy funders. Few if any in the Kingdom had much forensic experience. And as Prince Bandar had said in a *New York Times*/PBS *Frontline* interview, "Money leaves Saudi Arabia, goes to Europe and we can follow it, goes to the United States, America, and we lose contact with it."[12]

Tenet sat on a sofa next to Prince Mohammed bin Nayef, with Bandar in an upholstered chair. I sat on a straight chair across from them, separated by a coffee table. Massoud and my aide were in other straight chairs, though Massoud was in and out of the room. Tenet folded one leg under his seat, with the other leg dangling over the sofa, as if he were about to tell a long and entertaining story.

Tenet was especially concerned about the Bosnian branch of the Saudi-based Al-Haramain Islamic Foundation. In March 2002 a United Nations Security Council committee had listed that branch "as being associated with Al-Qaida, Usama bin Laden, or the Taliban for 'participating in the financing, planning, facilitating, preparing or perpetrating of acts or activities by, in conjunction with, under the name of, on behalf or in support of' Al-Qaida."[13] (Soon after receiving this designation the foundation had closed its operations in Bosnia. It resurfaced under a different name, Vazir, for a while, but that, too, closed. The main branch in the Kingdom, however, continued to operate.)

Reports said that Al-Haramain, a kind of Saudi equivalent in size to the United Way, was out of control. Al Qaeda was apparently holding cell meetings in Al-Haramain offices in Bosnia and Albania. The Saudi officials with whom I had spoken hadn't exactly denied this but claimed ignorance of its activities abroad. Instead they argued that they couldn't tell the foundation what to do outside the borders of Saudi Arabia. This excuse extended to all Saudi-based charities operating elsewhere. I thought this was a lame explanation.

So did Tenet. As our discussion went on and the excuses piled up, he grew increasingly agitated. Suddenly he lunged at Prince Mohammed from his seat on the sofa, rising up on his folded knee, jutting his jaw at the prince, nearly nose to nose. *You guys have to do this*, he shouted. *This is a matter of our national security and yours. You have to do better. What more do I have to say to you?*

Prince Bandar and I and the rest of the assembled kept our distance until the CIA director calmed down. I don't think anyone had ever spoken to Prince Mohammed like that. The prince, whom I liked and respected, was sincere in his efforts to help but did not have the strongest team assembled to do the job. He responded calmly in English that he understood, that there was more the Saudis could do, but that he was trying his best.

CIA directors, Treasury officials, ambassadors, and everyone else dealing with a foreign country need to understand the culture. Following the money was difficult because the Kingdom is, by and large, a cash culture. In the normal course of business, Saudis travel across borders with suitcases full of money.

This extends to charitable contributions. In the United States we make such donations via check so we can preserve tax deductions. Because the Saudis don't pay any personal income tax (thus no need for deduction), these contributions are often made in cash and are unmonitored. In a culture like this, you really need a network of informants to make a case.

Where does the royal family figure into this? It's true that several members would contribute to some of the charities that turned out to be suspect, just as Americans might contribute to the United Way. Even though some of these charities may have been providing some funds to terrorists—knowingly or unknowingly—I never saw evidence or had reason to believe that royal family contributions were made with strings attached. As far as I knew or know to this day, no one gave money to a charity and said, "Funnel this to Al Qaeda or some other terrorists." We never had even a hint of suspicion that members of the royal family, certainly not the senior members of the royal family, were engaged in any terrorist financing.

A few words about Tenet: As noted, I would visit him when I went to Washington. I found him very emotional, a big-picture guy who likes the grand gesture. He's also no political dummy, so, knowing I was friends with the president, I'm sure he wanted to stay on my good side. But we genuinely got along and became friends. It was clear to me that his organization at least understood how to operate in a foreign country—in tough conditions, a wartime environment, with a lot of nuances—much better than the FBI did. But it was also apparent to me that the CIA didn't trust the FBI, didn't like the bureau very well, and didn't share much information with it. That was mutual; the FBI didn't share anything with the CIA.

Our day at Bandar's house could have ended on a sour note due to Tenet's confrontation with the prince. Thankfully, order was restored. After the meeting we enjoyed a pleasant dinner.

Following dinner, Bandar invited Tenet and me to his private quarters for Scotch and cigars. This was not the first time a Saudi prince had offered me liquor or wine and a cigar. And it certainly didn't seem out of character for Bandar to make such a gesture. I guess it's the same as Southern Baptists whose conservative religious leaders frown on drinking or dancing but who can have a Jack Daniels and still show up in good faith for church on Sunday.

Keep in mind Bandar had been educated in England and in the United States at Johns Hopkins. He had been Saudi ambassador to the United States since 1983. More than any Saudi official whom I came to know, he moved at ease in both the East and the West. He had estates in Oxfordshire, Great Britain, and Aspen, Colorado, where he was a large contributor to the Aspen Institute, which holds seminars on public policy and leadership. When abroad he dressed in the finest British suits, and he socialized with several celebrated Americans in addition to the Bushes. I occasionally saw him at Dallas Cowboys games, where he was the guest of his good friend, owner Jerry Jones. His younger brother attended Baylor University in Waco.

The subject of terrorist financing was at the center of my threat to resign my post in early 2002. While not as infamous as the eighteen minutes missing on President Nixon's White House tape during the Watergate investigation, the twenty-eight redacted pages in the congressional report were and remain controversial. Speculation and leaks suggested these pages presented proof that Bandar's wife and others high up in the Saudi government and/or the royal family had contributed to one or more organizations that supported terrorism. Neo-cons and others suggested that the Bush administration was trying to protect its Saudi pals—even though those pals had helped finance the most deadly attack on America in history. The suggestions of such involvement were contrary to the reports I had been receiving. Still, as the point man in Saudi Arabia, I wanted to know, *needed* to know, if my government was indeed whitewashing the truth.

My initial requests to see the twenty-eight pages—relayed to Washington by Margaret Scobey—were denied. I found this unacceptable. Threatening to resign an ambassadorship is serious business. The implications extend beyond the individual. Even if the ambassador and the administration spin the move as stemming from "personal reasons," the press can sniff out a sham and then begin asking serious questions. *Why wouldn't you show your ambassador those pages? What are you hiding? The report must be incriminating.*

So when is it appropriate for an ambassador to draw a line in the sand and say, *Either you give me what I have requested or I'm leaving?* In my view it's when you so fundamentally disagree with a policy directly affecting your mission that you are unable to officially support it, or your superiors have placed you in an untenable position by withholding material facts necessary for you to function.

This was one of those times. I told Margaret that I was drawing a line in the sand. My message to Condi Rice, the FBI, the CIA, or whoever was calling the shots on this was simple: *All right, if you don't want an ambassador out here, send me home. But if you want an ambassador out here, I need to see those twenty-eight pages.*

Eventually word came back: *Okay, you can see them.* I suspect Rice or Tenet made the decision. But there were strings attached. The documents came in a courier package attached to a CIA briefer. He put me in a room with the documents. I was allowed to read them in his presence, but I could not copy them or take notes. To this day, I'm not at liberty to disclose the contents because they remain classified.

Because of all the speculation about the content of the redacted pages, President Bush wanted the pages released. So did Prince Saud, even though he had no direct knowledge of their contents. I agree. The pages should be declassified for all to see.

9

THREE MONTHS AND one week after telling me he was "fixin' to do a regime change in Iraq," George W. Bush followed through on his promise. A little after 10:00 p.m. Eastern Standard Time on March 19, 2003, the president announced that the United States and a handful of allies had launched Operation Iraqi Freedom. As the sun rose over Riyadh, where the time was nine hours ahead of Washington, Ann and I watched the bombing of Baghdad on CNN and Al Jazeera television. Soon it was reported that we had troops on the ground engaging the Iraqis.

The assault seemed to confirm what our preinvasion intelligence had predicted: Saddam Hussein's reign would soon be over. Although happy that the dictator would be out of power, I found little reason to cheer. This was a sobering experience. Innocent lives were being lost that morning.

Something inside me said that it shouldn't have come to this . . . at least not at this moment. Diplomacy and sanctions, the carrot and stick, had failed. But had they been given enough time? The inspectors looking for weapons of mass destruction (WMD) had yet to find any smoking guns. But maybe they, too, could have used an extension.

Still, like the majority of Congress and the American people, I supported what we were doing. Based on the reports I had seen, Saddam Hussein was going to be an existential threat to his neighbors and to the peaceful development of the Middle East. I concede, however, that while the intelligence I saw expressed certainty that Iraq possessed wmd, nothing suggested a connection between Iraq and Al Qaeda.

My caution about the timing of the invasion stemmed in part from listening to three great statesmen whose opinions I respected: Colin Powell, Brent Scowcroft, and Jim Baker. In our conversations before the war, Secretary of State Powell never expressed any doubts that Iraq possessed wmd. But he frequently questioned the wisdom of pulling the trigger before the inspectors had done their job. He also wondered whether the United Nations and the international community would be sufficiently supportive of an invasion. And, of course, as was well reported, he believed in the Pottery Barn rule, "If you break it, you bought it."

General Scowcroft, the former national security advisor to George H. W. Bush, was even more skeptical about going to war with Iraq. At the suggestion of the former president, Scowcroft and I occasionally met for breakfast or lunch at the Metropolitan Club when I was in Washington. The general was very kind to me and quite candid. We spoke about the turf battles going on inside the administration. It's no secret that he was supportive of Powell and dismissive of Cheney and Rumsfeld. Condi Rice had been his protégé, but their relationship grew strained as he became more and more critical of the president.

On August 15, 2002, the *Wall Street Journal* published Scowcroft's op-ed titled "Don't Attack Saddam." The general acknowledged that Saddam was a bad man and might have to go some point, but he cautioned that prosecuting a war against him would be "no cakewalk." Moreover, such an action would divert us from the real war on terrorism. Because Scowcroft was so close to Bush 41 and was questioning the policies of Bush 43, the piece gained widespread attention.

As previously noted, former secretary of state Baker was a friend and law partner. When the diplomat who put together the first Gulf War coalition writes an op-ed about Iraq in the *New York Times*, you pay attention. In his piece, which ran ten days after Scowcroft's, Baker didn't explicitly argue against an invasion. He focused instead on the conditions necessary to achieve our long-range objectives if and when we did invade. He warned that we needed to create a broad coalition, that we needed the American public to buy into the effort, and that we had to be honest from the outset that the war would be costly in terms of blood and treasure.

As the bombing began, I wasn't convinced we'd met those conditions. I suspect that when he wrote his op-ed piece setting out these conditions for an invasion, Baker knew we likely could not meet them. It was a subtle way of saying, "Don't do it if you can't do it right."

Something else weighed heavily on me as the invasion became imminent—a practical, as opposed to philosophical, reason for hoping that war could be avoided or delayed. Saudi Arabia was an obvious WMD target. The Kingdom was not only an ally of the United States, it was cooperating with our prosecution of the war. Riyadh was only about 850 miles from Baghdad—well within range of missiles carrying deadly chemical or biological components. As the U.S. ambassador, I had to worry about the safety of embassy personnel and the twenty-five thousand American citizens residing on this foreign soil. Protecting our people was my top priority.

Over the course of my daily intelligence briefings, I saw communication intercepts of Iraqi officers in the field saying, in effect, *Be sure when the fighting starts that you have your gas mask handy, because you're going to need it.* As a result I was convinced that the Iraqis would be lobbing Scud missiles into Riyadh. They had done so during the first Gulf War—a crater in the city remained as a frightening reminder. Those missiles were not WMD. Scuds are not particularly accurate, but if they have biological or chemical warheads on them, they don't have to hit a specific target to kill people.

Worried about our vulnerability, I scrambled to get gas masks for my embassy staff through our administrative officer. Believe it or not, I was told that masks were not available for civilians. Our military had preempted the entire supply.

Like most everyone else, the Saudis believed Saddam possessed WMD. I never received any pushback from any Saudi suggesting Saddam was bluffing. Not only was the Defense Ministry aware of our intelligence reports, it had its own sources, including intermarried tribes that moved back and forth between the Kingdom and Iraq.

As a result, Prince Khalid bin Sultan, the assistant defense minister for military affairs (and son of Minister of Defense Prince Sultan), asked me to get seventeen thousand gas masks for use by his troops and Ministry of Defense personnel. After failing, I apologized and explained that I couldn't even get them for my own people.

How can I say this diplomatically? I was extremely disappointed that my own government was unprepared to protect its embassy staff. Sad to say, I wasn't as surprised as I would have been a year earlier. During my tenure, I had already been exposed to a great deal of bureaucratic dissembling and ineffectiveness.

My fears for the safety of my staff and other Americans in the Kingdom were not limited to warheads coming from outside the country. We also were preparing for civil unrest within Saudi Arabia. Because it was quite possible that anti-American sentiment could boil over into violence against U.S. citizens, we considered a number of plans, including evacuation. We maintained a system of notices to the "wardens," as we called them—the civilian volunteers responsible for various units of the American community, including businesses and residential compounds. Warden messages would go out periodically advising of security concerns or travel alerts.

The wardens would be a key part of our preparedness for any attacks from Iraq. Each would phone a list of expat Americans. The expats, in turn, would phone those on their own lists—like the telephone tree used in American schools to advise of a snow day.

Evacuation would be a logistical nightmare, taking about three weeks. Because all military aircraft would be used in the war, we would have to rely on chartered private or regularly scheduled aircraft, both of which would become scarce the moment hostilities broke out. In all likelihood, therefore, we'd have to organize caravans to the desert or to the Eastern Province, which would be out of Scud range.

Gas masks weren't the only thing that our government didn't provide me. There was a paucity of information as well. My surrogates—Margaret, my political officer, my military people, and others—were for all intents and purposes stonewalled when they asked Washington about the invasion. I would occasionally go directly to my contacts at the State Department—Bill Burns, Ryan Crocker, and others—but they usually indicated they were in the dark as well. When I was in Washington, I would meet with Rice, but she, too, played it pretty close to the vest. Bottom line: I never really felt that my own government was opening the kimono to me—except when they wanted me to deliver something from the Saudis.

Why wasn't the beast returning the favor and feeding me? In part, I think, because of the secrecy that pervades all administrations when national security is involved. Also, turf-conscious Washington compartmentalized access to information in a way that, in my view, hindered what I was trying to do—which was to understand the big picture and then determine how what I was doing with the Saudis fit into that. Often State and Defense weren't any more cooperative with one another than the FBI and CIA.

Most of my good information about the war planning came through back channels from my senior advisor ("Bill"), who was regularly in touch with "Hassan," a top aide to Prince Bandar. (As the *Washington Post*'s Bob Woodward and others later reported, Bandar was privy to the invasion plans well before March 19.)

Fortunately the powers that be did give me a heads-up that the war was going to begin. On the afternoon before the offensive, my aide Bill—who had been briefed by his Washington sources—entered my office and whispered that the shock and awe would be starting soon. I wasn't surprised. For some time, there had been an air of inevitability. Buzz Moseley, the head of the air campaign, had also alerted me that the campaign was about to begin.

For better or worse, Operation Iraqi Freedom was facilitated by Saudi support. The Kingdom didn't like Saddam any more than the United States did. But Crown Prince Abdullah and his ministers had ample reason to sit this war out rather than help our nation intervene in the affairs of a Muslim neighbor. Instead, as the Associated Press, quoting "senior political and military officials from both countries" reported on April 25, 2004, "During the Iraq war, Saudi Arabia secretly helped the United States far more than has been acknowledged, allowing operations from at least three air bases, permitting special forces to stage attacks from Saudi soil and providing cheap fuel. . . . The American air campaign against Iraq was essentially managed from inside Saudi borders."

As our nation's man on the ground in Riyadh, I helped facilitate some of this support. I've been asked if in doing so I felt like I was helping write history. My answer then and now: I don't think that I was an author of history so much as part of the machinery that clanked into gear to make all this happen.

The machinery for invasion began gearing up more than a year before March 19, 2003. (Some might say it began a decade earlier!) In his memoir, *In My Time*, Cheney describes a private meeting with the crown prince in Jeddah in March 2002:

> I laid out for Abdullah the enormous impact of the 9/11 attacks on America. With 3,000 Americans dead, we could not wait for terrorists to attack again and then deal with them after the fact. As the president had said, waiting for threats to fully materialize was waiting too long. Saddam, his pursuit of weapons of mass destruction and his ties to terrorist groups, including al Qaeda, were of great concern. We intended to pursue a diplomatic resolution, but if we couldn't achieve one we would be compelled to act. And if war did come, I assured the crown prince we would prevail. The crown prince was concerned about Saddam, but skeptical about U.S. military action. He wanted more reassurance that we would in fact see it through.[1]

During the summer and early fall of 2002, the pros and cons of an invasion were being vigorously debated, but none of my contacts at the State Department, Pentagon, or White House told me that a decision had been made. As noted, my Saudi counterparts—including Foreign Minister Prince Saud and Prince Khalid bin Sultan—would caution me, "Don't win Iraq and lose Saudi Arabia" or "Do not win the war and lose the peace." Shades of Powell, Scowcroft, and Baker.

A timeline is helpful here. On October 11 the U.S. Congress passed a resolution authorizing the president to use armed force against Iraq if necessary. On November 8 the UN Security Council adopted resolution 1441, which stated that Saddam was in breach of a previous resolution related to WMD and other weapons. Resolution 1441 offered the dictator one last chance to "comply with its disarmament obligations." On November 18 the weapons inspectors, led by the UN's Hans Blix and the International Atomic Energy Agency's Mohammed El Baradei, returned to Iraq for the first time in four years.

During this period and the early days of 2003, the Saudi press, and for that matter Crown Prince Abdullah, expressed distaste for a U.S. invasion of Iraq and did not signal a willingness to help if we did invade. At the same time, they made clear that there was no love lost for Saddam.

Over these months several representatives from the State Department and Congress visited Riyadh. Many met with Prince Sultan to get some indication of his views of American military activity in Iraq.

Interestingly, Sultan never did say, "Don't invade." He would almost always say something like, *We are great allies of the United States and we believe our relationship is extremely important.* He was cryptic. But he was cryptic in a way that made me think that he was actually going to be willing to help us. In fact, during an August 2002 congressional staff delegation visit in Jeddah, Prince Sultan expressed his desire that the forward command center for Central Command remain in the Kingdom and not be moved to their Sunni Arab rival Qatar (as later occurred).

He went on to say that Iraq should be pressured to accept weapons inspectors but that, as in the first Gulf War, *If there is a need, we will cooperate.* He further approved Buzz Moseley's request to lift the restrictions on Operation Southern Watch that had prevented our use of the PSAB command center to assist fighters in striking back at Iraqi antiaircraft radar installations that had either locked on our planes monitoring southern Iraq or had fired at our jets. The gloves were off, and we would be permitted to respond in kind. I liked what I heard.

In September 2002 Franks and I met with Prince Khalid bin Sultan. The two reminisced about the first Gulf War, and Prince Khalid showed us the room in his military headquarters where he and General Norman Schwarzkopf bunked during the fighting. Prince Khalid expressed concern over possible Iraqi attacks on the Kingdom using chemical and biological warheads. We also talked about preparations for Operation Internal Look, to take place in December, potentially a dry run for war with Iraq using Saudi land and air facilities.

On the same day, in a meeting with Crown Prince Abdullah and Prince Sultan, the crown prince approved sending a Saudi liaison to Central Command headquarters in Tampa and adding more U.S. Air Force personnel at Prince Sultan Air Base outside of Riyadh. While I was aware of dissension within the royal family, including the articulate skepticism of the foreign minister, I was sensing signals that the Saudis were preparing for an American military confrontation with Iraq.

In late October, Bill Burns and I met with the crown prince. Burns indicated that we would continue to work the UN on Iraq but might need to return to discuss with him "military contingencies" to keep pressure on Saddam. The crown prince judiciously observed that military action would fuel more terrorist attacks against the United States and its allies.

In November I met with Prince Salman bin Abdulaziz, then the governor of Riyadh and later the crown prince and now king. A careful, deliberate man with decades of experience ruling Riyadh Province, he is one of the most respected senior royals. He bears a striking resemblance to his father, King Abdulaziz. While the focus of our meeting was the continuing crisis in the Palestinian Territories, Prince Salman expressed support for the removal of Saddam. The previous day, his nephew, Prince Khalid bin Sultan, had once again told me that, if the chips were down, the United States could count on Saudi Arabia regarding Iraq.

In December Prince Saud once again told me that the consequences of conflict with Iraq could be grave. He confided that the Arabs were considering going to Saddam to urge him to abdicate and that the group included some of Saddam's top lieutenants. Later in January, Prince Saud urged us to assure Saddam's potentially mutinous lieutenants that only the top tier of the regime would be taken out; the remaining officials could play a role in the new government.

In hindsight, the suggestion was worth considering, as the chaos that followed the invasion might have been averted if some vestiges of the regime, including some military officers, had been allowed a role in maintaining security and discipline after Saddam's fall. In any event, Prince Saud's proposal went nowhere, and Saddam remained firm in his insistence on remaining in power.

Also in December, I visited Adel al-Jubeir with Congressman David Price. Adel told us that in the event of conflict, the Saudis would provide us all we needed, though perhaps not all we wanted. As he was a close advisor to the crown prince, I considered Adel's signal reliable.

Still, the signals continued to be mixed. In January 2003 Tommy Franks and I met with Prince Khalid bin Sultan. His Highness was concerned about the impact on the region of a protracted war, which could stir up anti-Saudi sentiment in response to their assistance. In our meeting with the crown prince the same week, Abdullah was hoping against hope that something would intervene to make military action unnecessary.

He told us the story of a man with a donkey who bet his fortune that he could convince a villager that the donkey could tell the future. If the prediction came true, the donkey's owner would receive the villager's home; if the prediction failed, the owner would pay the villager half his fortune. The villager turned to one of the village elders, who advised him to defer making the bet. "Why?" asked the villager. The elder replied, "Maybe the donkey will die."

This was the crown prince's way of saying, *Maybe something will happen to Saddam. Maybe the decision will be lifted from our shoulders.* Despite this ambivalence and anxiety over the looming war, I remained confident that we would have the help we needed from the Saudis.

My assessment was contrary to the prevailing view in Washington, particularly that of the Pentagon. According to my military attaché, Bernie Dunn, and my aide Bill, the Defense Department kept repeating, *The Saudis aren't going to let us use their air bases; they're not going to let us use any of the assets that we've got; they're going to be a real problem.*

I was more sanguine. In addition to guessing that Prince Sultan would end up in our corner, I was pretty certain that Prince Bandar would press our cause. The prince was close to the Bush family and was dean of the Washington diplomatic corps. I felt he longed to be remembered as a statesman in the Kissinger mode and was invigorated by the opportunity to play a supportive role in our war on terror. He was fiercely pro-American and enjoyed unfettered access to the White House. In fact, the administration was later criticized for sharing the war plan for Iraq with him before the invasion began.

I failed to understand the controversy over the war plan. If an ally is providing logistical support for a military operation, you most certainly need to be sure the ally knows what plan it is supporting. The action had the further advantage of co-opting Bandar and other senior royals into the ground floor of preparation for the invasion, enhancing the chances of their continued support.

In my reports to Washington, I disagreed with the conventional wisdom that the Saudis would not cooperate. As I had told President Bush, we might not get everything we wanted, but we'd get what we needed.

Everything we wanted appeared on a laundry list that the Pentagon sent me in late January or early February 2003. Tasked as a negotiator, not a messenger, I was to try to secure such things as:

- Permission to enter Iraq from Arar, the main border crossing from the Kingdom into Iraq. (We wanted to put our special forces in there early to take out radar installations and forward observers.)
- Use of Prince Sultan Air Base to launch tankers and AWACS— surveillance aircraft based on the old Boeing 707, formally called the Airborne Warning and Control System.
- Access to the marine and oil terminal areas in the north on the Arabian Gulf, near Yanbu al Bahr. (We needed to be sure these facilities were secure, and I suspect that some had hoped to use these areas to stage troops or logistical assets.)
- Access to the air base at Tabuk, a city in the northwest not far from Israel.

This last item demonstrates the complex nature of geopolitics in the twenty-first century. The Saudis said that we could use the air base at Tabuk for the war effort . . . on one condition: if they could have an F-15 squadron there. That presented a problem because when we had first sold the F-15s to the Kingdom in 1982, Congress had insisted that we ban the Saudis from basing the fighter jets in Tabuk. This ban was in deference to nearby Israel, which feared that if the Saudis had warplanes there, they could launch an attack with virtually no warning. Fortunately, we were now able to gain approval from Congress to strike the deal, partly thanks to Senator Joe Biden, chairman of the Senate Foreign Relations Committee. We also advised Israel.

The list also included some requests that were, quite frankly, outlandish. One example: Washington wanted the Saudis to close their three largest commercial airports—at Jeddah, Riyadh, and Dammam—and let the U.S. military take them over.

Requests in hand, I went to see Prince Sultan and Prince Khalid bin-Sultan. "Here's our wish list," I said. But I also said—and this is where an ambassador has a certain amount of latitude—"You know, there are some things on this list that I think my government wants more than others. I understand how difficult it would be for you to close your commercial airports."

I had to keep my credibility with these leaders. If I came in pounding the table, saying, "By God, we have to have these airports," I would look like a complete fool—which is what I thought the Pentagon people would look like if they truly believed the Saudis would bite on every request, lock, stock, and barrel.

In the end we received Saudi approval and cooperation. The word was relayed to me by Moseley. We got basically all we had seriously asked for: border crossings at Arar; use of PSAB to launch tankers, AWACS, and support aircraft (but not fighters); and a squadron of F-15s at Tabuk, despite Israeli grumbling. The reaction in Washington was one of surprise and relief.

Questions have been raised about whether the Bush administration "sold out" to the Saudis in order to secure their cooperation. I saw no evidence that we softened our positions on terrorism, human rights, or religious freedom during this period. I continued to press for progress on counterterrorism, terrorist financing, and child custody issues and to urge the economic reforms necessary for WTO membership. Congressional delegations and cabinet or subcabinet visitors continued to press for similar reforms. For their part, the Saudis hinted that our path would be much easier if we gave them a sense of commitment to resolving the Israeli-Palestinian conflict. Their message essentially was, *Look, if we're going out on a limb to help you in Iraq, we need to show the Arab world, and especially our own people, that we are getting something in return on the Palestinian front.*

Fair enough. And for our part, I urged the Saudis to provide financial support for the Palestinian Authority and to encourage Yasser Arafat to support Mahmoud Abbas (known as Abu Mazen) in his tenuous hold on leadership of the Palestinian Authority. Abu Mazen was one of the few who were inclined to stand up to Hamas, which was gaining more traction in light of the corruption and ineffectiveness of governance by the Fatah party as well as manipulating popular anger against American support for the Israelis.

As the war in Afghanistan continued and the invasion of Iraq approached, I visited Prince Sultan Air Base at least once a week. What I saw at PSAB was almost surreal. There were two large video screens, about the size of commercial movie screens, in this massive Combined Air Operations Center. These screens featured electronic lights showing areas where we were either engaged with or targeting the enemy. Sometimes I'd actually see live video feed of a drone monitoring a target— say a convoy—and then releasing its bomb. Suddenly there would be an explosion . . . and no more convoy.

Some of our operations in the region were considerably less sophisticated than targeted drone strikes. On one occasion I was shown a tape of intelligence and special operations forces on horseback chasing through the mountains and the desert after the Taliban. I couldn't help thinking of the military campaigns of Genghis Khan some eight hundred years earlier. I was astounded that in this high-tech age we still had our people doing this sort of thing.

A final word about my visits to PSAB. First, it wasn't "our" base at all; it belonged to the Saudis, and we were their guests. I had to have an appointment and clearance ahead of time to get into the base. I couldn't just show up unannounced. Due to some problems that predated my arrival in the Kingdom, there was bad blood between the Saudi commander of the air base and our American contingent. As a result, every now and then the commander would hassle us a bit. I would arrive at the appointed time and be kept waiting for no reason. I would register my unhappiness, but to no avail.

One day when the Saudis kept me waiting outside the gate for over fifteen minutes, I blew my top. I told one of my people to call the commander and tell him we needed to get in immediately. Ten more minutes passed after the call. "That's it," I said to my driver. "We're leaving. Let's go back to the embassy."

We pulled out and started the forty-five-minute drive back to Riyadh. As we motored quickly down the highway, we saw through the rearview mirror a car chasing after us. Its siren was wailing. Its lights were flashing. When the car caught up with us, Saudis from the base emerged and breathlessly said the commander was ready to receive us. Would we please come back?

Several minutes later, I sat in the commander's office drinking tea with him. Pardon my French, but I chewed his ass up one side and down the other. I lost it with him, on purpose. I wanted everybody in the room to see the wrath that they would incur if they continued these gratuitous insults. I was the president's representative there, we had important business to do, and this little jerk was not going to get in our way. "If you ever do this again, I'm going to go to your government and I'm going to ask to have you replaced," I said.

It never happened again.

In addition to seeing our operations on the ground at PSAB, I took to the sea and air to familiarize myself with our military capabilities. In February I visited the aircraft carrier USS *Constellation* in the Arabian Gulf (most Americans call it the Persian Gulf, but that doesn't go over well in the Arab world, where they hate the Persians). Later I flew on an AWACS mission up to the Iraq border.

When the commanding officer of the *Constellation* invited me aboard, I jumped at the chance. I needed to have a better understanding of what our naval assets were doing in the region. In addition, as a navy man and the son of a navy man, I was just plain curious.

The flight from Riyadh to the Gulf took about an hour. We flew in a COD (carrier onboard delivery)—a propeller plane with about twenty seats. We wore helmets and faced the rear, and when we reached the carrier, we corkscrewed down to kill speed. As the plane landed on the deck, we were still traveling at 250 miles per hour. About three seconds later, we were down to 0 mph, as the plane's tailhook was caught by one of the three arresting wires on board.

"Awesome" is an overused word, but it's appropriate to describe the sight of a 1,088-foot carrier in the midst of some one hundred ships in a flotilla—destroyers, cruisers, and other naval craft. The *Constellation* is like a city, home to some six or seven thousand people and about seventy aircraft.

After a briefing by the commander, we spent the day watching the flight operations conducted at a 24/7 tempo to simulate the upcoming war. At this point, the pilots on board were participating in Operation Southern Watch, the enforcement of a no-fly zone in southern Iraq that began after the first Gulf War ended.

The pilots flew out to taunt or bait the Iraqis into shooting at them. This would allow them to execute the response option, under which we had three days to go back and take something out. The pilots were also trying to answer other questions: How do we get our support? Do we need to do midair refueling? How do we use the AWACS technology? They were doing a lot more than simply kabuki; they were out there operating.

My day on the *Constellation* brought home to me the massive military firepower of the United States. No other country in the world has a navy to match ours. We have, in effect, portable air bases in hotspots anytime we need them, and we have contingents of marines that can be deployed by airborne units almost at a moment's notice.

My opportunity to fly in, rather than just observe, an AWAC came courtesy of General Moseley. As head of the U.S. Central Command air component, Buzz was in charge of air operations over Afghanistan and Iraq. About a month before the invasion, he invited me to meet him at PSAB. There he presented me with a flight suit embroidered with my Drew Carey–inspired "name"—BADASSADOR JORDAN.

Buzz was quite a character. Interviewed on television after the war began, he delivered a classic response to the pundits criticizing our battle plan: "Retired military people from various grades, from major to general, seem to feel free to comment on a plan that they have never seen . . . or have any understanding of. I grew up in Texas, and a lot of these guys, I'm amused by the way they critique it, but in the end, it's a whole lot like listening to a cow pee on a flat rock. It just doesn't matter."[2]

The Saudi air base was the headquarters for Operation Southern Watch—the southern no-fly zone, south of Baghdad. Saddam's people were forbidden either to fly in that zone or to attack our aircraft that were conducting surveillance. One of our fighters had been shot at, and I was invited to participate in the response. The purpose of our mission was to control a fighter aircraft that would then attack an Iraqi radar installation; we would provide the air traffic control for that twelve-hour mission. The AWAC on which I flew stayed at the border, and then the fighter actually went into Iraqi airspace.

Was there a possibility of avoiding the war for which we were preparing? According to Harb Saleh al-Zuhair, the answer was *yes*. Zuhair, an Iraqi-born Saudi industrialist in his mid-sixties, periodically showed up at embassy gatherings and other business meetings I attended. He said that his tribe inhabited southern Iraq and that he was the grandson of the last emir of Basrah. We weren't friends, but I knew who he was.

In November 2002 he came to my office with a bombshell of an assertion: he said that he had it on good authority that Saddam would resign and go into exile if the Saudis would finance or otherwise help facilitate that. His source had asked that the United States simply say what we wanted. I realized that this was a far-fetched proposal with only a slim chance that it was for real. But I also realized that it wasn't up to me to dismiss it without advising our intelligence community that I had been approached. After we parted, I passed the information on.

Zuhair might well have been approached by someone pretending to be talking on behalf of Saddam. I think it is indicative of the fact that so many of these Saudis had very close family and business connections within Iraq. And so their communication lines were buzzing, and I'm sure there was a lot of back-and-forth among them about all these issues. It's certainly possible that there was more to it than that, and our people may well have had discussions with Bandar and others about it.

As Zuhair had significant business holdings in the Kingdom, he was no doubt worried about the impact of a war. The American expat businessmen in the Kingdom were also concerned. One thing about expats: those who live in a place like Saudi Arabia are tough as nails and not terribly fearful of geopolitical events. Those working in the oil industry are especially tough. Many have lived in far more dangerous places, like Angola or Chad. Still, they were curious about what was happening—if for no other reason than to keep their bosses back in the States or Europe advised. I would frequently meet with the American Business Group of Riyadh and brief their members and guests.

My fellow diplomats, particularly the EU ambassadors, were nervous. They kept track of the times I would go to see the crown prince or another high-level minister or travel to the United States. They saw me as the guy who had the most access to the leadership in Saudi Arabia and in Washington, so whenever I would blink an eye, some ambassador would call me up and say, "What's happening next?"

I learned what was happening next in late February when Moseley came to the embassy to brief me on the war plan. By the time our meeting in a secure room was over, I was hyperventilating, as I had after meeting with the president in the Oval Office some ten weeks earlier. *We were going to war.*

The plan was relatively simple. Through the "shock and awe" use of our airpower, we would quickly take out the Iraqi Air Force. We'd then bring several divisions of ground forces into various parts of the country at once. The Fourth Infantry Division, for example, would enter Iraq through Turkey to open up a front in northern Iraq and subdue any large efforts by the Iraqi military to escape over the border. This was important because air power alone could not pacify the country or create the conditions necessary for reconstruction.

Washington assumed that Turkey would grant us permission to send tens of thousands of our troops over its borders. Signals from Turkey's executive branch suggested this would be the case. But on March 1, by a margin of only a few votes, the Turkish Parliament refused to give the necessary approval.

To me this seemed another example of our government's dysfunction. Why didn't our diplomats on the ground see this coming? Didn't it make sense that an Islamist parliament less beholden to America than the Turkish president would vote this way?

Rebuffed at the eleventh hour, the military had to resort to a backup plan. Moseley and I hurried to Prince Sultan's office. *Look,* we told the prince and his son, *we aren't able to bring our Fourth Infantry Division through Turkey now, so would it be okay with you if we move some of our naval ships and submarines from the Mediterranean through the Suez Canal and into the Red Sea and then shoot Tomahawk cruise missiles over your country into Iraq?* They said yes.

During the two weeks between this meeting and the launch of the war, Prince Khalid bin Sultan, Prince Saud, and I discussed a number of day-after scenarios. What if Iraq launched WMD into the Kingdom? What if the Saudi "street" erupted in protest over the U.S. invasion? And, assuming neither of these occurred, what were we going to do if we toppled Saddam quickly?

The Saudis had their own list of preferences. After Saddam invaded Kuwait in 1990–91 and then menaced the Saudi oil fields in the Eastern Province, they joined us in going to war against Iraq. They hated Saddam and wanted him gone. But they were wary of creating a vacuum into which their mortal enemy, Iran, could move, especially with a large Shi'a population in Iraq. The Saudis wanted to keep their Sunni spiritual allies in charge, so a lot of what they would ask me about had to do with keeping that Sunni minority in control of the instruments of power. Their preferred strategy was for us to take out Saddam, take out his thirty or forty top lieutenants, and take out every military officer at the general level and above. But leave in place the ministers, leave in place the bureaucrats, many of whom had to join the Ba'ath Party simply to get a job. And don't take this society down to the stubs—which, of course, we ignored.

I relayed these conversations to Powell, Armitage, and Burns back at the State Department (and at times Rice as well). During this period, however, the president assigned the postwar responsibility to the Defense Department. This surprised me because State had a group that had been planning the postwar reconstruction of Iraq for about two years. (This didn't mean they knew were going to war all that time, but it meant they were doing a lot of thinking about the possibility.)

Soon reconstruction was on the front burner. Saddam's regime toppled almost as easily as his statue. The Saudis were not surprised by the ease with which we came in; I think they felt that the revolutionary guards had some allegiance to Saddam, but the rest of the military were largely conscripts who would not fight to the death. The Saudis also knew that we had massive air superiority and that Saddam had virtually no air force. (We were somewhat concerned about Saddam's antiaircraft capability, but that proved to be illusory. Also, we had taken out a lot of Iraq's forward observer sites and missile-launching capabilities with our special forces in the weeks leading up to the invasion.)

When the president appeared on the uss *Abraham Lincoln* on May 1 in front of the infamous "Mission Accomplished" banner, the Saudis paid little heed. Like the rest of us, they knew that we had a lot more to do. Also, they probably realized that Bush's people were not directly responsible for putting up the banner, which, while taken out of context, was nevertheless inappropriate.

In its postinvasion planning, the State Department had already identified Americans who would be assigned to help the various ministries of Iraq maintain traction and stay up and running. All of this was thrown aside by Rumsfeld. Instead, he had his handpicked minions come in. Sadly, these were individuals who didn't have adequate training and had not been preparing for two years to maintain stability.

Neither General Jay Garner nor Paul "Jerry" Bremer, the first two heads of the war reconstruction effort, proved successful in getting basic services and security restored or in preventing the looting of the art museums and other Iraqi sites. Garner did his best with limited resources and was shoved aside. Bremer made what most now agree was the fatal decision to disband the Iraqi army and the Ba'ath Party. With that, as those at Foggy Bottom knew, any chance for stability was virtually destroyed.

The Saudis didn't quibble with how we carved up Iraq administratively, but they did second-guess our insistence on disbanding the Ba'ath Party and the military. Prince Saud and Prince Khalid each told me, in effect, I don't get it. "I don't either," I said.

The Saudi press was equally bewildered and more belligerent than the ministers. I read allegations that we Americans were missing the boat, were kind of buffoons, couldn't guarantee security. Some of this had to be taken with a grain of salt because many in the Iraq military and Ba'ath Party were, like the vast majority of Saudis, Sunni Muslims. The Saudi press, like the government, did not like the idea of Shi'a interlopers taking over Iraq.

This raises a question: Is the press in Saudi Arabia an extension of the government, an organ unwilling or unable to criticize the rulers? While there is no direct criticism of the senior royals, the Saudi press overall is more candid than most other news outlets in the Middle East. For example, when the fire at the girls' school in Mecca led to the tragic deaths of students because the religious police would not let them escape without their *abayas*, the Saudi press aggressively pursued the story, even though it was embarrassing to the establishment.

I conveyed to Washington the Saudis' bewilderment about our reconstruction effort, but never received responses. I wished I had. I wasn't feeding the beast just to cover my tail or seem important, I was doing it because I thought there was a reason to communicate. Too often, however, the beast is a machine that is not interactive.

In hindsight I think I probably should have spent more time on a secure telephone or other means of communication with people like Burns and Armitage and Powell, but I knew Powell shared my views, and so occasionally I would send cables back that I believed supported what I thought was his position on the situation. At this point, however, it was becoming clear that the State Department had lost the interagency battle for the postinvasion space and it was Rumsfeld's show. No one in the State Department was going to have much of a chance to overturn it.

What about Condi Rice? I did receive feedback from Powell and Armitage and others at State that they didn't feel that she was standing up to Rumsfeld and Cheney in the interagency principals' meetings and on policy in general. I don't want to put words into their mouths, but I sensed they felt that she wanted to be the president's pal, best buddy, to watch football games with him. They felt that she was enjoying that kind of access and she wasn't going to do anything to upset that.

That's not an entirely charitable analysis. I don't think Rice would ever selfishly try to cozy up to the president at the expense of doing what she thought was in the national interest. But I believe there were times when she could have asserted herself more if she had wanted to. Then again, it could be that she basically agreed with the decisions that were being made or decided there was nothing she could do about it. In that event, why waste your political capital, if you can't change the policy? Condi was in many ways acting less as a decision maker and more as a super-staffer, teeing up decisions for others to make and not trying to influence the process.

I've now had more than ten years to reflect on the invasion of Iraq. Today I feel the same way that Colin Powell, much of the American public, and many in Congress who authorized the war feel: if we had truly known that there were no weapons of mass destruction, I don't think we would have had the same justification for going in. I take issue with the hawks in the Pentagon and White House at the time, like Cheney, Rumsfeld, and others, who still argue, *Oh, no, the democratization agenda was a wise one.* That's not an agenda that I ever thought legitimized a full invasion, takeover, and subjugation of the country. And even though there are at times encouraging signs that some segments of Iraqi society and economic activity are improving, it's hard to identify a vital U.S. national interest that would, in hindsight, justify America's sacrifice of blood and treasure. With the rise of the Islamic State, the disintegration of the Iraqi security forces, and the continued dysfunction of the government in Baghdad, it is hard to see much hope for an Iraq that meets even the most modest of expectations.

10

Ambassadors, like parents, dread receiving unexpected late-night phone calls. And so I feared bad news when I was startled out of sleep by the ring of my private line on May 12, 2003. That fear was immediately confirmed by the tense, worried voice on the other end. Margaret Scobey was calling from her residence to tell me that around 10:30 pm there had been a bombing at the Al Hamra Oasis Village, an upscale Riyadh compound that was home to Americans as well as Saudis and other Arabs. There were many casualties, she said.

This was the moment I prayed would never come. My countrymen in the Kingdom had been attacked. I was prepared to face terrorism, but until this night it had not visited on a mass scale during my eighteen months as ambassador.

My mind started racing. Colin Powell was scheduled to arrive in the morning. Was the bombing related to the secretary of state's visit? Who did this? How many were dead? What next? An attack on the embassy? Riots in the streets? Were we at a tipping point? Was the regime going under? Did we need to evacuate the embassy? Seek military help from carriers in the Gulf or from Prince Sultan Air Base? We immediately dispatched a security team to investigate. The regional security officer would coordinate with Washington.

While this was going on, I called my friend Alphy Johnson, who lived in the Al Hamra compound. Alphy, the manager of the Rosewood

Faisaliah Hotel and a steadfast member of the Friday Group, answered the phone, his voice trembling. He was hiding in a closet with his two children. I could hear the sound of gunfire in the background. He said his windows and doors had been blown out. Outgoing cell phone calls were blocked, so he asked me to call his wife, Barb, who was visiting in the States. "Please tell her we're all right, at least for now," he said.

Minutes later Margaret called back. Two more compounds had been hit, with even more casualties. There were Americans at these locales as well, as both compounds were connected to U.S. military elements.

I asked Margaret to dispatch my driver and bodyguards. They arrived promptly and we raced to the embassy. I convened our Emergency Action Committee in my office and took reports on the nature of the attacks and the damage. The committee was composed of our senior management, including security, intelligence, and administrative support personnel.

Staff reported that several Americans in the compounds were believed dead. Many more were believed wounded. We sent foreign service officers, mostly from consular affairs, to the local hospitals to help the wounded, account for any who were missing, and contact family members.

Reports from the compounds confirmed that the attacks were all carried out with car bombs involving large quantities of explosives. The attackers were well coordinated and obviously knew a lot about each compound. They had shot their way into the center of two of the complexes before detonating their vehicles. The damage to two compounds was massive. The methods, the organization, and the high level of explosives bore all the hallmarks of Al Qaeda, according to our regional security officer.

Al Hamra was owned by the deputy mayor of Riyadh, whose own son was killed in the attack. Lushly landscaped with swimming pools and other first-rate amenities, the compound was rumored to be a socially active place, where local Saudis could attend parties in apartments far away from the scrutiny of their extended families or the religious police.

The terrorists obviously knew how the gates at Al Hamra operated. The unarmed civilian guards would wave residents through and lift a flimsy wooden bar so each vehicle could pass. We learned that on this night the terrorists simply pulled into the driveway behind a resident. When the resident drove into the compound, the bombers followed closely before the bar could drop. As the guards started yelling, the terrorists opened fire, racing into the middle of the compound. Later accounts told of terrorists on foot shooting at residents, including young girls running to their parents in horror. The car bomb exploded in the center of the compound near the pool and community center, destroying most of the nearby units and seriously damaging others for blocks.

The second compound housed employees of Vinnell Corporation, a Virginia-based defense contractor that provided advisers to the Saudi Arabian National Guard (SANG). This attack sent a special message. SANG is the elite fighting unit that protects the royal family and other major elements of the Kingdom. Its commander for many years had been Crown Prince Abdullah, who retained leadership even after taking over the reins of the Kingdom.

Unlike Al Hamra, the Vinnell compound was heavily fortified and guarded by SANG soldiers. A .50-caliber machine gun was posted at the gate. The only way to enter the compound was for the armed gate guard to lower a large vehicle barrier. As the terrorists were attacking the Al Hamra compound a few miles away, the Vinnell guards could hear the explosions and see the bursts in the night sky. With this modest advance warning, they scrambled to their posts just as the second group of terrorists arrived.

A young soldier raced to the machine gun as the terrorists advanced. Terrified, he fumbled to operate the weapon but did not know how to load it. The terrorists gunned him down. It was not hard to penetrate the guard post—push the button to lower the barricade and drive the explosive-filled vehicle into the midst of the barracks area. The explosion ripped the face off the midrise barracks building and the surrounding facilities.

The residents of the third compound were more fortunate. The Dorrat al Jadawel compound housed Western advisers and contractors to the Royal Saudi Air Force. Like Vinnell, it had a strong vehicle barrier. Unlike at Vinnell, the attackers were unable to find the button to lower the barrier and could not shoot their way in. Frustrated, they simply blew themselves up at the entrance to the compound. The only fatalities at Jadawel were the terrorists, and property damage was minimal.

Throughout the night I took reports on the damage. Embassy personnel scoured the hospitals for survivors and phoned in updates. Our security officers coordinated with the Saudi police and the Ministry of the Interior, evaluating the nature of the attacks and the danger that might remain. Roadblocks began to spring up throughout the city. Our Marine Corps security guards and other security personnel went to full alert, with flak jackets and weapons at hand.

I ordered the embassy to lock down and remain closed for business the next day. Only essential personnel were to report for work. Children of embassy staff would not be taken to school until further notice.

In the predawn darkness, I turned my attention to Secretary Powell. He was scheduled to arrive in Riyadh in just a few hours. I continued to wonder about the risk of further attacks. Was this just the beginning of a massive uprising? Could the Saudi police and military protect us and him? Would our motorcade from the airport present too inviting a target?

The reports coming in suggested that more attacks were possible throughout the day, but unlikely. After the Saudis assured us that no public disorder was imminent, I sent word to Powell's plane, now in the air, that it was important that he continue with his trip. He needed to show the world that the terrorists would not frighten an American secretary of state away from an important meeting in the Kingdom, that he would not be deterred from his mission.

I later chuckled to myself that Colin Powell did not need me to tell him that he should carry on. The battle-tested general had braved far greater danger. No doubt he would be seizing this moment regardless of the advice of a rookie ambassador.

As the reports from the hospitals filtered in and we took stock of the damage, I began to understand the enormity of the attacks. As we soon learned, there were some 35 dead and some 160 injured. The dead included 9 Americans and a dozen attackers.

My blood began to boil. In the weeks preceding the attacks, we had received intelligence reports suggesting that terrorists were in the final phases of planning an attack. Since 2001 we had seen communication intercepts suggesting that Al Qaeda was debating internally whether to launch an attack within Saudi Arabia. As Al Qaeda gained important financing from extremist sympathizers in the Kingdom, it had been reluctant to risk alienating these sources by an attack.

By early 2003 the traffic suggested the terrorists were rethinking this embargo on violence, which sounded alarms within our intelligence community. We believed that Western interests, including housing compounds and government buildings, were likely targets. As with most intelligence reports, there was nothing to identify the specific time or place of the threatened attack.

We had shared these reports with the Saudis. I had written three letters to the minister of the interior, Prince Nayef, asking for more armed security for American buildings and housing compounds. Our security officer had been told they were "working on it."

A week before the attacks the Saudis had sent a surveillance team to watch a house a block away from the Jadawel compound. Suddenly several men raced out of the house, firing weapons at the Saudi police unit. The men escaped in a car, shooting back at the police as they made their getaway. The police charged the house and found massive quantities of weapons and explosives. While law enforcement had taken out this safe house and routed the terrorists, I had wondered that day if the threatened attack really had been disrupted or if the house was just one of many bases in Riyadh from which future attacks were to be launched. Now we had the answer.

News of the attacks shocked the world. The media began to call the State Department and the embassy. State asked me to respond to the media requests for interviews, and the major U.S. networks clamored to be first with the story. I was not instructed what to say. As I've previously noted, up to this point of my tenure, I was told to speak off the record with the American press, providing only background. That restriction was no longer in effect, and I headed to a local television studio.

As I recall, Ted Koppel on ABC's *Nightline* was the first to go on the air. After getting the details from me, he asked the question that I'd been asking myself for several hours: why hadn't the Saudis provided better security for the compounds? My answer was simple: in light of the intelligence reports, we had asked for more security and none had been provided.

CBS News was next. "We continue to work with the Saudis on this, but they did not, as of the time of this tragic event, provide the additional security we requested," I said. I told others the same thing.

Later I learned from my press attaché, John Burgess, that the State Department was pleased with my performance. On other occasions Richard Armitage also complimented my dealings with the media. The only negative comment I ever received was from Condi Rice, who told me that I should be "more in the receive mode than the transmit mode." I respected her point of view but took that advice with a grain of salt.

While the Kingdom was tragically late in providing the needed security, some commentators failed to understand that the Saudis couldn't provide every compound with full-armed protection. There were over one thousand compounds in the country, and it was logistically impossible to have government soldiers at each one. One U.S. news anchor asked me why we didn't have the U.S. Marines guarding every Western compound, obviously an impossible fantasy in any foreign country. Another asked if we could use the air force personnel at Prince Sultan Air Base for security—as if aircraft mechanics, pilots, and support personnel could be taken away from their military missions to become local police.

The sad fact was that, as in the United States, most people believed it was the responsibility of the apartment complex owner, not the government, to provide gate guards and site-specific security for private property. In my view, the rules of the game changed when widespread terrorist threats arose. The security I had requested should have been provided before the attacks. Plain and simple.

The early morning sun began blazing well before 6:00 a.m. I finished the news interviews at the studio and headed back to the embassy. There I grabbed some black coffee and checked my emails and cables. After getting the latest casualty update and reports on the damage, I headed to Riyadh Air Base to greet Secretary Powell.

The secretary's plane appeared in its approach pattern, hit the tarmac, and taxied up near the private government terminal. As it pulled up, I saw again the blue and white paint, the government emblem, and the "United States of America" lettering across the fuselage. Each time I met one of our government planes and saw the emblem and lettering, I felt a rush of pride and anticipation. This time my feelings were tempered by my anger at the attacks and a sense of danger and foreboding. The plane's door opened and armed security officers climbed down the stairs to join other security forces on the ground, looking anxiously from side to side behind their black sunglasses.

The early summer desert winds were already gusting. Powell stepped out onto the ramp and moved quickly down the stairs. We shook hands, even more firmly than usual, and exchanged sober looks of acknowledgment. He asked how I was doing, and we hurried to my armored car waiting by the plane.

Having known him for almost two years now, I was immensely impressed with his personality and his policies. He knew this and frequently confided in me about his struggles with Cheney and Rumsfeld and his frustration at what he considered Rice's lack of leadership. He felt he would make progress with the president on a policy issue, only to have Rumsfeld come in later and have the president reverse it, often with Cheney's involvement. He was disgusted with the backstabbing and was growing tired of the travel. He also felt that the Middle East peace process was being hijacked by the hawkish neo-cons in the administration.

Powell seemed to think I could approach the president on his behalf on these issues. He probably overestimated my influence, but I tried to pick and choose my moments of candor with the chief executive. He knew where I stood.

As we left the airport on the morning after the bombings, Powell and I decided the first order of business was to visit one of the compounds, Vinnell. It had a strong U.S. leader, retired general Bill Matz, who was prepared to brief us. Our motorcade pulled out into the midst of central Riyadh's traffic. Saudi police cars escorted us, blaring their sirens and blocking intersections.

As we pulled up to the compound, we could see the barricades and guard posts. We saw the .50-caliber machine gun where the young SANG soldier had been shot trying to load his weapon. We continued to the barracks at the epicenter of the blast. The site reeked of gunpowder and explosives. The entire face of the building had been blown off, revealing dormitory rooms with beds and chairs in fragments. Pieces of the building hung loosely from shattered framing. I instantly thought of the pictures of the Alfred P. Murrah Federal Building in Oklahoma City after the tragic bombing there by homegrown terrorist Timothy McVeigh in 1995.

As we walked through the rubble with Matz, the wind began to swirl, blowing corrugated metal pieces and other debris into the air. Before long the gusts had turned into a real Arabian windstorm, with objects flying from the wreckage of the buildings. Sensing danger, our bodyguards closed in on Powell and me, pushing us to the ground and forming a human clamshell around us. We had seen enough for the moment. The guards forcefully tugged us along the road and into my car.

Our next stop was Al Yamamah Palace for a meeting with Crown Prince Abdullah. The palace, site of the royal court, was surrounded by guards, tanks, and armored personnel carriers, guns at the ready. Normally a heavily guarded compound, it now seemed in full-blown war mode thanks to extra soldiers and armaments.

After clearing several security checkpoints, we were ushered into the chambers of the crown prince. Secretary Powell was no stranger to Abdullah, and their greeting was warm but somber. Likewise, the crown prince looked me in the eye as he shook my hand, as if to say, *I know, we all are under siege right now.* I nodded a silent acknowledgment and took my seat next to Powell, as the other members of our delegation stepped up to meet the crown prince. Across the room from our row of sofas were members of the royal court—sons, nephews, and cousins of the crown prince or King Fahd, along with military and civilian advisers.

As the servants offered us Arabian coffee laced with cardamom, Powell thanked the crown prince for receiving us and conveyed President Bush's concern over the events of the past hours. Abdullah was visibly shaken. He expressed his horror at what had happened and his condemnation of the terrorists as "deviants" who did not reflect the true nature of Islam. He vowed to track down all who were responsible, including all who had given any assistance or support for the attacks. The crown prince also expressed condolences for the Americans killed and wounded, insisting that any foreigner living in Saudi Arabia was a guest of the Kingdom and deserved to be treated as such.

I was startled by Abdullah's candor in addressing the next topic, the lack of armed security at the compounds. In front of the secretary of state and the entire royal court, he humbly acknowledged that I had previously shared intelligence and requested additional security. He admitted that he had not seen the need for additional security and that it was a grave misjudgment. He took full responsibility for leaving the compounds without additional protection.

I admired his forthrightness as a true leader in admitting this terrible mistake. He assured us that enhanced, aggressive security would be mobilized immediately. I later learned that in a meeting of the royal court, he had publicly fired the head of SANG security and angrily rebuked the deputy commander of the guard, his own son.

Powell expressed concern about the security environment and welcomed the crown prince's assurances of additional protection. He then provided an update on developments in the war in Iraq, a topic that, for the moment, seemed less urgent than dealing with the Riyadh bombings and their aftermath. The secretary of state thanked Abdullah for the Kingdom's extraordinary assistance in the invasion of Iraq. He added that he knew how difficult the crown prince's decision to aid our war effort had been.

There was one more item on the agenda. Powell requested the crown prince's support for the president's "road map," a vision of two states, Israel and Palestine, living side by side in security and harmony. The subject would be addressed in detail in June at a summit meeting in Sharm el-Sheikh, Egypt.

Abdullah was polite but noncommittal. His own peace plan, announced in February 2002, offered a similar vision but had not been actively supported by the Bush administration. Versions of the road map had been shared with European allies before being discussed with the Saudis or any other leaders in the region. The Saudis found out about it from leaks in Europe and were furious at the slight. This was no way to enlist Saudi support for the plan.

As we headed back to Riyadh Air Base, I shared with the secretary my thoughts on steps needed to protect embassy employees and their dependents. The security situation was not good, and the Saudis had not demonstrated the ability, or the will, to adequately protect Americans. This meant I would probably have to issue an Ordered Departure—commanding our nonessential embassy staff and all embassy dependents to leave the Kingdom.

Ordered Departure would have consequences. We would operate with a greatly reduced staff at a time when the war in Iraq, the conflict in the Palestinian Territories, and the war on terrorism required all the personnel we could muster. Embassy staff remaining without their families would suffer a big decline in morale. Many dependents worked as staff in the embassy, and their departure would place an even heavier burden on the "essential" staff remaining. Private contractors would likely follow our lead and reduce their footprint or move to neighboring countries. The American School would face pressure to close early for the summer, perhaps never to reopen. And the Saudis would take my decision as a sign of no confidence, a significant loss of face. Powell understood all these issues and left it to me to sort them out—a reiteration of his policy to let the "generals" on the ground make the "battlefield" decisions.

After Powell was back in the air, I turned to the grim task of visiting the wounded in the hospitals. None of the doctors and nurses I saw were American, yet they all recognized the tragedy of the bombings and the loss we were experiencing together. At the first hospital, I was ushered in to the intensive care unit. An unconscious young man on life support lay on a gurney. As the doctors told me he was not going to make it, I felt enormous sadness. Here before me was but one example of the human toll of these attacks. I paused at his bedside, prayed silently for his soul, and continued on. After I left, they disconnected the life-support equipment.

As I visited the others, I saw injuries that I will never forget. One man lying naked on a gurney, tubes connected everywhere, with shrapnel and cuts all over his body. Blood, bandages, and sutures. Another man with half his face bashed in, an eye barely recognizable. A young woman, less severely wounded, met with me, clutching her three-year-old child. Her Jordanian husband, the child's father, had been killed. She was almost in a trance. Her loss was heartbreaking.

Our foreign service officers were doing a terrific job in the hospitals. They had located all American survivors and initiated contact with the next of kin of those who were killed. They provided comfort and attention to the injured, putting them in touch with relatives by using the officers' cell phones from the hospital rooms. From my office I made several calls to relatives of those who had died, extending my condolences and providing contact information so arrangements could be made.

I felt the same surge of empathy and sadness that I felt thirty years earlier when, as a young naval officer in Washington DC, I served as a casualty assistance calls officer detailed to knock on the doors of the families of naval personnel killed in Vietnam, tell them the terrible news of their sons' deaths, and preside over funeral arrangements at Arlington National Cemetery. Many of those killed or injured in Riyadh were veterans of combat and understood that life in the Middle East has its risks. I suspect none of them thought it would ever come to this.

On the following morning, I visited the Al Hamra compound—what was left of it. As we pulled up to the gate and I saw the flimsy wooden bar, I understood how the terrorists tailgated the car ahead of them and forced their way in. The entrance appeared to have no damage, but as we drove into the compound and through the winding streets, I saw broken windows. As we reached the epicenter of the blast, I saw more debris and damage. The explosion of the car bomb had left a large crater and gutted the buildings. The recreation center was nearly leveled. The swimming pool was empty and shattered.

As I climbed out of my car, the smell of gunpowder and burnt buildings reminded me of the scene at the Vinnell compound the day before. Some residents were packing up their belongings, with a number of trucks on the streets to help transport heavy items. Walking from unit to unit, I saw remnants of people's lives scattered throughout the rubble. An umbrella. Folding chairs. And a small doll and a teddy bear on the sidewalk, the beloved symbols of security of some child whom I prayed had survived the attack.

Returning to the embassy, I met again with our Emergency Action Committee. We assessed the latest security information and the state of readiness of the Saudi police and military. Our regional security officer, Greg Hays, was pessimistic about whether we would see an immediate improvement in their readiness or attitude. The chain of command was garbled, with at least three commanders of separate units in the Diplomatic Quarter.

Some of the police in the Diplomatic Quarter had been indifferent about security, to say the least. Greg reported soldiers departing their guard posts to go to prayer, leaving their weapons behind, out in the open in the abandoned kiosks! The state of readiness of the Diplomatic Quarter police had long been a sore spot for us. Repeated calls for improvement, like the calls for security at the compounds, had gone unheeded.

In light of these problems, I had no choice but to require an Ordered Departure for all embassy dependents and nonessential personnel. I telephoned Prince Saud to give him advance notice of my decision. He was disappointed that we were taking such drastic action, but I felt certain he understood I had no choice. I also called Prince Mohammed bin Nayef, the assistant minister of the interior and, effectively, the head of domestic security and law enforcement. Even though evacuating embassy personnel was basically a vote of no confidence in the security posture, he also understood.

Then began the difficult process of deciding who should go and who should stay. We considered charter flights and wondered about military aircraft assistance, but with the war in Iraq there was little hope of military transport. We were able to arrange commercial flights over the next three weeks to effect an orderly evacuation. In the meantime, Diplomatic Security teams made up of highly trained Special Forces and other military alumni had arrived to provide additional protection and to survey the danger presented to the embassy and its employees. Several team members took positions on the roof of my residence, wearing flak jackets and carrying automatic weapons.

After their initial security evaluation, Greg Hays brought them to me and gave a startling report: my own residence was not secure. Terrorists could climb down into the small canyon, or *wadi*, behind it and then scale the back wall. The residence lacked cameras or electrified fencing, and the Saudi guard posts were considered unreliable. While security improvements could be installed over time, these experts considered it too dangerous for me to stay in Quincy House at night. They reluctantly advised me that I would have to start sleeping at an undisclosed location.

Riyadh changed dramatically in the days after the May bombings. The capital resembled a city in a state of siege. Saudi soldiers were everywhere, with armored personnel carriers and tanks springing up throughout the city, even outside the front gate of Quincy House. Concrete barricades redirected traffic through checkpoints.

I began my sentence of "solitary confinement." Each night after dinner at Quincy House, I would put on my ball cap and a pair of jeans, and the security team would take me into the garage and hide me in the back of an armored Suburban. They'd then sneak me out the front gate, past my own guards and the Saudi soldiers. We would weave through back streets to lose any cars that might attempt to follow. All the while, the team held their weapons at the ready and looked around every corner as we approached one of the secret locations where I would spend the night.

On the floor of the Suburban, I couldn't get my bearings and couldn't see out the blackened and curtained windows. I knew I would be in big trouble if anyone found out about our subterfuge. Once inside the safe house I tried to get some sleep, not an easy task with guys in flak jackets and holding machine guns standing outside my door.

The next morning we would return to Quincy House in the same manner. Then I would have breakfast at home as if nothing had happened. This routine lasted about a month, until I returned to Washington for consultations and security upgrades were performed in my absence. Ann had been evacuated earlier, never to return during my tenure.

The shockwave of the bombings marked a turning point in the Saudi attitude toward Al Qaeda. Through his representatives, King Fahd condemned the attacks. Crown Prince Abdullah vowed on state television to track down the terrorists and bring them to justice. With striking emotion, he swore that those who gave aid or comfort to the terrorists, as well as those who tried to justify their actions, would be punished as harshly as the terrorists themselves.

The Saudi police started to crack down on suspected terrorists with a vengeance. Periodic shootouts between police and terrorists were widely publicized in the media. Pictures of most-wanted terrorists were published in the newspapers, a highly unusual tactic for Saudi Arabia. The cumbersome chain of command of the various police and military units in the Diplomatic Quarter was refined, with a single commander finally in charge. Inattentive soldiers were disciplined.

The results were evident. On June 7 the Saudis named a dozen suspects in the compound attacks. One week later the police broke up a ring of terrorists in Mecca. Among the finds were booby-trapped Qurans. As cNN.com reported on June 26, "Saudi religious leaders . . . denounced the plot for its double hypocrisy in allegedly plotting a terror attack in Mecca and in waging a holy war against infidels using Islam's holiest book."

On June 27 the alleged mastermind of the bombings, Ali Abd al-Rahman al-Faqasi al-Ghamdi, surrendered to Prince Mohammed bin Nayef. One week after this, another of the suspects, Turki Nasser al-Dandani, and several other militants died during a five-hour gun battle with Saudi police in northern Al Jawf. Each of these suspects was tied to Al Qaeda.

Despite these improvements in the security environment, the embassy evacuation of dependents and nonessential personnel took its toll. Before the bombings, the Marine Corps snack bar at the embassy, Uncle Sam's, had been filled on weekends with families having lunch, splashing in the pool with the kids, and joining in a weekly community night or a happy hour. As the families began to leave, I decided we should keep Uncle Sam's open every night to provide at least some sense of community where we all could gather. Over time, the faces at Uncle Sam's began to look increasingly sad and lonely.

And I kept thinking about the doll and teddy bear I had seen in the dust at the Al Hamra compound.

11

ALTHOUGH WE MOURNED the innocent victims of the Riyadh bombings, those of us who remained at the embassy had an assignment that required our immediate attention. On June 3 President Bush was to come to Sharm el-Sheikh, Egypt, for a summit with Crown Prince Abdullah, Palestinian Authority leader Mahmoud Abbas, President Hosni Mubarak of the host country, King Abdullah of Jordan, and King Hamad of Bahrain. He'd then be moving on to Jordan and a meeting with Israeli prime minister Ariel Sharon and Abbas.

The stakes were high. As the *New York Times'* David Sanger and James Dao reported on June 3, 2004, our commander in chief would be meeting "amid deepening Arab fears that the American presence in Iraq will be lengthy and chaotic. The Arab leaders also worry that Mr. Bush will be insufficiently tough with Prime Minister Ariel Sharon on the abandonment of Israeli settlements in the West Bank and Gaza, part of the phased peace plan Mr. Bush calls the road map." The reporters added, "Mr. Bush's personal involvement in the peace effort represents a considerable political risk, but one he said today that he was willing to take."

Rather than tamping down expectations, Secretary of State Powell seemed to place even more pressure on his boss's shoulders. As Sanger and Dao reported in the same article, he told ABC television that the president saw "new dynamics" in the Middle East "equation." With both the Palestinian and Israeli economies suffering, "Israel doesn't want to keep its troops deployed forever in the cities and towns. So I think all the pieces have come together, and we are here at Sharm el-Sheikh to take advantage of the new elements in the equation and this window of opportunity that has opened."

For those of us who had been at the summit with the president and crown prince in April 2002, there was also pressure. The White House apparatus, whether through malfeasance or misfeasance, had let Bush down in Crawford. No one had briefed him on Abdullah's talking points. As a result he had egg on his face and the Saudis were offended.

I didn't want that to happen again. Mindful of how bad the staff work had been, I made sure the president had direct access to any input that I had on what needed to be done at Sharm el-Sheikh. Margaret Scobey and I were in regular contact with the State Department to ensure that our views were received. As June 3 approached, we were becoming fairly optimistic that the crown prince was going to play a positive role going forward, that he would be encouraged by the president's animation on the peace process.

Unfortunately road maps can't chart each and every bump. About two weeks before Sharm el-Sheikh, we hit a pothole. It didn't threaten the summit, but it had the potential to make things uncomfortable.

Some background: The road map was "officially" the production of a group called "the Quartet"—the United States, Russia, the United Nations, and the European Union. It was no secret, however, that this was our plan—one that had been in the making since late June 2002, when President Bush had spoken of a two-state solution featuring a "secure State of Israel and a viable, peaceful, democratic Palestine."

The road map document might have been presented by the end of 2002—the EU lobbied for that—but the United States, Israel, and other interested parties imposed certain preconditions. Most notably, we wanted to negotiate with a Palestinian leader other than Yasser Arafat. The appointment of Abbas in mid-March 2003 seemed to meet that condition.

The road map was finally released on April 30, just a few days before our summit. That would have been fine, but for that pothole. As Mustapha Karkouti of *Gulf News* reported on April 17, 2003, Britain's Foreign Office "leaked" the draft of the document for all to see by putting it in the library of the House of Commons. Karkouti opined, "[This] seems to be a deliberate act by the government to pre-empt any attempt to further delay its formal release."

The Saudis went ballistic when they learned that the document was circulating and that they had not seen it. Foreign Minister Prince Saud was particularly offended that it would be shared with European allies before even being discussed with Saudi officials. Adding fuel to the fire was the fact that Crown Prince Abdullah had offered his own peace plan in early 2002 and had received only tepid support from the United States. As I told Washington in a cable, the Saudis were asking, in effect, *What the hell's going on here? Why are you sharing this with EU delegates and governments and you're not including us in the process? This looks very arrogant on your part.*

The Saudi officials with whom I spoke felt sandbagged. They believed the Kingdom was sincerely trying to cooperate with U.S. efforts to resolve the Israeli-Palestinian crisis—even if we didn't agree on everything that needed to be done. Toward that end, at our request, they had been providing financial support to the Palestinian Authority rather than the more stridently anti-Israel terrorist group Hamas. I had also urged Prince Saud to encourage Yasser Arafat to publicly support his successor, Mahmoud Abbas, and his new cabinet. Thus it was embarrassing that the draft got out before they had a chance to see it, even though they knew we were working on it. In fact, in March Prince Saud had emphasized to me how important it was to proceed with the road map, expressing skepticism that we were suddenly working on it at just the time we were preparing to invade Iraq with much-needed Saudi support behind the scenes.

It was ironic to me that American rhetoric in the war on terror emphasized that "you're either with us or against us." We were pursuing a peace plan for the Palestinian crisis, yet we didn't give the Saudis a chance to be "with us" on the road map. In the Arab world there is often a feeling of victimhood. This episode only reinforced the sense that, once again, the Americans and their European allies had snubbed a major participant in the peace process, Saudi Arabia. It wasn't simply an issue of bad manners; we needed their input and they needed to be part of the team seeking a solution.

Despite this bump, as far as the United States and the Kingdom were concerned, the Sharm el-Sheikh summit went exceedingly well. On June 4 Sanger and Dao of the *New York Times* reported,

> The summit meeting today was notable for two reasons: the absence of any public statements by the Arab leaders attacking America's role as the occupying power in Iraq and the very public way they were bucking up Mr. Bush's peace efforts.
>
> A high-ranking Saudi official tonight praised Mr. Bush's efforts as "marvelous." The official said he was optimistic that the president was committed to the plan, known as the road map, for the creation of two side-by-side states, Israel and Palestine, by 2005.

That same Saudi official—whom I suspect was Prince Bandar—also "insisted that the Arab leaders had gone further in condemning terrorism today than ever before." Agreed. As Sanger and Dao also reported, the Arab leaders promised to actively fight "'the culture of extremism and violence' that has undercut peace efforts in the Middle East for years, promising to stanch the flow of money to the terrorist groups that have carried out suicide bombings against Israel."

This promise was a breakthrough. We had been pressuring these Arab nations to condemn attacks and police the financing of terrorists since 9/11. In April I had been joined by Ambassador-at-Large for Counterterrorism Cofer Black and Treasury General Counsel David Aufhauser in meetings with Prince Saud seeking Saudi restrictions on Al-Haramain, the largest Saudi charity and one we believed was involved in terrorist financing. Prince Saud promised immediate action against anyone suspected of terrorist activity. Aufhauser wanted public exposure of a discernable number of entities providing terrorist funding, as he believed that the American "perception" was that much of the financing was coming from Gulf countries. Public exposure would have a deterrent effect, in his view. Prince Saud calmly replied that he was interested in substance, not mere perception.

The May bombings in Riyadh had moved us to push even harder. Now at least the Saudis were willing to go on record and announce the creation of a body that would oversee funds disbursed by Islamic charities abroad as well as within the Kingdom. We still had a way to go, but this was a good start.

What did I do at Sharm el-Sheikh? An ambassador's main purpose when his or her head of state is meeting with a fellow head of state is to facilitate the interaction, make sure that policy issues on the agenda are addressed, brief the president on the latest attitudes and pitfalls he might encounter at the summit, and be ready for any surprise that comes up. I also used the time to catch up with David Welch, U.S. ambassador to Egypt and a former chargé d'affaires in Riyadh, who was extremely helpful to me in understanding Saudi and Israeli-Palestinian issues.

We had a beverage or two with Mohammed Dahlan, the newly appointed minister of state for security of the Palestinian Authority. Dahlan was a reformer opposed to the corrupt rule of Yasser Arafat. A colorful and controversial figure, he was later booted out of his job, resurfaced numerous times in the struggles between Fatah and Hamas in Gaza, and occasionally was rumored to be a future leader of the Palestinian Authority.

One of my key roles was to participate in the separate meeting between President Bush and Crown Prince Abdullah. The meeting was scheduled to occur at the Four Seasons Hotel after the breakfast meeting and speeches of the president and the Arab heads of state. Prince Saud, Prince Bandar, and I waited outside the suite where the meeting was scheduled, sitting outdoors in golf carts while the ceremonies overlooking the Red Sea were concluding. As President Bush and Crown Prince Abdullah drove their golf cart down the path toward our meeting, we gathered at the door and alerted the room staff that they were approaching. The room was fairly small, and there were about eight of us. One of the Saudis was Abdulrahman Al Saeed, a highly respected senior counselor to the royal court and a good friend.

Also present, to my surprise, was the erratic and unpredictable youngest son of King Fahd, Abdul Aziz bin Fahd—the host for Lieberman's Christmas 2002 midnight dinner in Riyadh. Interestingly, he was not wearing Saudi attire but rather a three-piece business suit. He joined us at a table that included President Bush, Condi Rice, Crown Prince

Abdullah, Al Saeed, Bandar, and Saud. He obviously was jet-lagged and had a hard time staying awake at the table.

The five Arab leaders at Sharm el-Sheikh weren't the only ones looking for face time with President Bush. Before the trip, Prince Alwaleed bin Talal called me and asked for a meeting there with the president. The prince, listed by *Forbes* magazine in 2013 as the twenty-sixth-richest person in the world, is a savvy businessman (with a substantial stake in Twitter) and philanthropist. American educated, he is considered one of the most reform-minded members of the royal family.

Much of Alwaleed's philanthropy has been directed toward bridging the divide between the Western world and the Islamic world (including money for an Islamic study center at Cambridge). Sometimes, however, that generosity has created waves. After 9/11, for example, he donated $10 million to New York City. That money was eventually returned unceremoniously by Mayor Giuliani because of remarks the prince made when giving the donation: "At times like this one, we must address some of the issues that led to such a criminal attack. I believe the government of the United States of America should re-examine its policies in the Middle East and adopt a more balanced stance towards the Palestinian cause."[1]

There were several reasons to accommodate Prince Alwaleed's request for a meeting. First and foremost, he's an influential royal. For nine years in a row, the publication *Arabian Business* named him the most powerful Arab in the world because of the clout of his company, Kingdom Holding. He has an American presence, too. For example, he frequently appears on the *Charlie Rose* show to provide U.S. audiences a perspective on the Kingdom.

Born in 1955, Alwaleed is of the generation that will someday rule Saudi Arabia. In addition, he owned the Four Seasons Hotel where the summit was being held and considered himself a quasi-host of the summit. When the prince told me, *I would like to meet with President Bush when he's at my resort*, I passed the request on to the White House.

The response: *You know, this really is not doable.*

I pushed back a little: *Look, this guy can be a big ally for us. He's influential. Can't we find some moment where he could have just a brief interaction with the president?*

The president's people finally said, *Yeah, we can do it about 7:30 in the morning after the breakfast with Mubarak and all of the others he's dealing with. The president can probably do a pull-aside handshake on his way to the bilateral meeting with Abdullah.*

A pull-aside handshake is, as the name suggests, a courtesy and an occasional annoyance to high officeholders who are overscheduled and scrambling from one appointment to the next. Whether the president is on the road or in Washington, prominent figures clamor for the opportunity for a handshake, or a quick conversation, or a photo-op.

The motives vary. Ego. A request for some favor or policy. As I indicated earlier, I posted photos of myself with the president to show staff and visitors that I had some clout in Washington.

My favorite photo with President Bush was taken by a newspaper photographer in 1992, when we were together at a Texas Rangers baseball game during the time when he was president of the club. We're in the front row. He's in jeans with his legs crossed, and his cowboy boots with the Texas Rangers logo are protruding in the foreground. To say the least, we look much younger. Who could have known when that picture was taken what the future had in store for each of us?

I wasn't at the breakfast where the "handshake" with Prince Alwaleed was to occur. Instead, I was with Prince Bandar and Prince Saud in our respective golf carts awaiting the upcoming meeting between the president and the crown prince. As is often the case, the breakfast with Mubarak ran late. When Bush and Abdullah finally emerged, Prince Alwaleed was waiting. He joined the two leaders as they walked toward the golf cart that would take them to their bilateral. We could see him chatting with the president.

Bush never broke his gait. He and Abdullah climbed into the golf cart and then the president took the wheel. As the leaders drove off, the prince broke into a trot to keep up with the cart and to keep up the conversation, his white robe flowing in the breeze.[2]

For me there was one other item on the agenda at Sharm el-Sheikh. At a private meeting after Crown Prince Abdullah and his entourage had departed the suite, I told the president and Condi Rice that the time had finally come for me to leave my post, sometime in the fall. They were not surprised, as we had discussed my desire to return to the private sector many times over the preceding year.

I had stayed almost a year longer than I had committed to, and I needed to get back to earning an income and putting my kids through college and graduate school. That said, I would not have broached leaving before getting full Saudi cooperation for the Iraq invasion—something we had accomplished. With a couple of other missions also accomplished in recent weeks, I felt good about the decision and the timing—particularly because I didn't see any more events on the horizon for which I needed to galvanize Saudi support.

I did not mention another factor in my decision. The bickering between the Department of Defense (and its ally the vice president) and the Department of State was disheartening. I had already shared my dismay about this with Colin Powell. He understood, as it was something he lived with every day.

The two missions we had recently accomplished? Number one: our agreement to withdraw from Prince Sultan Air Base after a dozen years. Number two: a complicated prisoner swap involving Westerners being held in the Kingdom and Saudis being held at Guantanamo Bay.

After ten years of planning, in the 1980s the Royal Saudi Air Force built a colossal air base in the desert fifty miles southeast of Riyadh. It spans an area approximately twenty-five by forty miles, with a fifteen-thousand-foot runway. By the time Operation Desert Storm was underway in 1991, PSAB (named after the minister of defense, Prince Sultan bin Abdulaziz) was home to thousands of U.S. forces and substantial numbers of aircraft. But it was not an American air base—it was never "ours." It was built at Saudi expense, and the Saudis even fed our troops.

Ironically, when Saddam Hussein invaded Kuwait, the Saudis knew they would need help to repel the invasion and protect their own oilfields. King Fahd rejected the pitch to lead the campaign made by one of his own countrymen with a highly experienced militia—Osama bin Laden. Instead, the king invited the Americans to join forces to liberate Kuwait. Bin Laden's reaction was one of shock and hatred.

The Americans moved into PSAB as guests of the Saudis and comrades in arms against Saddam. Later, after attacks against U.S. forces in Riyadh and Al Khobar in 1995 and 1996, units previously assigned there relocated to PSAB for security reasons. The American military presence on sacred Saudi soil became a rallying cry for Al Qaeda.

After Saddam was defeated in 1991, American fighter jets patrolled southern Iraq to monitor Iraqi compliance with a UN-mandated no-fly zone to protect the vulnerable Shi'a population from Saddam's air attacks. This Operation Southern Watch was based at PSAB. Under Southern Watch air patrols had flown over 286,000 missions. Bin Laden continued to rail at the way in which the House of Saud had capitulated to the American infidels.

Beginning in 2000 articles began to appear in the media suggesting that the Department of Defense and Prince Sultan were discussing reducing troop levels at PSAB. The Pentagon issued strong denials and asserted that Prince Sultan was perfectly happy with current troop levels. By the time of my arrival in late 2001, bin Laden's drumbeat was gaining favor among elements of the population and the religious establishment, and there was little enthusiasm among Saudi leadership for any increase in troop levels. In fact, we required special permission to add any personnel, even in conducting operations against the Taliban in Afghanistan. That permission was often not forthcoming.

The media continued to darkly predict our eviction from PSAB. Despite all the pessimism about our future at the base, I never once received a request from any Saudi official to draw down our troops or withdraw. We developed an alternate site for air operations at Al Udeid Air Base in neighboring Qatar, but not at the insistence of the Saudis.

In late April 2002 I met with Prince Sultan shortly before the presidential summit meeting in Crawford. He was optimistic about the crown prince's upcoming visit and expressed hope that Dick Myers, chairman of the Joint Chiefs of Staff, would come to Riyadh for a joint planning meeting later in the summer. We discussed the importance of the U.S.-Saudi relationship, and His Highness remarked, in the words of an Arab proverb, that our bumps in the road had been the result of a "slight wind" that cleared the land and made it ready for the rain to come and bring forth the land's bounty.

Then Prince Sultan turned to the subject of PSAB. He noted the increasing speculation that we would be removing our assets from the base. If the rumors were untrue, he asked, why were there so many stories? I replied that I did not know and added that the U.S. military was a guest in the Kingdom, staying at the pleasure of its host. Sultan then remarked that we had shed blood together in the liberation of Kuwait, signaling a bond that ran deep between our two countries.

A few months later General Tommy Franks and I met with Prince Sultan's son, Khalid bin Sultan, assistant minister of defense, at his office in Riyadh. This was the same office he used during Operation Desert Storm when he was commander of Islamic forces. He proudly showed us the room where he and General Norman Schwarzkopf bunked together during the war. We discussed using PSAB for the joint exercises called Operation Internal Look, scheduled to kick off in December. These exercises were the subject of much speculation over whether they would be a dress rehearsal for an invasion of Iraq in the spring. It also was reassuring during the meeting that there was no mention of curtailing our activities at PSAB. To the contrary, the base would play a large role in our joint exercises and in the potential invasion of Iraq looming on the horizon. It was at this time that Prince Khalid expressed concern to me that Saddam had chemical and biological weapons and inquired whether the United States could provide him with seventeen thousand gas masks in the event of a chemical or biological attack.

In October 2002 we kicked off a strategic joint planning conference with the Saudis. I was joined by Peter Rodman, assistant secretary of defense. During the conference Prince Khalid acknowledged that our use of PSAB was necessitated by the threats in the region, that its use was determined by mutual agreement with the Saudis, and that U.S. troops could continue there. Prince Khalid was in a cheerful and hospitable mood. We discussed the relocation of Central Command forward headquarters to Al Udeid Air Base in Qatar, and Prince Khalid interposed no objection to our strategic decision to relocate those elements.

The camaraderie was tempered, however, by Prince Khalid's concerns over the treatment of Saudi military trainees by immigration authorities in the United States, who in episodes of post-9/11 zeal had harassed a number of them in a manner that infuriated Khalid. The prince saw this as playing into the terrorists' hands by harming the U.S.-Saudi relationship. His words of caution: "Don't let bin Laden win."

As we headed into spring 2003, the specter of war was in the air.

Our carrier fleet and warplanes were operating 24/7 in the Gulf. PSAB was humming with activity. The "shock and awe" of the air attack that we ultimately unleashed in March was theatrical and effective. Then began the long slog toward pacification and reconstruction. PSAB had served us well. With Saddam's air force decimated, there no longer was a need to enforce a no-fly zone in Iraq, and thus Operation Southern Watch could come to an end. Our uneasy tenancy at PSAB would no longer be required.

While some in Washington urged us to sharply pull the plug and evacuate PSAB immediately, I felt we needed a more gradual approach. On April 16 I met with Foreign Minister Prince Saud and, knowing we would end up leaving, extended him the olive branch of asking his opinion on how it should be addressed. I suggested a consultative approach with the Saudi leadership. Prince Saud agreed, saying we should not "make hasty decisions." In his elegant way, he was joining me in an exchange of politeness even though we both knew we were choreographing a graceful exit that both sides wanted.

On April 21 I met with Prince Khalid. I told him that we had successfully removed Saddam as a threat, that the Iraqi air force was in shambles, and that we no longer needed Operation Southern Watch. We could draw down our troops there, secure in the knowledge that the air base had served its purpose. Prince Khalid agreed that a troop reduction made sense. I asked him how soon he would like for us to begin the reduction, and he replied that we could begin at any time that was convenient for us. He had met with his father, Prince Sultan, the day before and conveyed his views that we did not want it to appear that we were being evicted nor that we were leaving in dissatisfaction. We were leaving as friends.

On April 29 Secretary of Defense Rumsfeld and I met with Crown Prince Abdullah and Prince Sultan. Rumsfeld offered a major increase in U.S. training of Saudi military personnel, including ground forces, through our training mission in Riyadh. This was significant because we felt that ground forces at all levels of seniority who train together develop bonds over the years that preserve and enhance the bilateral relationship. Rumsfeld went on to say that we would be "rearranging" our forces in the region. Prince Sultan agreed with this approach and expressed his desire that the expanded joint training would show the world that our relationship was strong.

Rumsfeld and Sultan made the announcement at a press conference that day. "It is now a safer region because of the change of regime in Iraq," Rumsfeld said. "The aircraft and those involved will now be able to leave." The next Monday the air operations center for the Middle East moved to Al Udeid Air Base in Qatar. By summer nearly all our aircraft and troops were gone and our slice of PSAB was in mothballs.

A final observation on this subject: Ironically, Osama bin Laden's hatred of the United States and the House of Saud stemmed in large part from our occupation of PSAB. Our withdrawal was supposed to satisfy the extremists in our midst. Yet two weeks after Rumsfeld's announcement, as described in chapter 9, Al Qaeda suicide bombers attacked those three Western housing compounds in Riyadh.

Mission number two—the prisoner swap—was accomplished around the same time. One of my reasons for writing this book is to take readers behind the scenes of the diplomatic world. The prisoner swap offers an opportunity to explain how the diplomatic wheeling and dealing took place

While in Riyadh, I became good friends with Britain's senior diplomats in the Kingdom. We saw each other at diplomatic gatherings, spoke on the phone regularly, and met for drinks or lunch periodically.

In the late summer of 2002, one of them invited me to lunch. As we ate outside by his perfect English garden in a setting that looked like it was drawn from *Downton Abbey*, he said that the British foreign minister, Jack Straw, had been pressuring him to do something about countrymen held prisoner in the Kingdom for about eighteen months. Five Brits, a Belgian, and a Canadian were accused of deadly car bombings directed at other Westerners.

Although the attacks looked like they might be the work of Al Qaeda, the Saudis insisted they were linked to a bootleggers' turf war over the distribution of illegal alcohol. After the arrests, the suspects confessed, then recanted, saying that they had been tortured. In July 2002 they were found guilty by a Saudi court and given sentences varying from twelve years to death. (Although the party line was that the Westerners were innocent, some in the British and Belgian camps were uncertain.)

My British friend explained that British prime minister Tony Blair was concerned that negative press in Britain about the failure of his government to get the prisoners released was going to impair his party's efforts in the upcoming 2003 by-elections to fill empty seats in Parliament and could hurt Blair's own political ambitions. Pressured by Blair and Straw to arrange a release, my friend had tried without success. Then the ask: "Bob, could you help?"

Maybe. For several months the Saudis had been pressuring me to encourage the release of a number of Saudi prisoners held in our Guantanamo Bay prison. As I recall there were well over one hundred Saudi prisoners there, constituting a sizable percentage of the entire population. I'd looked into this but hadn't pressed the issue with Washington.

My embassy advisor Bill had told me that many of the detainees we'd captured on the battlefield were "low value"—teenage Saudi boys who might have thought it was cool to go to Afghanistan and had then ended up in the wrong place at the wrong time. To be sure, there also were many hardened Al Qaeda or Taliban combatants at Guantanamo. They weren't trade bait, but maybe a few of the "low-value" kids were. The Saudis had never given me specific names of individuals they wished us to free.

I didn't say anything to my British friend, but I thought to myself, *Let's see now, the Brits want these five guys released, and the Saudis want some of their own guys released. There might be a deal here.* I went back to Bill. He assured me there indeed were a fair number of detainees who could be released without harm, and we could probably even get the Saudis to monitor them or detain them in the Kingdom so they would be available to us for questioning. This was important, as one of the concerns was that even if we didn't have any evidence that they had done anything, they might have information valuable to us in understanding what was going on in Afghanistan and how Al Qaeda was working. In essence, some of the low-value prisoners were currently being held as material witnesses.

As I started thinking about helping the Brits, a few scenarios seemed plausible. Short of a straight-up prisoner swap, there might be the possibility of "repatriation." Here, prisoners from each side would be returned to their home countries and prosecuted there. Assistant Minister of the

Interior Prince Mohammed bin Nayef was in the early stages of insti-
tuting a reprogramming program in which young jihadis who were
returned to the Kingdom would meet with a moderate Islamic cleric
who would show them passages in the Quran that demonstrated that
what they were doing was completely un-Islamic.

After I reached out to Washington for guidance, Pierre Prosper, a terrorism expert serving as ambassador-at-large for war crimes in the State
Department, was assigned to work this issue and determine whether
there were detainees who could be released. I also discussed the matter
with Rice, whom I believe discussed it with the president, because they
were looking for ways to support and reward Tony Blair, our staunchest ally in the Iraq invasion.

Weeks passed without a definitive answer. Whenever I checked in
with Prosper, he would say, *Yes, we're working on it.* Whenever I checked
in with Bill, he would say there was no visible progress and it was probably going to have to be decided by Secretary of Defense Rumsfeld.

In late April 2003, a little more than a month before the summit in
Sharm el-Sheikh, Rumsfeld flew out for a tour of the region. I flew with
him from Abu Dhabi to Jeddah on what I recall was a C-17. The plane
had a pod for seating and conferencing and was filled with communications gear. This was no luxury liner like Air Force One, but at least we
didn't have to sit on the floor, as was the case in other military aircraft.

Among the passengers were generals, Pentagon spokesperson Torie
Clarke, and the usual array of aides to the secretary. Seated next to
Rumsfeld, I grabbed the opportunity to share the idea for the prisoner
swap formulated some six months earlier. "Condi Rice tells me the
White House supports this," I said. "And my staff tell me that these
guys can be released without compromising our safety. Is there a way
we can move this along?"

Rumsfeld shook his head and said the Saudi prisoners were "bad
guys" and that he didn't see how we could release them. Since they were
in Guantanamo, they had to be dangerous.

"Well, that's not what my advisors tell me," I said.

To his credit, he called over an aide with one or two stars on his col-
lar and told him to look into the matter. Within about twenty minutes,
the unknown was known. The aide said we could release the Saudis.

And the secretary gave the deal his blessing. Sometimes in diplomacy, as in real estate, the three things that matter are "location, location, location." Who knows what would have happened if I hadn't been seated next to the official with the power to make a decision?

In the end we returned five Saudis to their homeland. Two were clearly of no value and had no threat profile, and they could be let go. Three needed to be watched or detained and reprogrammed for a while. In August 2003 the Brits happened to get their five men back as well. The releases were never characterized as a swap, and the timing occurred several months apart. The two ideas "converged," as they say. (As soon as the Brits got home, they went on television, claiming that they'd been beaten and tortured. The Saudis, of course, didn't like that.)

Looking back, I consider this one of my most satisfying achievements during my ambassadorship. We were able to do a favor for our loyal ally Tony Blair. More important, we were able to improve U.S.-Saudi relations at a time when those relations had become very frayed and we were trying to put them back together. Over the course of my two years, I'm proud that, at least for the moment, we salvaged the relationship with the Saudis, preventing a permanent rupture that could have had devastating consequences for U.S. interests.

President Bush was not surprised when I told him that I was ready to leave. After the first year, he frequently asked me how much longer I planned to stay. Now, at Sharm el-Sheikh, he said something to the effect of, *Bob, thank you so much for your service to our country. You've stayed longer than you committed to, and I very much personally appreciate it.*

As I left our meeting, I thought, *That went smoothly.* Little did I know that before I left my post we'd have a tempest in a teapot—all because of some innocent remarks.

12

THIS IS HOW the Washington rumor mill works. On July 9, 2003, a London-based, pan-Arab newspaper asserts that remarks I made regarding Saudi succession in the Kingdom have angered the royal family. That paper, *al-Quds-al-Arabi*, is not a friend to the United States nor to Saudi Arabia. Indeed, according to the Washington Institute, it "has long been critical of Riyadh and . . . has published communiqués by both Osama bin Laden and Saddam Husayn."[1]

Ten weeks later, the now-defunct Saudi Information Agency—described by the Center for Media and Democracy as a "dissident independent news agency based in Washington, DC"[2]—picked up the story: "[The] U.S. ambassador has been declared persona non-grata in the Kingdom by . . . members of the ruling family fearful of American involvement in local Saudi politics. . . . Ambassador Robert Jordan was asked to leave after he made controversial comments regarding the political future of Saudi Arabia. . . . Jordan's comments came in two dinner parties sometime . . . [in] late spring."[3]

Three days later, the mainstream media, including the wire service UPI, repeat the story. In the *Washington Times*, the Embassy Row column of September 24, 2003, reports, "Saudi Arabia has demanded the removal of U.S. Ambassador Robert Jordan. . . . [He] angered several branches of the royal family when he [said] that Washington wants the next crown prince to come from a younger generation instead of the princes in line for the title, according to the unofficial Saudi Information Agency."

To summarize: the *Washington Times* quotes the Saudi Information Agency, which—inspired by another newspaper—apparently found its own anonymous source. I don't present this here because of sour grapes; I'm still standing. Rather, I offer this to demonstrate how stories gain "legs." Next time you read a newspaper report, be aware that it might be akin to a public game of "telephone," in which "news" changes as it is conveyed from one source to the next.

In the pre-Twitter days of 2003, the diplomatic world became atwitter at this report. The Saudis reacted. One day later, on September 25, Embassy Row tried to set the record straight: "Prince Bandar bin Sultan yesterday denounced the 'baseless and false' reports that his government demanded the expulsion of U.S. Ambassador Robert Jordan. . . . '[He] has been one of the most distinguished U.S. ambassadors to serve in the Kingdom,' Prince Bandar said. 'He served at a critical time in our bilateral relations and contributed greatly to the relationship.'"

Bandar added, correctly, that I was leaving for personal reasons.

End of story? Kind of. It doesn't take a great deal of Internet research to find sources that still erroneously insist that I was ousted from the Kingdom and forced to resign, when the truth is that I had stayed a year longer than my initial promise and in June had told the president at the Sharm el-Sheikh summit of my intention to step down in the fall.

I'm not saying that *parts* of the various reported iterations of this story weren't true. I did go to dinner parties in the spring, and Saudi succession was among the many topics discussed with my hosts and their guests. But the notion that I was meddling in the internal politics of Saudi Arabia is totally false. In setting the record straight here, I hope to shed some light on the role of a U.S. ambassador and on the perils that can befall a diplomat as he or she tries to carry out that role.

As I've previously written, I was frequently invited to dinner parties at the homes of Saudis. For educated people, my fellow guests had an incredibly naïve view of the world. They looked at the way the United States had exerted power and influence in the latter half of the twentieth century and assumed we still had the capability and will to do so in the twenty-first century. Two examples:

The Saudis pointed to 1956, when President Dwight Eisenhower stared down the French and the British during the Suez Canal crisis, saying, in effect, *No, you're not going to take over the canal. I'm siding with the Egyptians on this.* They also remembered the Yom Kippur War of 1973. In that conflict, the Egyptians were routing the Israelis until the United States intervened with Operation Nickel Grass, an airlift of enough equipment and armaments—more than twenty thousand tons—to allow the Israelis to prevail.

At the time of the war, King Fahd was the minister of the interior. He called all of his senior people in and said something like, *There's only one nation on earth that can do this, the United States. And if we ever get in some sort of existential peril, these are the guys who can bail us out. Don't ever forget this.*

Conventional wisdom at these dinners, some thirty-five years later, also held that the United States could snap its fingers and determine whom the next crown prince would be. And so it was that I found myself involved in the discussion about Saudi succession that gave grist to that rumor mill.

One dinner was at the home of Abdul Rahman Abdulaziz Al-Tuwaijri, the secretary general of the Supreme Economic Council. He was a well-respected, likable guy, with whom I had previously traveled to Geneva to advance the WTO cause. I considered him a friend and was pleased to accept his invitation. I knew there would be a very interesting and eclectic group of people at dinner.

Abdul Rahman lived in a nice section of Riyadh in a home with high ceilings and large rooms filled with sofas and chairs to accommodate gatherings of substantial size. By American standards this was quite a mansion; by Saudi standards this was a comfortable upper-middle-class dwelling.

After a dinner of Arabian *mezze* (small dishes); *fatoush* salad; lamb, beef, and chicken skewers; and a wide array of desserts, we adjourned to the *diwan*, the long, living room–like area where cushioned sofas lined all four walls. I should add that, thankfully, cocktails were also offered. Contrary to popular opinion, some Saudis do partake of alcohol at private gatherings. Drinks served include gin, vodka, Scotch, bourbon, and rum.

Abdul Rahman's *diwan* also featured several chairs. I sat in one of these, with about twenty-five pairs of eyes looking at me and twenty-five pairs of ears waiting to hear my thoughts on current events. Just as Americans are obsessed with presidential politics, the Saudis are obsessed with the royal succession. With Fahd incapacitated, the question du jour in 2003 was, Once Crown Prince Abdullah becomes king, whom will he appoint as the crown prince? As Abdullah was approaching eighty, the reality was that the next crown prince might ascend to the throne relatively quickly.

When the question came up at Abdul Rahman's home, I turned it around: "Who do *you* want to be the crown prince?" I asked as we sat in the *diwan*.

The answers varied. Several guests mentioned the usual suspects, members of the "second generation"—the sons of the first king, Abdulaziz. These included Prince Sultan (thought to be the next crown prince and heir apparent), Naif, Miteb, Salman, and others.

Someone in the room said, "We can't continue to be ruled by these old men."

Someone else responded, "The only way it will happen is if the United States makes it happen."

"How do you think we can do that?" I asked.

Another guest, whom I don't think necessarily spoke for the group, said, "America has that kind of power. America can dictate those terms."

I confess that in asking my question, I was not just making small talk. I was on duty there. My job was to act as an American intelligence officer and find out what the elites were thinking. This is one way in which we gain a lot of our intelligence. We don't necessarily gain it through the CIA. This is why we need diplomats out in the field talking to people every day.

I kept probing. *All right, well, what about this guy? What do you think of him? Why do you like him over this guy? And how do you think this could really happen? Have you thought of trying to make it happen within Saudi Arabia?* My questions were proactive, but by no means was I herding the group toward a particular result or asserting that America was capable of making any of this happen, even if we wanted to.

The tempest began a day or two later. I started hearing rumors from my staff that they were hearing that someone went to Prince Sultan and told him that the American ambassador was saying that the next crown prince should come from the next-younger generation and the United States was going to make that happen.

I was flabbergasted. More accurately, I was flabbergasted and angry. "I never said anything of the kind," I told my staff.

Why would someone spread such a falsehood? Perhaps he wanted to discredit me with the presumptive successor, Prince Sultan. Perhaps he wanted to curry favor with Sultan—at my expense.

Over the next few days, the rumor gained steam, and I steamed. Finally, I paid a visit to Foreign Minister Saud. "I'm hearing these stories," I said. "I want you to know, number one, they aren't true. And number two, I'm really concerned about it and I think we need to deal with it."

Saud responded that he had heard the same rumors and that, of course, he knew they weren't true. Then he said something slightly gratuitous. *You know, anytime an American ambassador starts talking about these topics, it's going to be the subject of great conversation.* I took that to mean he would have preferred that I had never even had the conversation, in the same vein that Americans might not appreciate a Saudi diplomat in Washington speculating with a group of Americans over whom the next president should be. The reality is, however, that such discussions happen around the world. It was appropriate for me to hear what they had to say. That was my job.

Although the Saudi press did not write about the rumors, the story finally broke in early July in *al-Quds-al-Arabi*. Sometimes the medium is the message. The newspaper is funded by the state of Qatar. At the time, the Qataris and Saudis were bitter rivals who had almost broken off diplomatic relations. As a result I don't think the Saudis gave much credence to the report. They didn't consider it a reliable or an unbiased paper. They knew, too, that some of the facts were wrong on their face— most notably the assertion that I had been declared persona non grata and had been expelled from Saudi Arabia.

As I recall, both the Saudis and the State Department offered denials after the story was reported in July. Yet there it was in September in the wire services and the conservative *Washington Times*. The good news was no one appeared to give the articles credence—at least not in the circles in which I was traveling—and then Bandar shot the story down the next day. In the end, the stories never got in my way of doing what I wanted to do. Both Abdul Rahman and Usama Al Kurdi, who was alleged to have hosted another dinner at which the topic was discussed, have confirmed to me that I said nothing inappropriate at either dinner.

Although I didn't express my personal opinion to the Saudis about their royal succession—that was not my role and would have been inappropriate—I did have some thoughts on the subject. I believed that at some point in the not-too-distant future, the Saudis were going to have to come to terms with their aging leadership and the importance of the next generation. My view was that this was something for *them* to decide; the last thing the United States needed to be doing was dictating or trying to manipulate the royal succession in Saudi Arabia. Meddling would be foolhardy and would backfire on us. (Imagine the outcry if we tried to do something like that in Great Britain.) At the same time, I felt that, for our own interests, we should indeed be identifying the emerging leaders and learning as much about them as possible. It's no secret that our intelligence community does this across the globe.

I left the Kingdom and my post in October 2003, almost exactly two years after I had first arrived. By the time I departed, President Bush had already asked Jim Oberwetter to succeed me—though the formal nomination did not come until November. I thought Jim was a great choice. A fellow resident of Dallas, he had served as press secretary to then-congressman George H. W. Bush. He was currently working for Hunt Consolidated, an oil company. He would have the president's ear, as I had. The Senate confirmed him in December 2003.

I knew, too, that Margaret Scobey's days in the Kingdom were numbered. She would soon be nominated and confirmed as U.S. ambassador to Syria.[4] That meant we had to find her successor as deputy chief of mission. I tried to persuade Deborah Jones to seek the position, but she demurred, citing the fact that she had two young children. Deborah was the director of the State Department's Office of Arabian Peninsula Affairs and one of my reliable backstops if I needed something in Washington. She eventually became ambassador to Kuwait and later made the courageous move to succeed Chris Stevens as ambassador to Libya.

Before leaving I was privileged to be feted at farewell parties hosted by the Friday Group and the American Business Group of Riyadh and at a few private Saudi dinners. Margaret emceed a lovely event hosted by our embassy. All staff, from maids and drivers to section heads, were there, as were friends from the Friday Group and the American business community. There were a lot of laughs and a few tears.

Tears also flowed in one-to-one goodbyes with the staff. One of the things that I've always admired about the Bush family, both elder and younger, is how they treat everyone with respect and kindness, whatever their position. I've tried to live my life that way as well and think that's one reason I was attracted to the Bushes. We share the philosophy that one should never act like he is lord of the manor.

Before leaving, I also said farewell to Crown Prince Abdullah. We had a very warm meeting in the Royal Palace with many of his entourage present. As I left he said, "I want you to promise me one thing."

"What's that?" I asked.

"I want you to promise me that you'll come back and see me three times a year."

"Your Royal Highness, I'll certainly look forward to that," I said.

The crown prince then grabbed my hand and held it as he escorted me past the throne room and down the royal carpet to the reception area. There he kissed me on both cheeks.

13

JIM BAKER TELLS a great joke about his return to private life after serving a dozen years in the Reagan and Bush 41 administrations. As he spins the yarn, on the day on which he was to return to his law practice, he got into his car and nothing happened. The vehicle did not move. After a minute or so, he realized why—*he was sitting in the back seat.* Accustomed to being driven everywhere for so long, he'd forgotten he was on his own again and was waiting for his driver to take his place in the front seat. That car wasn't going anywhere unless Baker was behind the wheel.

I'm not equating being an ambassador with being White House chief of staff, secretary of the treasury, or secretary of state, but I understand the point of Jim's anecdote. In Saudi Arabia, I had people who drove me everywhere. I had bodyguards who protected me, and I had a deep staff that ran errands, cooked meals, and did many other things for me that "civilians" normally do for themselves. I even had an agenda on my desk first thing every morning. Not so when I came back to Dallas in the fall of 2003.

After I returned home, I did not return to my old law firm immediately. First off, I needed some time to decompress and resolve personal matters, including going through a divorce after over thirty years of marriage. I won't say I had post-traumatic stress disorder, but there was certainly a period of just kind of exhaling and catching my breath, of getting used to things . . . and people. I had to get reacquainted with folks I hadn't seen in two years.

As I readjusted to life back home, I realized there were some things I missed about being ambassador to Saudi Arabia and some things I didn't miss at all. Some of what I missed had to do with my fascinating, often maddening environment in Saudi Arabia. It's a place my deputy, Margaret, once called an *Arabian Nights* trip into the seventh century, complete with costumes, camels, and melodious calls to prayer from the minarets. Some of what I missed also had to do with the job. Despite all my frustrations, I missed the excitement of occupying a front-row seat to history, interacting with American and Saudi top leadership, and occasionally doing some good. As I look back, I think of my top ten (actually, eleven) things that I miss and my top ten list of what I don't miss:

What I Miss

1. The sense of mission and noble purpose. I don't think anyone takes a job eight thousand miles from home in a dangerous location without having a sense of purpose. Public servants certainly don't do it for the money. I was proud to represent my country, even at times when I did not fully agree with our policies or tactics.

2. Playing a role in historic and occasionally productive events. Arriving in the aftermath of 9/11 was a sobering experience, but also one that filled me with adrenaline. Being in charge of my country's interests in Saudi Arabia thrust me into many of the major events of the day. Fighting terrorism in my midst; working for religious freedom, human rights, and women's equality; moving forward on World Trade Organization accession; participating in two presidential summits; seeking the release of political prisoners; working on the invasion of Iraq (with decidedly mixed results); and repairing a fractured bilateral relationship—these were challenges and opportunities that few of our citizens get a chance to experience.

3. The people I served with in the embassy and our consulates. It's often fashionable to stereotype the "striped-pants set"—our diplomats abroad, who aren't treated with the same respect as our soldiers in uniform. But our foreign service is made up of brave men and women

who risk their lives every day to serve our country. Some, like Chris Stevens, have paid the ultimate price. Many of my colleagues made me look good, protected me, and taught me all I knew (but not all they knew). Margaret Scobey and others were a joy to work with. I truly miss them. And I also miss the military component of my mission, many of whom became good friends. These folks were magnificent professionals trying to get it right, and they usually did.

4. My Saudi friends. Despite Secretary Baker's admonition to avoid getting "clientitis," it's impossible to serve abroad without making some friends among the locals. Yes, you can preserve your objectivity; no, you don't become a cheerleader for the other team. But despite serious disagreements with my government over many of our policies and practices, many Saudis welcomed me into their homes, shared their thoughts and aspirations with me, and treated me as a friend. I still am in touch with a number of them, like Abdullah and Khalid Alireza and Hassan Alkabbani. Yes, they would often bark at me as they vented their anger, but among them were a number who would say, "A true friend is one who speaks the truth to a friend."

I also miss my professional friendships with many in the Saudi government, especially King Abdullah, Crown Prince Salman bin Abdulaziz, Foreign Minister Prince Saud Al Faisal, current minister of the interior Prince Mohammed bin Nayef, former ambassador Prince Bandar bin Sultan, and current ambassador Adel al-Jubeir. I see them occasionally but enjoyed our more frequent interaction in the "old days," even when we were miles apart on policy.

5. Many colleagues from our government. Working in an intense wartime environment is a galvanizing experience. I had known President George W. Bush for ten years before going to the Kingdom, but our relationship reached a new level during my time as ambassador. I am grateful for the confidence he reposed in me, for his leadership in difficult times, and for his friendship. Likewise, I developed enormous respect for Colin Powell, Condi Rice, Rich Armitage, Bill Burns, Ryan Crocker, George Tenet, Bob Mueller, and many others at senior levels in our government. I also miss the periodic chats

I would have with those whose views I sought out, including Brent Scowcroft, Chuck Hagel, and others.

6. The Friday Group. On a day-to-day basis, these were my pals. After a week of crisis upon crisis, I relished our weekend afternoons hanging out by the pool, playing tennis, having a few drinks and dinner. More importantly, I relished the human contact that had little to do with work. For a few hours, the most important thing was whether I could return Franz's serve or whether the dog would jump in the pool. This group was a lifesaver.

7. The military. As I learned from my first encounter with General Tommy Franks, a lot of our military officers are among our best diplomats. I miss seeing Tommy, as well as Buzz Moseley (later to become chief of staff of the Air Force), Marty Dempsey (later to become chairman of the Joint Chiefs of Staff), and many others. Working with our military, I had the experience of landing on an aircraft carrier and flying on an AWACS mission to the Iraq border, exciting stuff for a civilian. I also miss the Marine Corps security detachment at the embassy, mostly young guys who had served one or more tours in combat and were rewarded with a "luxury" tour in Saudi Arabia. They would sometimes invite me to join them for horseback riding in the desert, and they ran Uncle Sam's, the popular off-the-record bar and cafe at the embassy. Solid and dedicated, these young men give you faith in America's youth.

8. The desert. Isabel "Dede" Cutler, the wife of former ambassador to Saudi Arabia Walt Cutler, is a renowned photographer who in 2001 published a beautiful work, *Mysteries of the Desert*. She gave me a copy of her book when I took my post in Riyadh. I had never seen such stunning pictures of Saudi Arabia. During my time there I rarely tired of the ever-changing desert landscape, with the light playing across the dunes and the colors so vibrant.

My off-road trip through the desert along the route of the Hejaz Railroad from Jeddah to Aqaba was a real highlight. Spending time in the desert also increased my respect for the Bedouin tribes that have eked out a living in this harsh environment for centuries. They remind me in some ways of the independent spirit of many of my fellow Oklahomans and Texans who pioneered the American Southwest.

9. The food. After I arrived in Riyadh, I gained twenty pounds. Enough said. Middle Eastern food is fabulous, although Saudi hosts will try to gorge you like a goose being fattened for foie gras.

10. Saudi reformers and journalists. During my time in Saudi Arabia, objective journalism came a long way. Freedom of the press increased, even though the progress was uneven. One journalist wrote a piece modeled after Martin Luther King Jr.'s "I Have a Dream" speech. He described a fictional dream of his daughter's in which she imagined being educated, getting a law degree, and—gasp—driving a car. He lost his job at the newspaper, only to be rehired by another patron. To this day he successfully provides commentary on reforms that are ongoing in Saudi Arabia.

    Courageous editors and writers are increasing. Women are agitating more for the right to drive, to control their own lives, and to operate their own businesses. Most reformers don't want Saudi Arabia to morph into a Western-style society but rather want to expand freedoms within the context of their Islamic faith.

11. The diversity. In my youth I lived abroad for periods in Peru and Hong Kong. I never tired of the exotic blend of cultures, smells, and sounds. So it was natural that my *Arabian Nights* experience would also present a diversity of cultures that I would find fascinating. The Nejdis in the conservative heartland of the country are as different from the cosmopolitan Hejazis in Jeddah as Kansas wheat farmers are from cappuccino drinkers in San Francisco. The expat community is equally intriguing, and I found the mix of Indian, Pakistani, British, French, African, Dutch, and other cultures to be a real treat. In many cases I was outside my comfort zone, and that was a good thing.

What I Don't Miss

1. Our dysfunctional government. While the rivalries and backbiting among the White House, State Department, Defense Department,

FBI, and CIA hold a certain academic interest, I found it debilitating. It's one reason I decided to leave in 2003. At least in those days we had a Congress that had a semblance of public responsibility and a president willing to work with them. I took small comfort in the comment of a friend who served in the administration of George H. W. Bush, who said that the backstabbing was equally bad in those days and simply "goes with the territory." Reports from within the Clinton and Obama administrations suggest that much of it is endemic to the high-stakes pressures of American government, regardless of party. Former secretary of defense Bob Gates's recent book, *Duty*, repeats these concerns in spades.

2. Their dysfunctional government. Many Saudis, especially business leaders, frequently complained to me about poor governance in their own land. Despite reaping huge sums from the world's largest oil reserves, for decades the Saudis neglected their infrastructure. Roads, bridges, schools, and hospitals were ignored. Floods in Jeddah and Riyadh have killed countless citizens due to inadequate drainage and corrupt or incompetent contracting practices. When Crown Prince Abdullah pressed us on helping the Kingdom join the WTO, his commerce minister ignored the order and subverted every effort to move forward until he was replaced by another minister. The Saudi royal court does not have even a rough equivalent of the White House staff that could direct the ministries and monitor compliance with royal decrees. An insistence on consensus often led to gridlock at the highest levels. The Tea Party would love it.

3. Congressional delegations. Long before public opinion rated Congress's popularity below that of serial killers, I got a glimpse up close and personal. While there were many in Congress who served with distinction and honor, my experience with CODELs was not pretty. Whether they were on a witch hunt to humiliate excellent officers who had the misfortune to innocently issue visas to Saudis who turned out to be terrorists or attempting to subvert our efforts to return a kidnapped child to her mother, our elected representatives' grandstanding and selfishness reflected poorly on the institution.

4. Religious intolerance. I have always believed that people have a right to their own religious preferences, but I have never understood how they could legitimately interfere with another person's freedom of worship. It's a very American sentiment, upon which our country was founded. So I found the Saudi intolerance of any religious practice other than Sunni Islam to be a problem. In their schools the textbooks would denigrate Jews in coarse terms. Proselytizing a Muslim is punishable by death. Recent studies suggest that little progress has been made, despite King Abdullah's establishment of centers for dialogue and understanding and the firing or "reprogramming" of many imams in the mosques.

5. Saudi treatment of women. The typical American perspective is, Why can't they let Saudi women drive? Driving isn't the half of it. Elite Saudi women drive all the time on vacation in Beverly Hills or Monaco, and women also drive in the rural areas of Saudi Arabia. Driving is a proxy for the control exercised by men over women in the society. It's not an essential element of Islam but instead springs from tribal customs that will not die. I also will not miss the tragic child custody cases in which American women lost access to their children who were either kidnapped by Saudi fathers or were otherwise held incommunicado from their mothers.

   In fairness, progress is being made. Agreements on visits of expat mothers to their children have modestly improved access. Women make up the majority of college graduates and thirty women now serve as members of the Majlis Al Shura. They are finding some job opportunities. But there is a very long way to go.

6. Death and destruction. The images of the aftermath of the bombings of May 12, 2003, are forever etched in my consciousness. Witnessing videos in the CAOCC of drone attacks on Afghan houses, hearing of beheadings or shootings of American citizens, the carnage in the Palestinian Territories and attacks on innocent Israelis, and the loss of so many American and allied lives in the wars we fought—all are part of a world I was happy to leave behind, but I doubt the memories will fade.

7. Claustrophobia and security paranoia. Being the American ambassador has its privileges, but privacy is not one of them. I do not miss

the suffocating cocoon in which I had to travel, nor the constant tension of my bodyguards, looking suspiciously at every car we would pass and every door we would enter.

8. Separation from family and friends. I missed my son's senior year in high school and many other family events. I rarely saw close friends from back home. I lost touch through common experience with many friends and colleagues. Despite the 24/7 crush of work and collateral activities, I will not miss the loneliness.

9. Micromanagement and secrecy. This dysfunction gets its own category. In earlier times, ambassadors were truly plenipotentiary and had the freedom to operate on a day-to-day basis. With the ongoing expansion of the White House staff, ambassadors and even secretaries of state have had less room to maneuver. Presidential (and vice presidential) aides, some with little experience and less common sense, inject themselves into functions previously delegated to those in the field, using the name of the president as if the boss really knew what they were doing. They hoard information like chestnuts for the winter. Knowledge is power. The silo mentality was nearly impossible to penetrate, and one hand often did not know what the other was doing. I will not miss having to ask Saudi officials what my own government was planning to do on major policy issues.

10. The traffic. Some have said that, per capita, more Saudis die in traffic accidents than residents of any other country. While the poor infrastructure and lack of modern highways contributes to the toll, there seems to be a cultural marker that requires everyone to drive like maniacs. Tailgating is common. Impatient with a slower car in front of you? Just pass it on the shoulder at ninety miles per hour (commonly called the "Saudi Swipe").

There was another factor preventing a quick return to Baker Botts. I was no longer affiliated with the firm. Fearing conflicts of interest, the government had mandated that I resign from the law practice upon confirmation as ambassador. In addition to resigning, I'd had to sell all stocks in my retirement plan and personal portfolio that had anything to do with the oil industry because of that sector's association with Saudi

Arabia. As a large percentage of my holdings were in Exxon, this was a major transaction for someone like me.

I've heard some pundits opine that ambassadorships are generally cushy rewards to presidential friends and financial supporters. There are indeed great benefits—the opportunity to serve one's country, the prestige, and, yes, the potential to leverage the position into postambassadorial lucre. But for a guy like me, who was not independently wealthy and who wasn't going to an embassy in Western Europe or a sunny island nation, there was a downside as well. I'd left a well-paid position with a certain amount of influence to travel to a place that even boondoggling congresspersons studiously avoid. I'd taken a significant cut in pay at a time when I was sending three kids through college and graduate school.

Although my contacts and standing in the Middle East might make me an attractive practitioner, I would be returning to Baker Botts (or joining any new firm that might want me) with little or no business. Upon my departure, I had referred all my clients to my highly competent partners. Unless unhappy with their new lawyers, none of these folks were going to return to me, and it would have been unfair for me to ask.

I am not complaining. If I could go back in time, I'd make the same decision to become an ambassador. I bring this up, however, to remind readers that many of the people who serve in government—long term or short term, elected or appointed, department heads or bureaucrats—make certain sacrifices in the name of country.

What I thought would be a two-to-three-month decompression period ended up being about five months. I wasn't a couch potato. I weighed job opportunities. I did some preliminary research and writing on what eventually became this book. And I became an academic of sorts.

During this time, the John Tower Center for Political Studies at Southern Methodist University in Dallas approached me and asked if I would become its "diplomat-in-residence." This was an unpaid position, but a nice opportunity to work with students and faculty. Already on the board of the Tower Center and friends with some of the political science faculty, I accepted.

Soon I had another title and well-defined duties. As adjunct professor of political science, I taught an undergraduate senior-level course called

Current Problems in Middle East Politics. As the name suggests, we combined readings with what was happening on the ground. Because the region was rife with fascinating eruptions every week, the course became quite popular. One week we might discuss a presidential summit meeting. Then the next week we might discuss the death of Yasser Arafat or the role of women in Saudi Arabia. I taught every year from 2004 until 2010 and returned to teaching in 2015.

Early in 2004 I said "thanks, but no thanks" to a handful of law firms making overtures and returned to Baker Botts. This was no slam-dunk. First, we had to settle on a role for me. We agreed that I would no longer primarily be a litigator handling lawsuits and arbitrations but instead would focus more on business transactions in the Middle East. I was anxious to use my unique knowledge of the region for our clients' benefit, and, frankly, it seemed like an enjoyable specialty to pursue at a time in my life when I could make a choice.

Just as the government worries about conflicts of interest while an ambassador is serving, so, too, does it worry about postservice private-sector conflicts. Washington imposes a lifetime ban prohibiting involvement with anything that one specifically worked on while ambassador. As with other ambassadors, I was also banned from working on anything that fell under my global authority or supervision—even if I didn't personally work on it—for two years.

Example? Ambassadors often are asked to engage in commercial "advocacy" for American bidders on government contracts abroad. If more than one American bidder is involved, the ambassador can't choose sides and must stay on the sidelines. Let's say that, as ambassador, I had advocated to the Saudis that they acquire a particular counterterrorist technology, say some kind of a drone aircraft. In that event, I probably couldn't ever work for the drone aircraft manufacturer who sold it to the Saudis and try to sell them more drones or otherwise work on the contract that I might have worked on as ambassador.

I support reasonable efforts to avoid a "revolving door" so that former government officials don't cash in on their experience by joining private-sector institutions to peddle their connections and influence. It is a different matter when it comes to providing advice on how to comply with laws and regulations in a foreign country or in understanding the geopolitical or regulatory environment that may affect the way business is conducted in a country. If former government officials have skill sets useful to the private sector, they should be able to use them if no improper influence is exerted and they are not working both sides of the street. Our current laws strike the right balance.

As noted, Baker Botts had an office in the Middle East and later added two more. I felt no pressure to base my practice there, however. The firm seemed comfortable with my traveling there with some regularity, say one week every other month. Ultimately our managing partner did request that I stay for a month or more at least once a year, rather than just five or six days at a time.

On some of these visits, I'd find time to reconnect with my old friend Hassan Alkabbani at his beach house in Jeddah. During this period, there was an attack on the U.S. consulate in that city. Several suicide bombers in a car actually made it through the wall and shot up the place, killing the driver whom I used when I was in Jeddah. This act and other violence led Baker Botts to move all of our Western lawyers out of Riyadh and to relocate them to Dubai. We left our Saudi lawyers and a British lawyer in Riyadh. I then started visiting Dubai as well.

Dubai was, as they say, "a happening place." In 1999 they completed the Burj Al Arab, the big luxury hotel shaped like a sail. By 2005 the place was booming, at over $1,500 a night. They were going great guns on building iconic skyscrapers, an indoor ski slope, the world's largest shopping mall—things that might be described as Texas-sized, out of the Jerry Jones and the Dallas Cowboys' school of spare no expense on our monuments. Even more ambitious than Jerry's World (as the Cowboys' stadium is often called) is the Burj Khalifa, the world's tallest structure, half a mile high. Construction began in 2004 and the building opened in 2010.

Because I was no longer an ambassador/automatic terrorist target, I was able to travel much more freely in the region. On visits to the Kingdom, I could actually go on my own to restaurants, hotels, markets, and malls. I could walk the streets in anonymity—a much appreciated change.

Still, I can't say that I spent much time with the average person on the street. My work brought me in touch with the same business elites that I'd dealt with as ambassador.

There was one big change in dealing with the Saudi business community. I certainly felt less necessity to advocate for U.S. policy or defend it, and my conversations with these people reflected that they no longer expected me to do that either. It was nice that I was a bit less of a target for them to vent over U.S. policy, and we could simply talk more about business or even exchange an "How's the family doing?"

On each visit to Riyadh, I'd call on my successor, Jim Oberwetter, and later his successors as well. We'd have very nice chats and sometimes dinner at Quincy House. It was great to see my old staff at the embassy and the residence.

Jim and I also spoke by phone with some regularity. It was important to me to keep abreast of developments in the Kingdom and to obtain Jim's measured and astute perspective. The WTO accession was still progressing, the Israeli-Palestinian conflict was still festering, and the aftermath of the Iraq invasion was becoming a quagmire. The Saudis were in an "I told you so" mood, and Jim was doing a yeoman's job juggling all these balls. His wife, Anita, was making great inroads with the Saudi female population, the half of the country that Jim could not access. Her background as a nurse came in handy in dealing with health care issues that were pressing in the Kingdom.

Jim was not only competent, he was gracious. As previously mentioned, I had worked hard to revive the effort to admit Saudi Arabia to the World Trade Organization—a move that I thought would lead the Kingdom to accelerate its human rights efforts. Initially, each government had resisted, but by playing the right political cards, I was able to get talks going. Jim and I often spoke about this. When the Saudis finally gained admission in 2005, Jim went the extra mile and called me in Dallas from Washington.

"Bob, I'm sitting here in the Office of the U.S. Trade Representative with the Saudi delegation," he said. "We're signing the documents for the accession of Saudi Arabia into the WTO, and I just want to pass the phone around the room and let everyone congratulate you on this tremendous accomplishment." Class act. The lead Saudi negotiator, Deputy Commerce Minister Fawaz Al Alamy, also got on the line, along with some of the U.S. Trade Representative staff. They made my day.

While I saw Ambassador Oberwetter whenever I was in Riyadh, I also fulfilled my promise to Crown Prince Abdullah that I would visit him when possible. Soon the crown prince had a different title. After the long-incapacitated King Fahd died, Abdullah ascended to the throne on August 1, 2005.

I did not see President Bush or my contacts at the State Department every time I was in Washington—two or three visits a year to attend conferences or speak to think tanks like Middle East Institute or the Washington Institute for Near East Policy. I didn't expect to be invited to the White House or Foggy Bottom; these are busy people. After you leave your post, the government takes your diplomatic passport, punches holes in it, and gives it to you as a souvenir; you can't use it anymore. A fitting metaphor.

I did run into State Department contacts on occasion, and I saw the president at a couple of receptions during his second term. He was his usual amiable self, posing for photos and telling those around us, "This guy was one of the best ambassadors I ever had."

My diplomatic passport did open the door to life as a talking head. Whenever something momentous happened in the Middle East, the media called on me for commentary and perspective. Fox News, CNN, MSNBC, Bloomberg, and others put me on air or in print.

By 2009 the firm had opened another office in the Middle East, this one in Abu Dhabi. More important from a personal standpoint, that same year I had remarried. After my divorce I had been lucky enough to meet Kathy Donovan, a smart, gorgeous businesswoman in Dallas, through mutual friends. As we were planning our wedding in late 2008, she was diagnosed with colon cancer. We attended her chemotherapy sessions together, and she was halfway through chemo when we were married on January 17, 2009. She is now cancer-free, and life is good.

Under Baker Botts' rules, I was scheduled to take mandatory retirement at age sixty-five in 2010. I had plans to travel and sail with Kathy and work on my neglected golf game. Instead, the firm asked me if I would stay on and take charge of our Middle East practice. This would involve a permanent move to the region.

I was as uncertain about taking this post as I had been about taking the ambassadorship some nine years earlier. Not so my new wife. When she had first heard that the partner heading the three offices was returning to the States, Kathy had said, "You know who needs to take that job?"

"No," I said.

"You do."

"Well, you've been married a year to me and want to get rid of me already?" I said with a laugh.

I didn't have to lobby her. After the firm asked me to take the job, Kathy was very supportive. We decided she would remain in Dallas, where she had three offices providing title insurance to the real estate industry. The firm agreed to see to it that she and I could meet once a month—either in Dallas, the Middle East, or somewhere in between. That was the only basis on which I would take the job.

I re-upped for another two years in 2012. I divided my time between Riyadh, Abu Dhabi, and Dubai, with my principal residence in a modern apartment overlooking the beach in Dubai. Kind of a Malibu with minarets. It's not unusual to see a woman in a bikini walking down the beach arm in arm with an Emirati woman in full *abaya*. The beach brings all cultures together, young and old, rich and poor. My morning walks along the surf cleared my head and refreshed my soul. Back in Dallas for good now, I am absorbed by my work at Southern Methodist University, give a few lectures and interviews, serve on some boards, and enjoy our new granddaughter.

In the next (and final) chapter, I look at Saudi Arabia today and try to project its future, especially as it pertains to the United States. My focus is on domestic politics and international relations. Before doing so, however, a portrait of the current and future business climate of the Kingdom and the region is in order.

Saudi Arabia has been at the crossroads of commerce for centuries. Traders in Jeddah would meet the pilgrims coming from all over the world to Mecca for the hajj, the religious journey that every Muslim is expected to undertake at least once in his lifetime. The discovery of the world's largest oil reserves changed not only their economic outlook but their culture as well. No longer did most citizens have to live by their wits, making deals and trading. Instead, the oil money began flowing and the younger generation had less pressure to learn a trade or study subjects in school that would qualify them for employment. Expatriate labor was imported to do the jobs that the newly affluent Saudis now felt were beneath them, swelling to over 9 million foreigners. Saudi Arabia became the world's largest source of outward remittances, payments the expat workers would send home to their families in India, Pakistan, the Philippines, and many other countries.

With the nation having one of the highest birthrates in the world, 50 percent of the Saudi population is under the age of twenty-five. That number continues to increase. The largest part of the youth bulge is the age group between ten and sixteen. It's a nation of kids. Kids without jobs, and often without the education or skills sufficient to hold a job. By the end of 2012, overall unemployment jumped to 12.1 percent, according to the International Monetary Fund. Among the growing category of fifteen-to-twenty-five-year-olds, it's closer to 30 percent. Among women it's 35 percent. In the region women make up only 22 percent of the workforce.

This youth bulge is a ticking time bomb. The Arab Spring mostly bypassed Saudi Arabia, as the government had the resources to subsidize utilities, gasoline, housing, health care, and education. Two-thirds of working Saudis are employed by the government, but the public sector has no room for further expansion. Under current conditions, as these kids move through the school system and more and more enter the job market, their expectations will not be met. The result could be a petri dish breeding social upheaval and dissent. It could turn nasty. Think of *Les Misérables* in white robes and checkered headscarves.

The other side of the coin is not all gloom and doom. Reform has a chance to succeed. The Internet, Facebook, YouTube, and Twitter have allowed Saudis to communicate about ideas, including improving education, job opportunities, and governance. As Tom Friedman reported in the *New York Times* on December 1, 2013, "Saudi Arabia alone produces almost half of all tweets in the Arab world and is among the most Twitter- and You Tube-active nations in the world."

This communication genie is out of the bottle and can't be stuffed back in by government censorship. The government will face a challenge to its legitimacy if it cannot deliver on jobs and a more vibrant private-sector economy. King Abdullah pushed for economic reforms, some of which have shown promise. Accession to the World Trade Organization already has produced a significant increase in foreign investment and trade. Between 2010 and 2012, over 240 American companies exported to Saudi Arabia for the first time. Nondefense exports to the Kingdom climbed by double digits.

During my time as ambassador, Saudi travel to the United States dropped to nearly nothing. Due to visa and immigration hassles, Saudi students gave up on education in America and headed for Australia, Singapore, and the UK. That is now turning around. Nearly 132,000 Saudis applied for visas to visit the United States in 2012. Over eighty thousand Saudi students attend American colleges and universities, and over 25 percent are women.

King Abdullah has provided scholarships for 150,000 Saudi students to study throughout the world. He understood the connection between education and a viable economy. He saw, too, the connection between a jobless, failing private sector and civil unrest. I believe King Salman will continue in the same direction.

Despite some encouraging statistics, WTO accession has not been all it was cracked up to be. One of the key features was supposed to be the elimination of the requirement of a local Saudi partner or agent. Foreign investors were to be free to set up their own companies without giving a local Saudi a cut of the action. In reality, some Saudi agencies require a foreign investor to use a local agent. This is a flagrant violation of the WTO accession agreement. Likewise, I continue to hear complaints about corruption from well-established Saudi businessmen, some of it involving one of the six thousand or more minor Saudi princes in the Kingdom.

There also appears to be a disappointing decline in the quality of service provided by the Saudi Arabian General Investment Authority, the main foreign-investment arm of the government. What was intended to be a user-friendly system for market entrants now has morphed into an agency interested only in major corporate investment. The small and medium-sized businesses wanting to enter the market get short shrift.

While King Abdullah did not take on the cause of women's rights as forcefully as the reformers would like, he introduced incremental change, some of it in a clever way. His principal economic aim was to assist the progress of women through education. He promoted the recent found-ing of Princess Noura University, which sits on a gigantic campus near the Riyadh airport. The all-female university houses about forty thou-sand students.

I have wondered what the effect on the Saudi economy will be when ten thousand female graduates a year descend on the labor market with high hopes, if not expectations, of a job. And I have wondered if, some-where in the back of his mind, King Abdullah intended the pressure-cooker effect that this pent-up job demand will create, as a means of forcing the economy to adjust and make room for more women in the workforce.

Other episodes in the struggle for women's participation in the economy have been frustrating. In 2012 the Saudi government proudly announced that female lawyers would henceforth be allowed to appear in court and would no longer be relegated to the "legal consultant" work of legal research and office practice. In 2013 licenses were issued to women allowing them to represent clients in court. Yet when women attorneys showed up for their court appearances, judges turned them away because they were not accompanied by a *mahram*, or male guard-ian. Apparently the judges did not get the memo.

I initiated the hiring of women lawyers in our office in Riyadh. We hired several interns from King Saud University, the only university with a law school for women in the Kingdom. We had good luck with the women and invited them to participate in firm meetings and events. Technically, we were required to have separate space for them to work in, where they would not mix with our male employees. In reality, they came and went as they pleased. In order to avoid controversy, we made sure that they, and their parents or husbands, were comfortable with this environment. By contrast, in far more liberal Dubai, almost half our lawyers were women.

Saudi women have struggled for years to work as clerks in retail stores. Believe it or not, until recently women's lingerie was sold only by male salesclerks. Imagine the embarrassment of a Saudi woman wanting to buy unmentionables and having to deal with a man. This practice often led husbands to go to these stores and attempt to buy undies for their wives, only to find upon arrival at home that the size or style was com-pletely wrong. At long last, the forces of progress have outlawed the use of male clerks in women's lingerie shops, and women have been allowed to take their rightful places behind the sales counter.

Saudi Arabia is the only country in the world in which women are not allowed to drive. For many years the local women said that the real issue was economic opportunity, not driving. Dr. Isobel Coleman of the Council on Foreign Relations has found that these attitudes are changing. More women are willing to risk arrest by driving in public to make a point. They can communicate more easily with like-minded women by text message. And they see the connection with economic opportunity.

Their husbands should see this connection as well. Unless a Saudi family has the resources to hire a driver (usually an Indian or Pakistani, who, for some reason, are viewed as perfectly appropriate companions for the lady of the house for much of the day), the husband must take the kids to school, leave work to bring them home, and take the wife shopping. This leaves little time for productive work. It also discourages women from entering the workforce, as they would be at the mercy of a primitive taxi system or a husband who would have yet another round of driving to undertake.

The toll on the Saudi economy of excluding women from the workforce, and forcing husbands to tote around all other members of the family during working hours, is incalculable. Near the end of my tenure as ambassador, I facetiously asked Prince Saud, the foreign minister, if he would permit American female embassy staff to drive on official business, as it would assist them in their diplomatic duties and would save us significant dollars spent on a massive motor pool operation. He simply smiled and rolled his eyes.

The Saudis are facing another cold reality of their economy: we don't need their oil so much anymore. American energy independence is no longer simply a slogan. The shale boom and expansion of U.S. oil and gas production, combined with the effects of conservation and clean technology, have revolutionized our attitudes toward Middle Eastern oil. Yet in 2012, ironically, American oil imports from Saudi Arabia actually increased. This is largely due to the grade of crude needed by American refineries, for which Saudi crude is more suited than some grades of American oil.

Over the long haul, the Saudis are losing their biggest customer and are transitioning primarily to the Asian market. They were aided in maintaining oil prices by the loss from the market of crude oil due to sanctions imposed on Iran and by the slowness of Iraqi production to ramp up after the fall of Saddam Hussein. However, they have been severely affected by the collapse of oil prices in 2015.

At a current volume of slightly over 9 million barrels a day, some reports suggest that the Saudis need to maintain oil prices at around ninety dollars per barrel in order to balance their annual budget. I suspect the number is somewhat lower. Of course, they also have massive currency reserves and can run a budget deficit for several years. But over the longer term, they must hope that world demand increases and can absorb the likely production increases that would occur upon the lifting of sanctions against Iran, an uptick in Iraqi production, and robust American and perhaps Brazilian production, among other factors. A significant decline in Saudi oil exports, or continued low prices, could have a real impact on the economic subsidies they bestow upon their population.

Another threat to Saudi oil exports is closer to home; domestic demand is increasing. The population explosion requires vast amounts of oil and gas for power plants, desalination facilities, and transportation. Some have predicted that by 2030 the Saudis will be consuming nearly all the oil they produce, sharply impairing their financial position. The Saudis are aggressively working to develop solar and potentially nuclear-power technology in anticipation of this drain on their export capacity. The Saudi Electricity Company recently has switched an upcoming massive power plant project from oil-fired to gas- and solar-fired in order to conserve oil for export.

An emerging concern for American businesses may be the increasing hostility of Saudi leaders toward American foreign policy, especially under President Obama. Members of the royal family, including former ambassador to the United States Prince Turki al Faisal, ambassador to Great Britain Prince Mohammed bin Nawaf, and former head of Saudi intelligence Prince Bandar bin Sultan, have been highly critical of Obama's policy missteps, from ill-advised support for the Muslim Brotherhood in Egypt to fecklessness on the Israeli-Palestinian conflict to about-faces on whether to provide support to the rebels fighting the regime in Syria to the emerging effort to reach detente with Iran over its nuclear program. These princes have called loudly for Saudi Arabia to distance itself from the United States.

In my view, while their policy concerns are well grounded from the standpoint of Saudi national interests, the effect on business with the United States should be minimal. Even as America grows more energy independent, we will continue to have a national interest in the rest of the world's access to Middle Eastern oil. And I doubt that the Saudis will stop buying Patriot missiles or F-15s any time soon. Their military officers train with ours and attend our advanced service institutions. While there may be an increase in awards of construction contracts to Chinese or Korean companies, I expect little change in the economic relationship between our two countries. Pepsi, Starbucks, and Pizza Hut should have little fear.

14

I HAVE LIVED half of the last thirteen years in the Middle East. My work has immersed me in the politics, business, and culture of Saudi Arabia, the United Arab Emirates, and occasionally other states of the Middle East. I've seen up close the aftermath of the most horrific attack on American soil in history. I've negotiated with, cajoled, and threatened officials standing in the way of the pursuit of American national interests, and I've supported many of the same people when they have been unfairly dismissed, ignored, or stereotyped by American bureaucrats, congressmen, or journalists. I've seen a war commenced with noble purpose but pathetic planning—brilliant in its initial execution but totally bungled in the attempted transition to peace. I've seen my own government try to do the right thing and too often the clumsy machinery of government, egos, ambition, and miscommunication prevent us from succeeding.

I've seen an Arab Spring that has turned into a dark winter for many who had high hopes for fundamental political change. I've seen American leaders abandon a longtime ally in Egypt who refused to go gracefully, only to embrace a Muslim Brotherhood regime that promoted extremism and failed to govern competently. I've seen a bloody civil war erupt in Syria, with Iran and Saudi Arabia waging a proxy battle for control, and a baffling series of miscues on the part of the American administration in dealing with Syrian strongman Bashar al-Assad's use of chemical weapons and the criminal slaughter of his own people. And I have seen Iran's looming threat to develop a nuclear weapon and the excruciating pace of negotiations to keep it from the brink while it extends its influence in Iraq, Lebanon, Yemen, and Syria.

Morning Joe, one of my favorite morning talk shows, ends each day with the participants asking, "What have we learned today?" It's a fair question to ask about my last thirteen years. It's also fair to ask, with all humility, what advice I would give to my successors as ambassador, to the policy makers in Washington, and to the leadership in the neighborhood in which I have been living.

Forecasting the future is fraught with peril, especially in the Middle East. You can take it with a grain of salt, but if you've read this far you may want to see if there is indeed something to take away from these stories. Fair warning—it can't be tied up neatly in a bow.

So how do the stories in this book inform our view of the future? What lies ahead? How do American policy makers manage challenges in the Middle East with diminishing resources, waning popular support, increasing energy independence, and a mentality of "leading from behind?"

I'd start with the realization that it's not just about us—it's also about them. As I told President Bush and Colin Powell, we've had a history of parachuting in and making demands of the Saudis without developing an overall vision of what the relationship should be from the standpoint of both parties. First, the Saudis feel increasing tension in their relationship with the United States and a gnawing sense of isolation. The Israeli-Palestinian conflict has troubled the Saudis for decades, and they remain highly critical of the lack of American leadership on the issue. Then came the ouster of longtime ally Hosni Mubarak in Egypt, which infuriated the Saudis. *If you will do this to Mubarak*, the Saudis ask, *what's to stop you from throwing the Saudi regime over the side as well?*

But perhaps the greatest concern for the Saudis is Iran, their longtime rival for primacy in the Middle East. The Saudis view Iran as a major strategic threat. They view the Shi'a religion as politically driven by Tehran and blame Iran for the dissent in their Eastern Province and the uprisings in Bahrain. The catastrophe in Syria, the assassination of Rafiq Hariri in Lebanon, the continuing violence promoted by Hezbollah, and the threat of nuclear proliferation all are traced back to Iran's designs on the Saudi circle of influence. So the Saudis shudder at the thought of a "grand bargain" between the United States and Iran, potentially involving an accord on nuclear development in exchange for lifting economic sanctions and softening on the agenda of regime change in Syria. Since 1945, the Saudis have believed we had their back. Now they are not so sure.

The Saudis have lashed out at American and Western capitals in reaction to these cascading concerns. After campaigning for a seat on the United Nations Security Council, and after triumphantly announcing their selection, the Saudis abruptly rejected the seat, claiming that the UN had shown no ability to act on Syria and Iran. The Saudi ambassador to the United Kingdom castigated President Obama for declaring a "red line" on Syria's use of chemical weapons, only to back down once that red line was crossed. One Saudi wag from Jeddah viewed these uncharacteristic outbursts and was quoted as saying, "We used to be known for riyalpolitik, but now what we do is piquepolitik."[1]

Let me add one more factor that makes the future with Iran a problem for the Saudis. Economic competition. When Iran ultimately emerges from crippling economic sanctions, it has the potential to be an economic powerhouse. With abundant natural resources, Iran also enjoys a comparative advantage in human capital. Iranians are industrious, aggressive, and well educated. Much of the world is waiting for the opportunity to do business there. King Abdullah recognized that a Saudi workforce that is better educated with a stronger work ethic will find it easier to compete in the marketplace, and the new monarch is working hard to achieve this as well.

For all the talk of American energy independence allowing us the luxury of telling the Gulf Arabs to pound sand, the reality is quite different. Even if the United States were never to import another drop of Middle Eastern oil, the rest of the world will depend upon a reliable flow of oil for decades to come. That oil drives economies that produce goods and services for a global market, including the United States. And the cost and availability of those goods to the United States is directly tied to the flow of oil from the Middle East. So even if American oil imports were reduced to zero, we'd remain indirectly dependent on the world oil market to drive a world economy in which we so heavily participate.

Saudi Arabia remains important to America for other reasons as well. While much can be said about the incubation of global terrorists by the bin Laden network in Saudi Arabia and Afghanistan, the Saudis turned out to be important partners in fighting violent extremists. In fighting these battles, Saudi royals such as Minister of the Interior Mohammed bin Nayef have been targets of terrorist assassins. Al Qaeda cells in the Kingdom have been wiped out and countless terrorist leaders killed or imprisoned, often at the cost of lives lost by Saudi police and soldiers themselves.

As the birthplace of Islam and the home to two of the holiest sites in the Muslim world, Saudi Arabia plays a key role in the eyes of over 1.3 billion Muslims. And as one of the world's fastest-growing economies, at a crossroads of the world, the Saudis are increasingly participants in markets and transactions of major significance, including the purchase of staggering amounts of American goods and services.

While the United States cannot turn its back on the Saudis and their Gulf neighbors, we have no choice but to leave increasing responsibility for the region to those who live there. America's finger on the scale cannot determine outcomes. When President Obama drew a "red line" over the use of chemical weapons in Syria and then failed to act when that red line was crossed, his wobbliness was noted in capitals across the world, both friend and foe. Presidents cannot afford to box themselves into bold declarations unless they are prepared to back them up. Likewise, when President Obama earlier declared that the expansion of Israeli settlements in the West Bank had to stop, and the Israelis refused to comply, his credibility was shredded throughout the region. This vacillation has been a particular irritant to the Saudis, who feel increasingly insecure in the face of perceived American weakness.

Bold talk is also no substitute for a strategy. While the Saudis have announced that they are "going their own way" on Syria, providing lethal weapons to rebel groups, such aid is unlikely to lead to regime change. Certainly the humanitarian disaster has sickened the world and intensified the pressure for American intervention. Yet one lesson from Iraq and Afghanistan is that noble objectives to "liberate" an oppressed people can have unexpected consequences. Launching a military attack has many more moving parts than the Sunday talk show pundits recognize.

Marty Dempsey, chairman of the Joint Chiefs of Staff, has expressed skepticism over the prospect of military action against Syria. Even limited air strikes would have enormous cost and risk of involving Iran and Russia. As David Lerman and Terry Atlas reported for Bloomberg on July 23, 2013, Dempsey said, "We have learned from the past 10 years . . . that it is not enough to simply alter the balance of military power without careful consideration of what is necessary in order to preserve a functioning state." The reporters also noted that Dempsey has further warned, "Once we take action, we should be prepared for whatever comes next. . . . Deeper involvement is hard to avoid."

Dempsey has estimated that air strikes could launch us onto a slippery slope requiring hundreds of aircraft, ships, and submarines, endangering the lives of pilots with little guarantee of success against the regime or of fulfilling any realistic political objective. I think he and I learned some of the same lessons over the last ten years.

Another lesson I learned is the power of personal diplomacy. At the presidential summit in Crawford in 2002, Crown Prince Abdullah and President Bush were primed to square off at each other. Powell, Rice, Bandar, and many others of us had a feeling of foreboding about the meeting. Yet when Bush took Abdullah on that pickup ride through his ranch, much of the tension melted and we had a productive meeting. It paved the way for many more personal exchanges, both direct and through intermediaries like me.

My own experience with the crown prince and his senior cabinet reinforces my view. After many midnight meetings with Interior Minister Prince Nayef, I had established the personal relationship and credibility to ask him to help me save Michael Baba Yemba from a certain death if he were deported to Khartoum. Marty Dempsey managed close personal relationships with the top echelon of the Saudi Arabian National Guard, including Crown Prince Abdullah himself. I sometimes worry that President Obama has remained aloof from many world leaders and the lack of a personal connection inhibits diplomatic progress. Just because President Bush and King Abdullah were photographed holding hands according to Arab custom in 2005 didn't mean they were going steady—but it signified that they could do business together.

In this vein it's important to note that appearances matter. The optics of President Bush calling Ariel Sharon a "man of peace" shortly before our summit meeting nearly sabotaged the trip. When Crown Prince Abdullah became king, his first trip outside the region was to China. Important symbolism. A congressman grandstanding by attempting to bring Mike Wallace to Saudi Arabia for a television opportunity undercut long-standing groundwork on child custody issues.

My time in the Middle East also has taught me that domestic affairs both at home and in the region are intertwined with foreign policy. Richard Haass, president of the Council on Foreign Relations, points out in his excellent book *Foreign Policy Begins at Home* that "many of the foundations of America's power are eroding. . . . The effect, however, is not limited to a deteriorating transportation system or jobs that go unfilled or overseas owing to a lack of qualified American workers. To the contrary, shortcomings here at home directly threaten America's ability to project power and exert influence overseas, to compete in the global marketplace, to generate the resources needed to promote the full range of U.S. interests abroad, and to set a compelling example that will influence the thinking and behavior of others."[2]

Becoming entangled in wars of choice, or even undertaking major humanitarian interventions, ignores the lessons of the last ten years and is beyond the reach of America today. Our crumbling infrastructure, income inequality, education deficits, and expensive social programs all need our focus, and we cannot remain a superpower without attending to these needs.

I also would argue that the foreign policy of the states of the Middle East begins at home as well. Egypt, once the dominant foreign policy force in the entire region, is mired in a struggle between Islamism and military rule. Its economy is in shambles. Bahrain, once the banking center of the Gulf, has lost billions in the midst of its Sunni-Shi'a clash. Iraq, awash with oil and human capital, has failed thus far to overcome sectarian strife and corruption. When Iran ultimately emerges from crippling economic sanctions, its domestic strengths in resources and human capital will enhance its influence throughout the region.

Despite their wealth, the monarchies of the Gulf are not immune from many of these forces. Perhaps America's most steadfast ally in the Gulf, the United Arab Emirates, remains a beacon of stability and resistance to the forces of the Arab Spring. Life is good there and the Ferrari market is booming. I've occasionally joked that the only protest we will see in Dubai is if they close the local Gucci store. Yet its leaders maintain a watchful eye on sources of dissent. The UAE has a relatively small indigenous population and is occupied by a vast majority of expats who depend on visas and work permits to remain.

Saudi Arabia is a more complex case. Apart from its challenges in job creation and its unsustainable increase in consumption of its own oil production, detailed in the preceding chapter, the Saudis face other internal hurdles. Thankfully the royal succession unfolded smoothly.

Over the past fifty years it was not unusual for a highly placed royal to enter cabinet service in his twenties (or occasionally even earlier). Because these ministries have been held by one person for generations, the leadership and experience have not been passed down to very many of the "kids" in their fifties and sixties. The next generation of leaders may have a steep learning curve, and a number of them may decline to pursue government service altogether.

While I once was restrained from speculating on future generations of Saudi leadership, I can now state that there is a promising bench of younger royals. We are starting to see some of them filter into diplomatic and deputy ministerial ranks. Some, like Crown Prince Muqrin and Interior Minister Prince Mohammed bin Nayef, have even more experience in government. Many others are less experienced, but able. They haven't yet been given the keys to the car, but they are well educated and have a broad view of the world. They may lack top ministerial seasoning, but they should be up to the task.

I also learned that even though the nation is an authoritarian monarchy, Saudi Arabia's leaders operate as often as possible by consensus and are keenly aware of the importance of their own legitimacy in the eyes of their people. The king doesn't visit remote areas of the Kingdom merely to take a stroll; he wants to be seen as caring about his people. King Abdullah was considered the first king to actually visit a Saudi slum, when previous regimes denied there could even be such things. Walking among the crowds, he reminded me of a Lyndon Johnson kind of figure, enjoying pressing the flesh.

A greater problem, one that troubles many in the Saudi business community, is poor governance and corruption. There is little follow-through on major royal decrees and no staff apparatus that monitors compliance. Stories of petty corruption at local levels are unfolding to an alarming degree.

One of my Saudi friends told of his exasperation with the level of competence in public services. An acquaintance of his fell desperately ill and an ambulance was called. The man needed oxygen, and the attendant put the mask over his face. He turned the valve, but there was no airflow—the oxygen tank was empty. Needlessly, the patient died. My friend told the story not as an example of tragedies that could befall any of us but as an example of simple incompetence that is an every-day occurrence. As with Richard Haass's view of America's internal vulnerability, the Saudis will not be able to maintain their prosperity at home and influence abroad if their levels of governance and freedom from corruption cannot improve.

King Abdullah addressed these issues. He appointed a commission to root out and punish corruption. He launched billions of dollars' worth of public projects to address inadequate infrastructure, education, and health care. For example, grandly ambitious health care cities are planned in several parts of the Kingdom. These involve thousands of beds, campuses, and amenities. While I wonder how the Kingdom will find the health care professionals to staff this momentous expansion, it's a significant step toward taking care of its growing population.

Finally, my time in the Middle East taught me a few things on a personal scale. First, I learned that agreeing to enter public service doesn't mean you get an instruction manual. You don't realize the depth of intrusion into your life that federal background checks and security clearances can impose. You will be exposed to a media culture that is even more intrusive and less objective.

When I returned from my service in Saudi Arabia, a friend said, "Bob, have you seen this movie called *Fahrenheit 9/11*?" I hadn't, and he proceeded to tell me that I'm actually in the movie. Apparently it was director Michael Moore's attempt at a "documentary" on President Bush's supposed failings after the attacks of 9/11. A couple of months passed, and my curiosity finally led me to drop into a theater and view it.

After sanctimonious indictments of the Bush family and Jim Baker for relationships with the Carlyle Group, in which the bin Laden family (not Osama) invested a small fraction of their wealth, the movie then focuses ever so briefly on me. I'm portrayed as a lawyer who "got off" George W. Bush from a securities investigation and was "rewarded" with the diplomatic plum of becoming ambassador to Saudi Arabia. Sure enough, there is a shot of me in a television studio in Riyadh, preparing to go on American talk shows to discuss the bombings in Riyadh in 2003. I'm scratching my nose in an outtake. It certainly didn't feel like a plum assignment as I was walking through the death and destruction of the Al Hamra compound the day after the bombings. After viewing the movie, I was reminded of Buzz Moseley's crack that media criticism is about as meaningful as "a cow peeing on a rock."

Also on a personal scale, I learned how much I care about family, friends, and faith. I missed my sons desperately and treasured moments when they were with me. I can now look forward to the joys of grandchildren and a loving family life. I was blessed to have my Friday Group friends and many others as well, some of whom I still see frequently. I also was blessed to have many professional friends, my embassy colleagues who served so bravely and taught me so much. I came through spiritual challenges with a stronger faith.

The lessons learned from the stories in these chapters continue to resonate with me. I don't claim to have all the answers. My father served on a naval ship on D-Day at Normandy and with the Agency for International Development in Saigon during the Tet Offensive. Like his experiences, mine have colored the next phases of my life. So far it's been an amazing ride.

NOTES

Chapter One

1. This story, along with an astute analysis of U.S.-Saudi relations, can be found in Rachel Bronson's important book *Thicker Than Oil: America's Uneasy Partnership with Saudi Arabia* (New York: Oxford University Press, 2006).

2. When I agreed to take the position, I had to arrange to resign from my law practice to avoid any conflicts of interest. With three sons to put through college and an 80 percent reduction in income staring me in the face, we put our house on the market and rented a small bungalow less than half its size. We closed the sale of the house on September 10, 2001.

3. The Kingdom remains a feudal environment, and the recent history of its monarchy calls to mind medieval England. King Faisal, for example, seized power in the early 1960s when his older brother King Saud was out of the country. Faisal, in turn, was assassinated in 1975 by the son of a half brother.

4. "Dallasite Embraces Post as Saudi Envoy," *Dallas Morning News*, October 5, 2001, 35A.

Chapter Three

1. At the time, Prince Mohammed's father, Prince Nayef bin Abdulaziz, was minister of the interior. In 2011 he became crown prince, but he died less than eight months later. Prince Mohammed became minister of the interior in late 2012 and deputy crown prince in 2015.

2. The State Department has an office that arranges for ambassadors to speak in their hometowns and other cities when back in the United States for a visit. On subsequent trips to Dallas, I spoke to clubs, churches, and synagogues. Audi-

ences at houses of worship were generally less trustful of the Saudis than those at, say, the Rotary Club.

3. "Saudi Police 'Stopped' Fire Rescue," BBC News, March 15, 2002, http://news.bbc.co.uk/2/hi/1874471.stm.

4. Later the crown prince actually had a meeting with the merchant families and told them that this was a very important agenda item for him and they had better fall in line, which they did. While some saw the loss of their monopolies over the distribution of goods and services, others recognized that the pie would be getting larger and they'd still have a role to play—because even if it weren't legally required it would still make sense as a practical matter to have some sort of local contact at a high level in that country.

5. On May 26, 2004, a *New York Times* editorial would acknowledge that such reporting had relied too heavily on an unreliable source, Ahmed Chalabi. Unfortunately, such reporting created a climate that made it easier to go to war. Judy Miller also spent some time in jail a few years later for refusing to reveal her sources in connection with another article.

Chapter Four

1. Waveney Ann Moore, "Sailor Was the Piper of History," *Tampa Bay Times*, February 12, 2005, http://www.sptimes.com/2005/02/12/Southpinellas/Sailor_was_the_piper_.shtml.

2. Martin Bilbert, *Churchill and the Jews: A Lifelong Friendship* (New York: Henry Holt, 2007), 232.

3. Parker T. Hart, *Saudi Arabia and the United States* (Bloomington: Indiana University Press, 1999), 236.

4. Brian Knowles, "Sharon Is Praised as 'a Man of Peace,'" *New York Times*, April 19, 2002, http://www.nytimes.com/2002/04/19/news/19iht-prexy_ed3_.html.

5. Dick Cheney, *In My Time: A Personal and Political Memoir* (New York: Threshold Editions, 2011), 377.

6. *Time*, April 29, 2002.

Chapter Five

1. According to reporter Mike Dorning's story in the *Chicago Tribune* of May 12, 2004, Chairman Hyde came under criticism for deciding to take his committee of thirteen legislators and twenty-three staffers to Ireland and Hungary. Some thought the congresspersons should have gone to Iraq; almost everyone agreed that the trip was staff heavy, particularly with respect to Hyde's own entourage of staffers and the presence of his personal physical therapist.

2. One exchange with a fellow ambassador in January 2002 proved particularly unsettling. Assad Durrani, a retired general serving as ambassador of Pakistan, was a charming fellow with whom I enjoyed conversations about regional politics. I asked him about rumors of potential renewed hostilities between India and Pakistan. I gasped when he said, "Sometimes a little war is a good thing. We take a little of their territory, or they take a little of ours. It can clear the air. We would only use nuclear weapons if one side or the other appears to be winning too decisively." Thankfully his scenario didn't come to pass.

Chapter Six

1. Joel Mowbray, "Visa Express Derailed," Townhall.com, July 7, 2002, http://townhall.com/columnists/joelmowbray/2002/07/11/visa_express_derailed; emphasis in original.

2. Mowbray, "Visa Express Derailed"; emphasis in original.

3. Douglas Jehl, "Once Trusting, Saudis Are Now Leery of U.S.," *New York Times*, December 7, 2001, http://www.nytimes.com/2001/12/07/world/a-nation-challenged-visas-once-trusting-saudis-are-now-leery-of-us.html.

4. "U.S. Department of State: Marriage to Saudis," *Middle East Quarterly* 10, no. 1 (Winter 2003): 74–81, http://www.meforum.org/520/us-department-of-state-marriage-to-saudis.

5. "U.S. Department of State: Marriage to Saudis."

6. "U.S. Department of State: Marriage to Saudis."

7. U.S. Department of State, Country Information, Saudi Arabia, "Local Laws and Special Circumstances," n.d., http://travel.state.gov/content/passports/english/country/saudi-arabia.html.

8. U.S. Department of State, Country Information, Saudi Arabia, "Entry, Exit & Visa Requirements" and "Local Laws and Special Circumstances," n.d., http://travel.state.gov/content/passports/english/country/saudi-arabia.html.

Chapter Seven

1. U.S. Department of State, 2011 *Report on International Religious Freedom*, July 30, 2012, http://www.state.gov/j/drl/rls/irf/2011/nea/192905.htm.

2. The per capita wealth of Saudi Arabia is far less than that of Dubai, where Ferraris, Rolls Royces, and Lamborghinis are a dime a dozen. Yet the elites in Riyadh were as logo-happy and status conscious as hedge fund czars on the Riviera, affecting Rolexes and Gucci and Prada loafers for the men and handbags for the women—all the trappings of material success. The men usually wore silver or stainless steel watches and little jewelry. The women found gold the accoutrement of choice and were granted custody of their gold jewelry in any divorce.

Chapter Eight

1. Mohammed Alkhereiji, "Lieberman Wants Saudi Peace Plan Reinstated," *Arab News*, December 27, 2002, http://www.arabnews.com/node/227048.

2. "The Arab Peace Initiative, 2002," Al-bab.com, http://www.al-bab.com /arab/docs/league/peace02.htm.

3. Alkhereiji, "Lieberman Wants Saudi Peace Plan Reinstated."

4. Robert Baer, "The Fall of the House of Saud," *Atlantic*, May 2003, http://www .theatlantic.com/magazine/archive/2003/05/the-fall-of-the-house-of-saud/304215/.

5. Matthew Levitt, *Tackling the Financing of Terrorism in Saudi Arabia*, Policy-watch 609 (Washington DC: Washington Institute, March 11, 2002), https://www .washingtoninstitute.org/policy-analysis/view/tackling-the-financing-of-terrorism -in-saudi-arabia.

6. Levitt, *Tackling the Financing of Terrorism.*

7. Al-Qadi has never been convicted of illicit financing. But despite the Saudi business community's defense of this multimillionaire, he remains a "specially designated global terrorist" under U.S. law. In March 2012 a U.S. federal judge found that the Department of Treasury's Office of Foreign Assets Control had provided "sufficient reason to believe" that the Saudi had supported terrorists and/or their associates. I met with him once in Jeddah during a visit to a Saudi women's college; he asked me to get him off the list, which I did not do.

8. Testifying before Congress in 2004, Aufhauser characterized Saudi Arabia as the "epicenter" of terrorist financing. Understandably, his remarks greatly offended the Saudis. As the comment was certain to be taken out of context, Aufhauser should have been more careful. But if you look at it in context, it was sort of like saying Miami's South Beach is the epicenter of drug trafficking in the United States. It doesn't mean that the political leadership in Miami is casting a blind eye to what's going on, it means that's where the bad guys are.

9. This congressional inquiry and report should not be confused with the inquiry and report of the bipartisan 9/11 Commission chaired by former New Jersey governor Thomas Kean.

10. In the same article the *Guardian*'s Borger also noted, "The leaks . . . are a symptom of rivalry in Washington. Congress is preparing a report into the September 11 investigation criticising the administration for failing to pursue leads that point to the Saudi establishment. The FBI is also frustrated that its inquiry into the Saudi role was stymied for political reasons."

11. George Tenet, *At the Center of the Storm: My Years at the CIA* (New York: HarperCollins, 2007), 105.

12. Bandar quoted in U.S. Senate Subcommittee on International Trade and Finance, *Hearing on the Role of Charities and NGOS in the Financing of Terrorist Activities*, August 1, 2002 (statement of Matthew A. Levitt, senior fellow, Washington Institute for Near East Policy), http://www.banking.senate.gov/02_08hrg/080102/levitt.htm.

13. United Nations, Security Council Committee, "Pursuant to Resolutions 1267 (1999) and 1989 (2011) Concerning Al-Qaida and Associated Individuals and Entities," available online October 30, 2009, http://www.un.org/sc/committees/1267/NSQE07102E.shtml.

Chapter Nine

1. Cheney, *In My Time*, 377.
2. "General Amused by Analysts," *Dallas Morning News*, April 6, 2003, http://www.freerepublic.com/focus/f-news/886389/posts.

Chapter Eleven

1. Jennifer Steinhauer, "Giuliani Says City Won't Accept $10 Million Check from Saudi," *New York Times*, October 11, 2001, http://www.nytimes.com/2001/10/11/nyregion/11CND-PRIN.html.
2. Later Alwaleed sent me a video of President Bush's visit. The video was edited so artfully that to some it may have appeared as if the president had actually come to talk to the prince and that their conversation lasted far longer than it actually had.

Chapter Twelve

1. Simon Henderson, *Inconsistent Representation in Saudi Arabia: A Continuing Problem*, Policywatch 789 (Washington DC: Washington Institute, October 2, 2003), http://www.washingtoninstitute.org/policy-analysis/view/inconsistent-u.s.-representation-in-saudi-arabia-a-continuing-problem.
2. "Saudi Information Agency," SourceWatch.org (Center for Media and Democracy wiki), last modified October 2, 2006, http://www.sourcewatch.org/index.php/Saudi_Information_Agency.
3. Ali Al-Ahmed, "U.S. Ambassador to Riyadh Persona Non-Grata," Saudi Information Agency, September 21, 2003, http://maximpost.tripod.com/bulletin/index.blog?start=1075413126.
4. Margaret was pulled from her post in Syria in 2005 after the assassination of former Lebanese prime minister Rafiq Hariri. Many experts believe that the Syrian government was behind the murder. Margaret went on to serve in Bagh-

dad and was named U.S. ambassador to Egypt in 2008. She served there until 2012, during the controversial ouster of Hosni Mubarak.

Chapter Fourteen

1. "Despite Their Immense Wealth, the Saudis Are Not Happy," *Economist*, February 6, 2014, http://www.businessinsider.com/saudi-arabia-politics-no -satisfaction-2014-2.

2. Richard Haass, *Foreign Policy Begins at Home: The Case for Putting America's House in Order* (New York: Basic Books, 2013), 3.